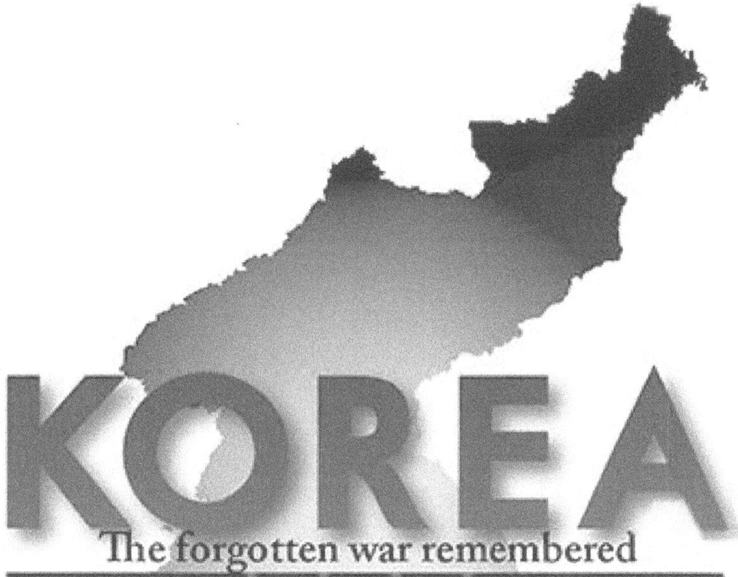

KOREA
The forgotten war remembered

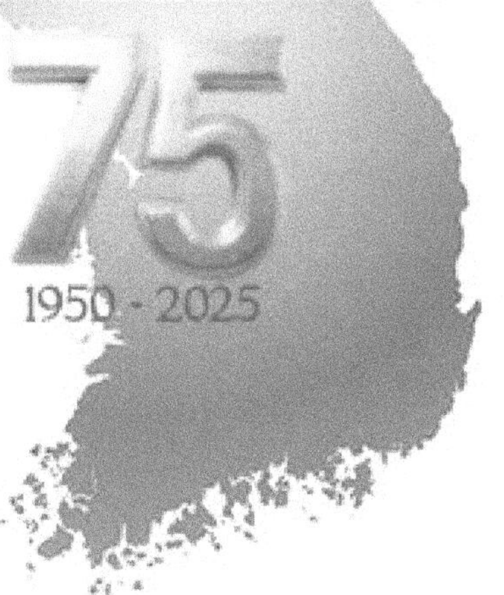

75
1950 - 2025

WHEN HELL FROZE: A MARINE COMBAT PHOTOGRAPHER AT THE CHOSIN RESERVOIR

Frank Kerr, former SSgt., USMC

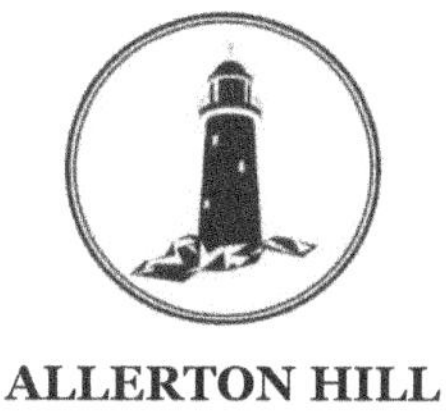

ALLERTON HILL

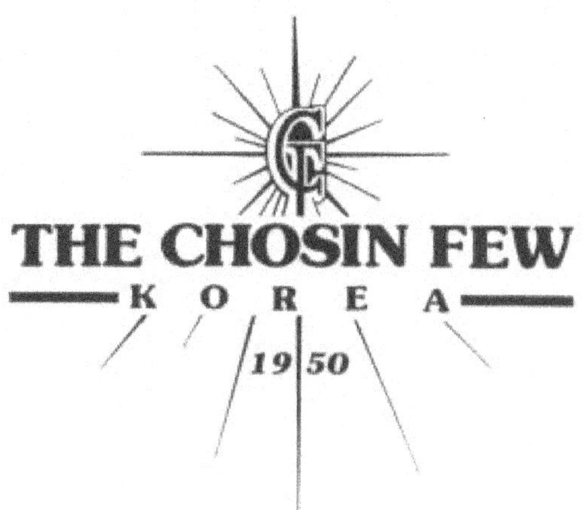

To the Chosin Few:

Whatever we were in that frozen long-ago and whatever we are now, we are bound as one for life in an exclusive fraternity of honor. The only way into our ranks is to have paid the dues of duty, sacrifice and valor by being there. The cost of joining, in short, is beyond all earthly wealth.

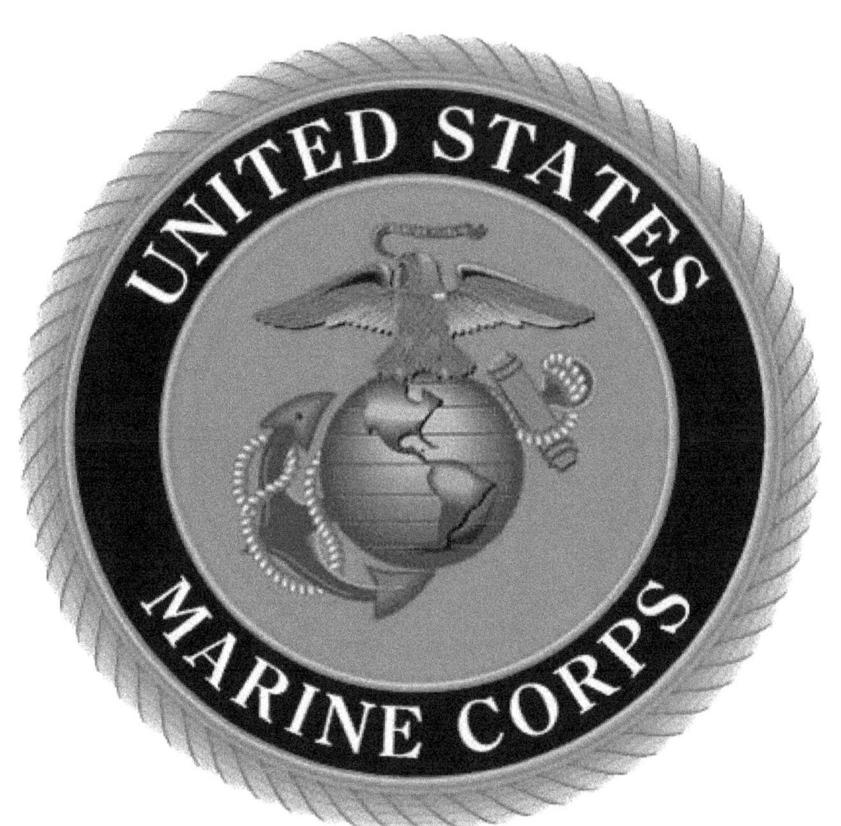
UNITED STATES
MARINE CORPS

FOREWARD

During our father's lifetime his experiences were many; hard rock miner, newspaperman, documentary filmmaker, corporate executive, community organizer, beloved husband and father. But no chapter seemed to define him more than his service as a Marine combat photographer covering the Korean War from 1950 to 1951, particularly the First Marine Division's extraordinary breakout from the Chosin Reservoir in the late fall of 1950—one of the most storied engagements in United States military history.

Fought from November 27th to December 11th, the Battle of the Chosin Reservoir pitted 12 Chinese Divisions, over 120,000 men, against a vastly outnumbered force of U.S. Marines, soldiers, British Commandos and South Korean troops under the United Nations command of General Douglas MacArthur. Surrounded in the mountains of North Korea by an enemy determined to annihilate them, the men of the First Marines fought for fifteen days in arctic-like cold to escape the communist trap. So profound was our father's experience at Chosin that he later co-founded "The Chosin Few", an international brotherhood of veterans who served in that legendary campaign.

Not long after dad passed in March, 2007, a treasure trove of his combat photographs and personal memorabilia was discovered in the attic of our family home in Massachusetts, including wartime letters to his mother and three typewritten drafts of a memoir describing the harrowing days he spent with the U.S. Marines at the Chosin Reservoir—the first written in 1952, just one year after his return from Korea. Because dad never spoke of the war, the story he told in those brittle, yellowed pages was a revelation to us all.

With the 75th anniversary of that historic battle coming in November 2025, we felt it was time to share dad's remarkable story with others. *When Hell Froze: A Marine Combat Photographer at the Chosin Reservoir* is not about the personalities and military strategies that helped shape that epic campaign, rather it is the story of a 20-year-old Marine sergeant who carried a camera into battle and was forever changed by the experience.

To honor our father and the Corps he proudly served, all profits from the sale of this book will be donated to the Marine Corps Heritage and Marine Corps Scholarship Foundations. And one final note: While certain language in this memoir might be considered offensive today, bear in mind that it reflects the context and culture that existed at the time it was written.

Thank you for reading *When Hell Froze*, and to all United States Marines here and gone, God bless and Semper Fi.

The Kerr Family
September, 2025

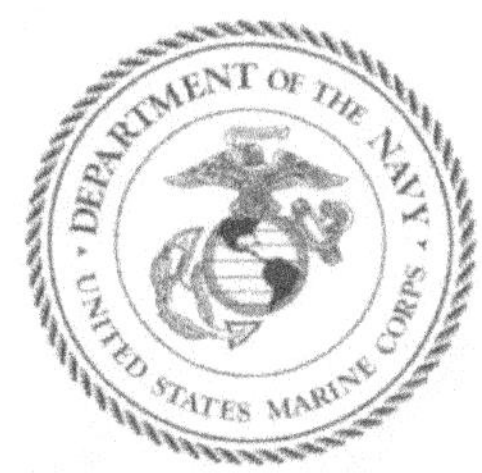

CITATION for COMMENDATION RIBBON WITH COMBAT "V"

The Commanding General, 1st Marine Division takes pleasure in commending

SERGEANT FRANK KERR
UNITED STATES MARINE CORPS

for service as set forth in the following

CITATION:

"For excellent service in the line of his profession while serving with a Marine division during operations in Korea from 7 September to 11 December 1950. Sergeant Kerr displayed great ability, courage and confidence in the performance of his duties as a combat photographer. During the fighting on the Pusan perimeter, the Inchon-Seoul campaigns and the continuing advance into North Korea, he repeatedly exposed himself to accurate enemy fire in order to film combat operations. During the Chosin Reservoir operation, where extreme weather conditions sometimes rendered his camera inoperable, he was nevertheless able to secure many extraordinary still photographs depicting the entire withdrawal from Yudam-ni to Hungnam. His overall performance was so outstanding that he was officially recognized as the ablest military photographer of the Korean theater. The wide coverage accorded his photographs contributed materially to the national attention directed to the exploits of the First Marine Division. Working long, tedious hours under the most adverse weather conditions, he failed to display any regard for his own personal safety or fatigue, thereby setting an example for all who served with him. Sergeant Kerr's conduct throughout was in keeping with the highest traditions of the United States Naval Service."

OLIVER P. SMITH, Major General, U.S. Marine Corps

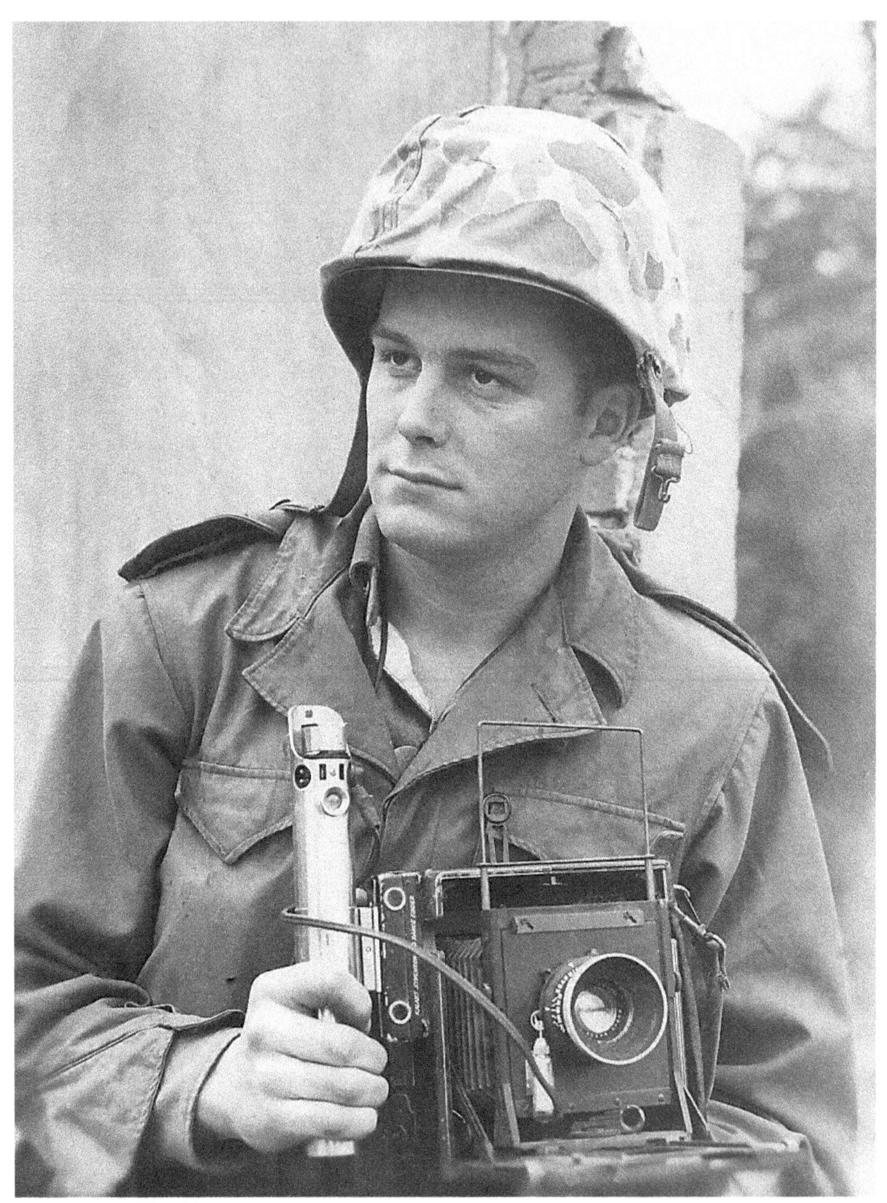

Marine combat photographer Sgt. Frank Kerr in Masan, South Korea holding the Graflex 4x5 Speed Graphic camera used during his wartime service. *(Photo by Sgt. James Powers, USMC)*

WHEN HELL FROZE: A MARINE COMBAT PHOTOGRAPHER AT THE CHOSIN RESERVOIR

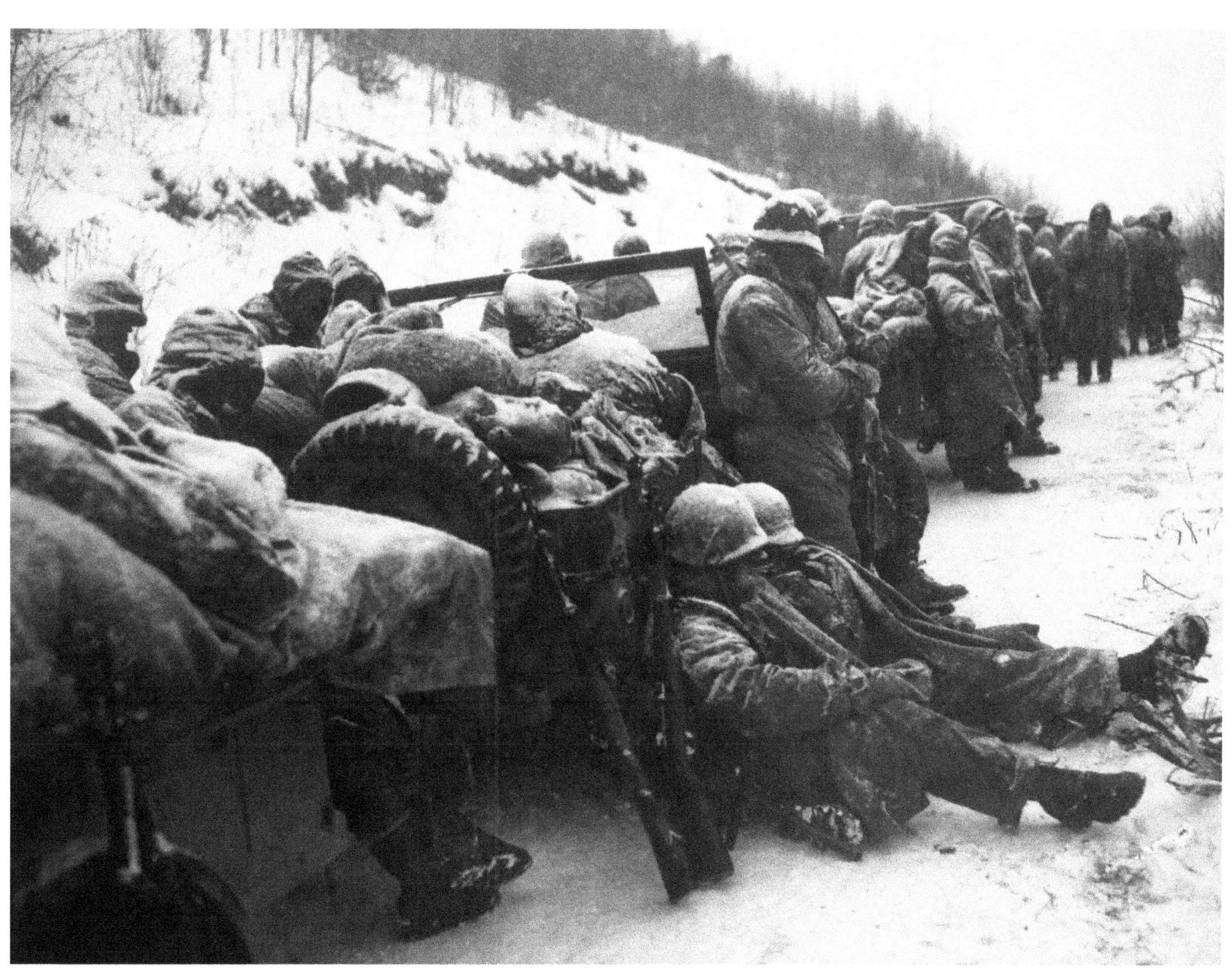

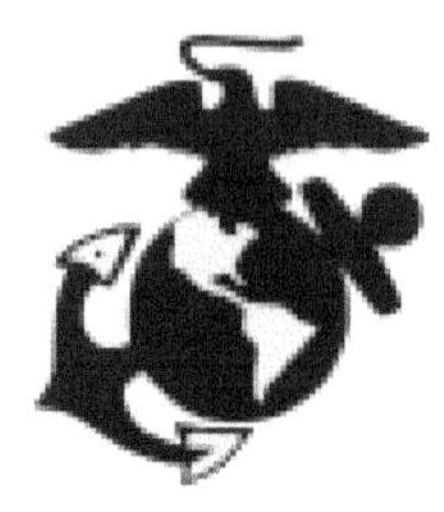

June 1950, Camp Pendleton

Dear Mom,

Well I'm pretty sure of going over now, as a matter of fact I think I'll be leaving sometime next week... We're not sure of where we're going—by "we" I mean all of us so called peons in the outfit. We might go to Japan and train or go right into Korea. I do know that we photographers are in for a heck of a lot of work though. We've had several conferences so far and we've found that Washington wants the best possible coverage of this thing with both stills and movies. Keep an eye on the papers, maybe you will see some of my pictures.

--Excerpt from a letter home to Sgt. Kerr's mother, Ida, from his personal collection.

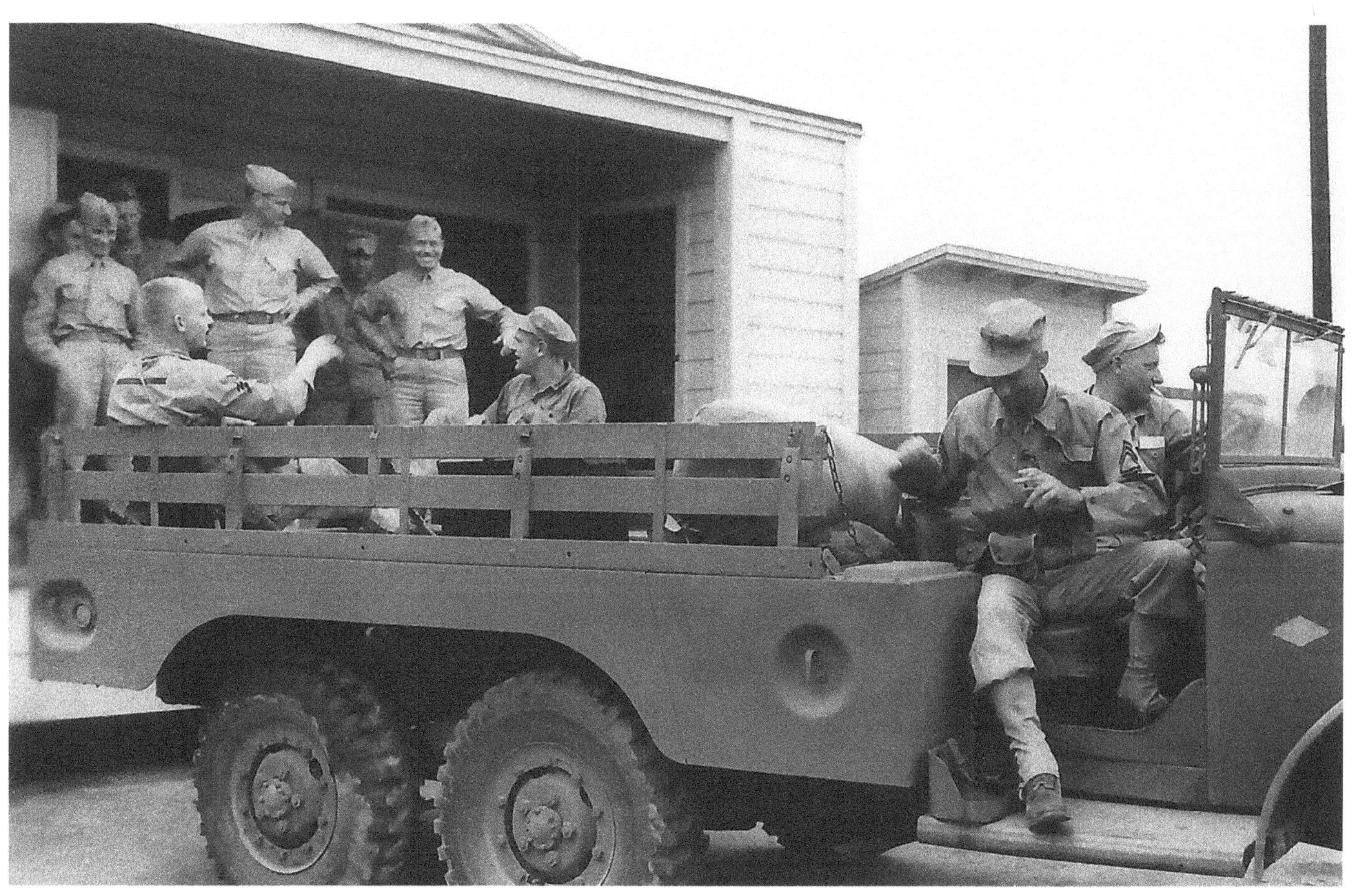

Departing Camp Pendleton for Korea, July 1950. Seated in the bed of the weapons carrier on their way to board the transport ship *USS Clymer* are, from left, Cpl. Jake McKay and Sgt. Frank Kerr of the Photo Section, 1st Provisional Marine Brigade. *(National Archives Photo, USMC)*

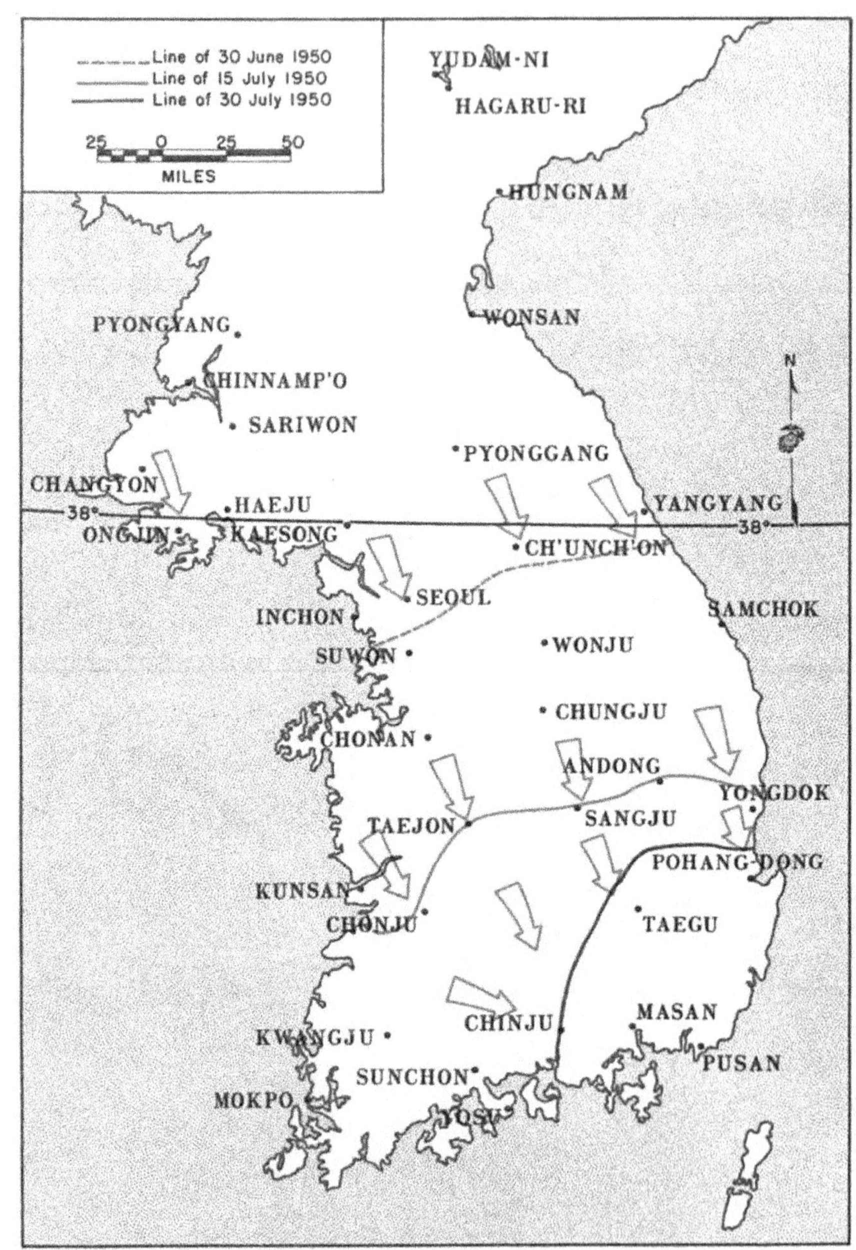

Invasion of South Korea by the North, showing North Korean
Army advances from June-July 1950

4

PRELUDE TO CHOSIN

Winter had come early to the North Korean high country. As our regiment pushed deeper into the mountains along an unpaved, ice-encrusted road, the temperature hovered near zero and would soon plunge lower. I was a 20-year-old Marine combat photographer when I carried my camera into that frozen hell. Some of what I experienced over the coming days would be captured on film, but how do you capture the horror of watching men die, or fighting in weather so brutally cold that breath freezes and flesh turns black, or seeing an enemy soldier come screaming from the night as you try to reload your rifle before he does? You can't. Not really. To truly understand is to have been there in the late fall of 1950, at a cold and forbidding place known to history as the Chosin Reservoir.

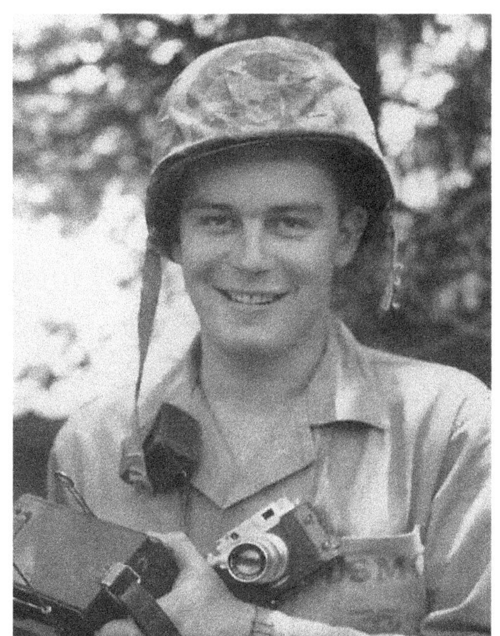

Cpl. Kerr at Camp Pendleton, 1949

When I quit school to join the Marine Corps in 1948, fighting a war in some godforsaken landscape on the other side of the world was the furthest thought from my mind. I was eighteen and looking for direction— any direction other than working on highway road crews or in the suffocating heat of an Idaho silver mine. So I left my mom and three younger siblings in Yakima, Washington, and started life anew as a United States Marine, learning the photographer's trade with the Reproduction and Photographic Service Section at Camp Pendleton in San Diego.

After communist North Korea invaded the South in June 1950, and the United Nations voted to send troops to drive them out, I was deployed as a combat photographer with the 1st Provisional Marine Brigade, organized as a placeholder while the 1st Marine Division—demobilized after World War Two—was hastily reassembled. The Brigade's mission in those early days of the war was straightforward; reinforce beleaguered U.N. troops, including the U.S. Eighth Army, under siege by the North Koreans at the southeast tip of the Korean peninsula—a 140-mile-long defensive position known as the Pusan Perimeter.

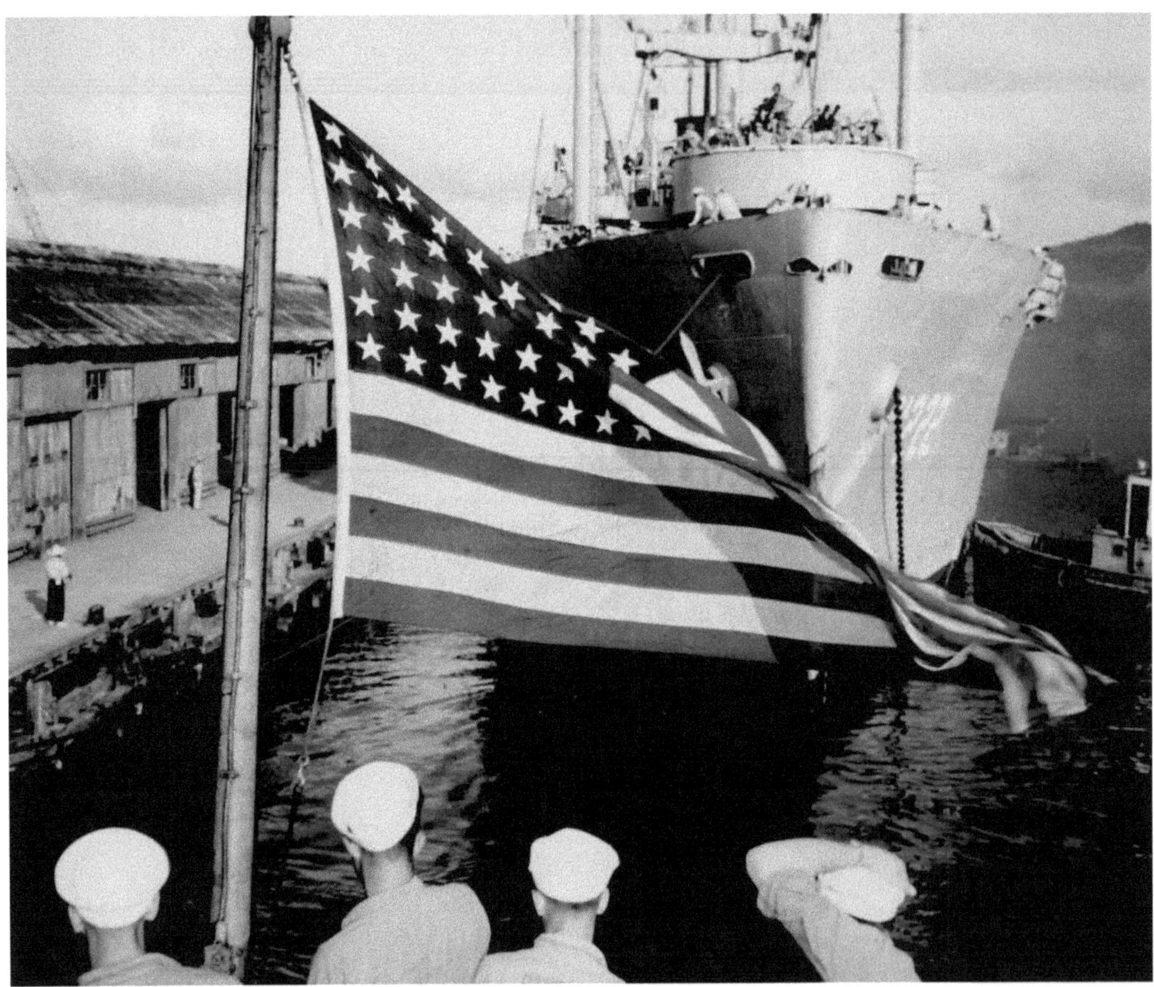

The American flag waves from the stern of the *USS Clymer* as the Clymer and *USS Pickaway* arrive at the docks in Pusan, South Korea with troops and equipment of the 1st Provisional Marine Brigade. *(Photo by Sgt. Frank C. Kerr, USMC)*

THE PUSAN PERIMETER

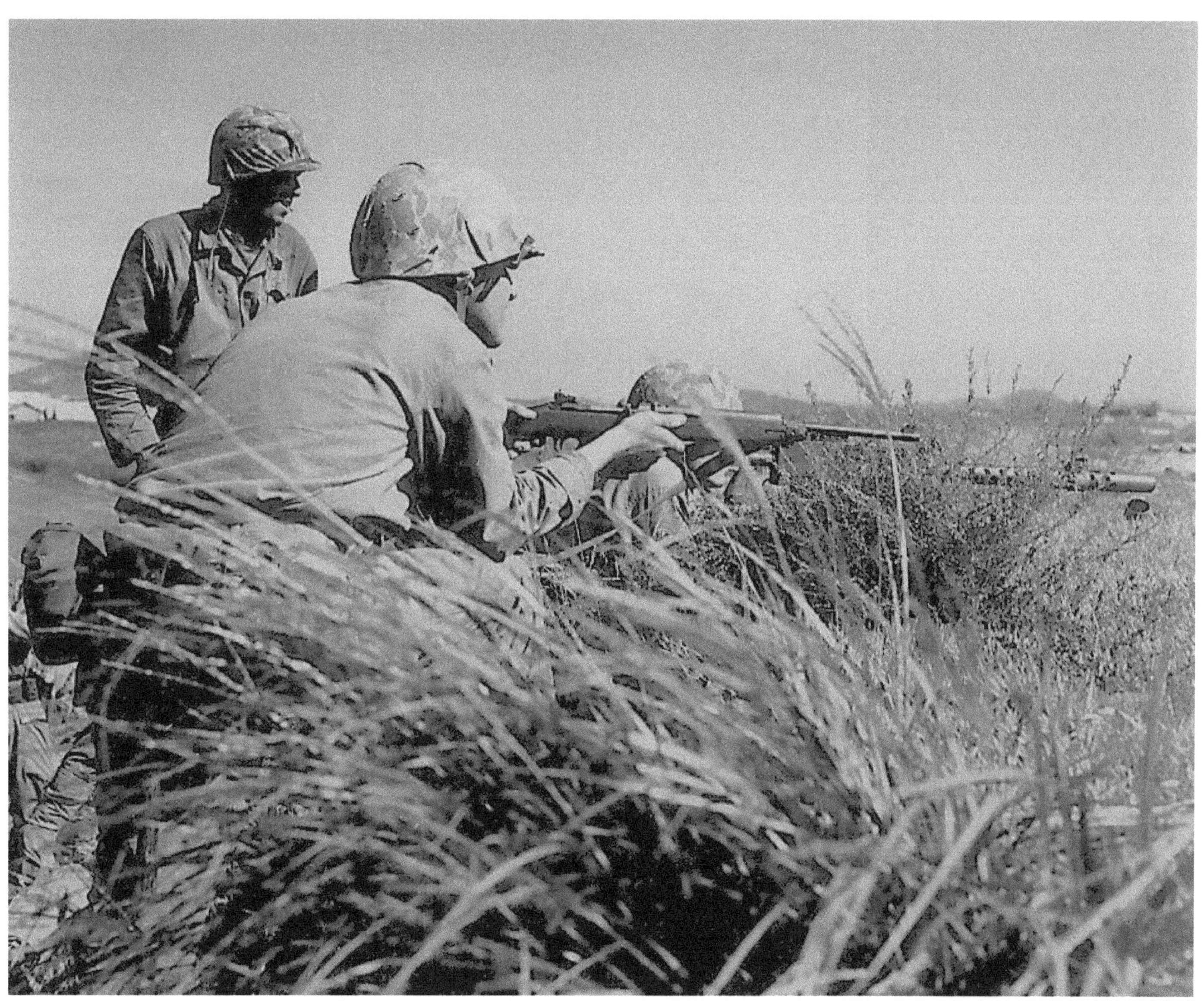

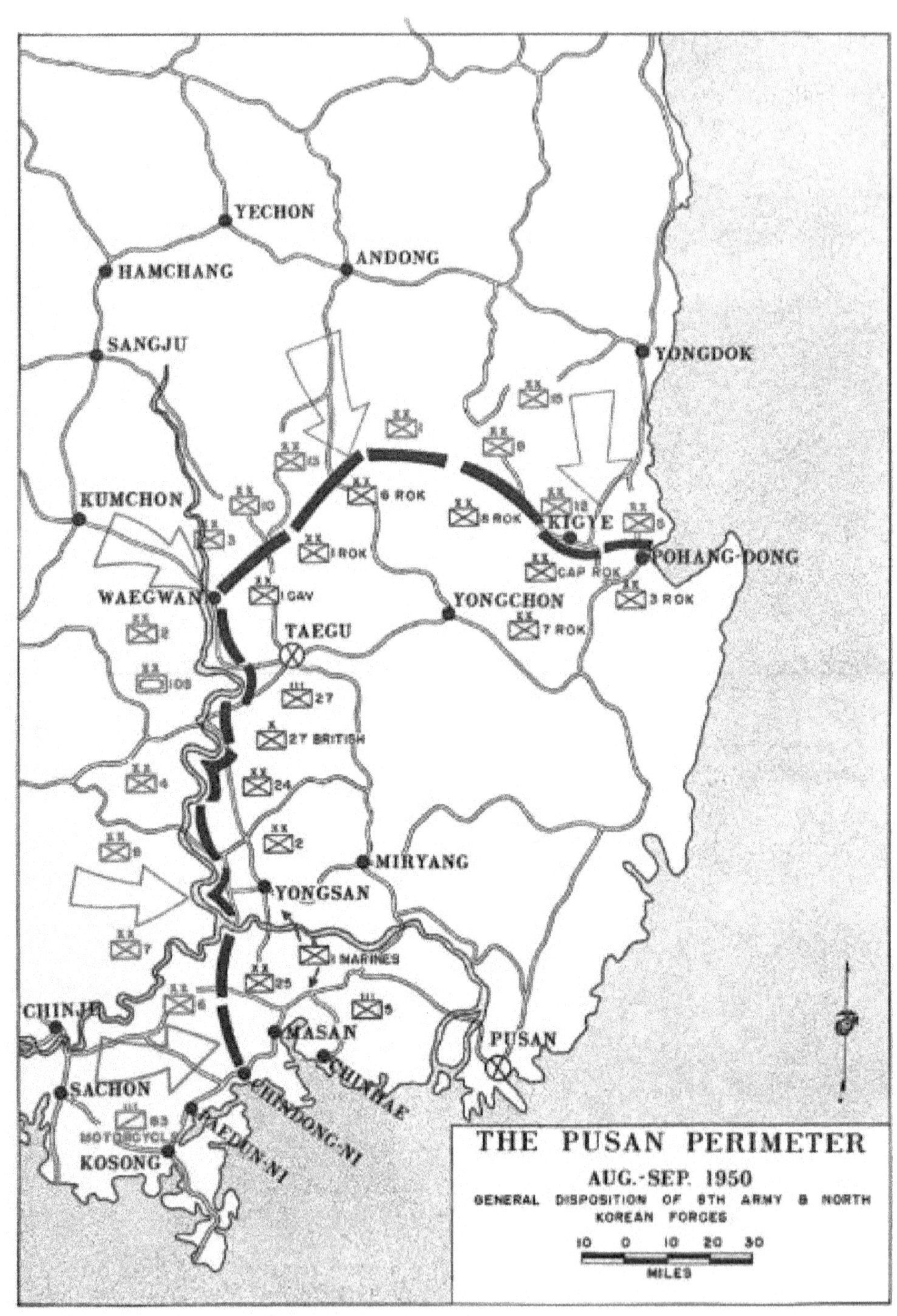

YECHON
HAMCHANG
ANDONG
SANGJU
YONGDOK
KUMCHON
6 ROK
8 ROK
12
5
KIGYE
1 ROK
POHANG-DONG
WAEGWAN
1 CAV
CAP ROK
3 ROK
TAEGU
YONGCHON
7 ROK
2
108
27
27 BRITISH
24
2
MIRYANG
9
YONGSAN
7
1 MARINES
25
5
6
CHINJU
MASAN
PUSAN
SACHON
CHINHAE
63
MOTORCYCLE
CHINDONG-NI
KOSONG
HAEDUN-NI
THE PUSAN PERIMETER
AUG.-SEP. 1950
GENERAL DISPOSITION OF 8TH ARMY & NORTH
KOREAN FORCES
10   0   10   20   30
MILES

Not long after the brigade landed at Pusan on August 2nd, 1950, I was given my baptism by fire with the men of Third Platoon, Dog Company. Pinned down in a ditch by a North Korean machine gunner camouflaged with branches, my initial thought was the enemy looked a lot like the bad guys in movies. The next was to get focused and do the job I was trained for. As things developed, the first photograph I took in combat was godawful. The one I should have taken was of the platoon's mustang second lieutenant, a battle-tested World War Two vet named Dutch Emmelman, who stood over his men as bullets whistled past, exhorting them (and me) to stop cowering and act like Marines.

It was during combat at Pusan that I discovered how surprisingly difficult war is to photograph—not because of the danger involved, but because even the most savage firefight can appear tame in a picture. The key to capturing combat, I would learn, was to freeze in time those moments that declare, without question, that this is war; from infantrymen passing a burning building to taking enemy prisoners at gunpoint.

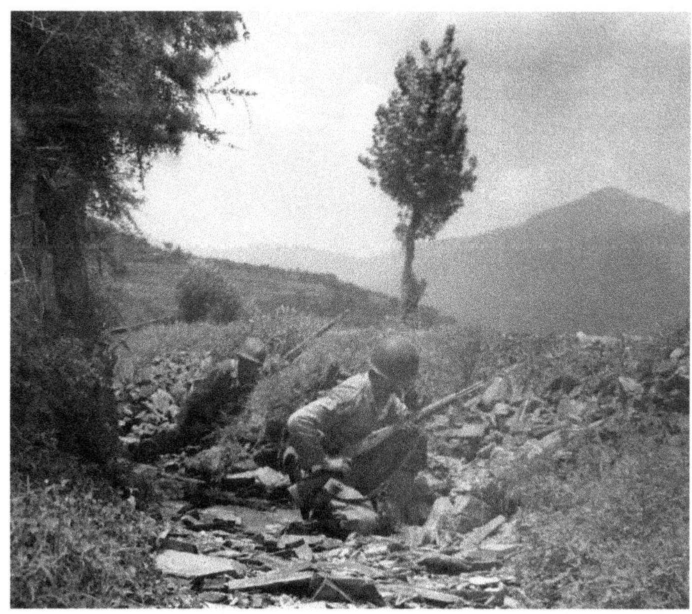

Marines of the 1st Brigade take cover during a North Korean ambush in the Pusan Perimeter. (Photo by Sgt. Frank C. Kerr, USMC)

When the brigade was folded into the reactivated 1st Marine Division and inserted behind the communist lines at Inchon, I applied those lessons on Wolmi-do, a heavily fortified island in Inchon Harbor that our ground forces captured after a merciless bombardment from the air and sea. With the Marines now sweeping inland from Inchon to retake the South Korean capital of Seoul, and the 8th Army finally breaking free of the Pusan Perimeter, the decimated and demoralized North Korean Army fled north, chased by United Nations forces toward the Yalu River on the Manchurian border.

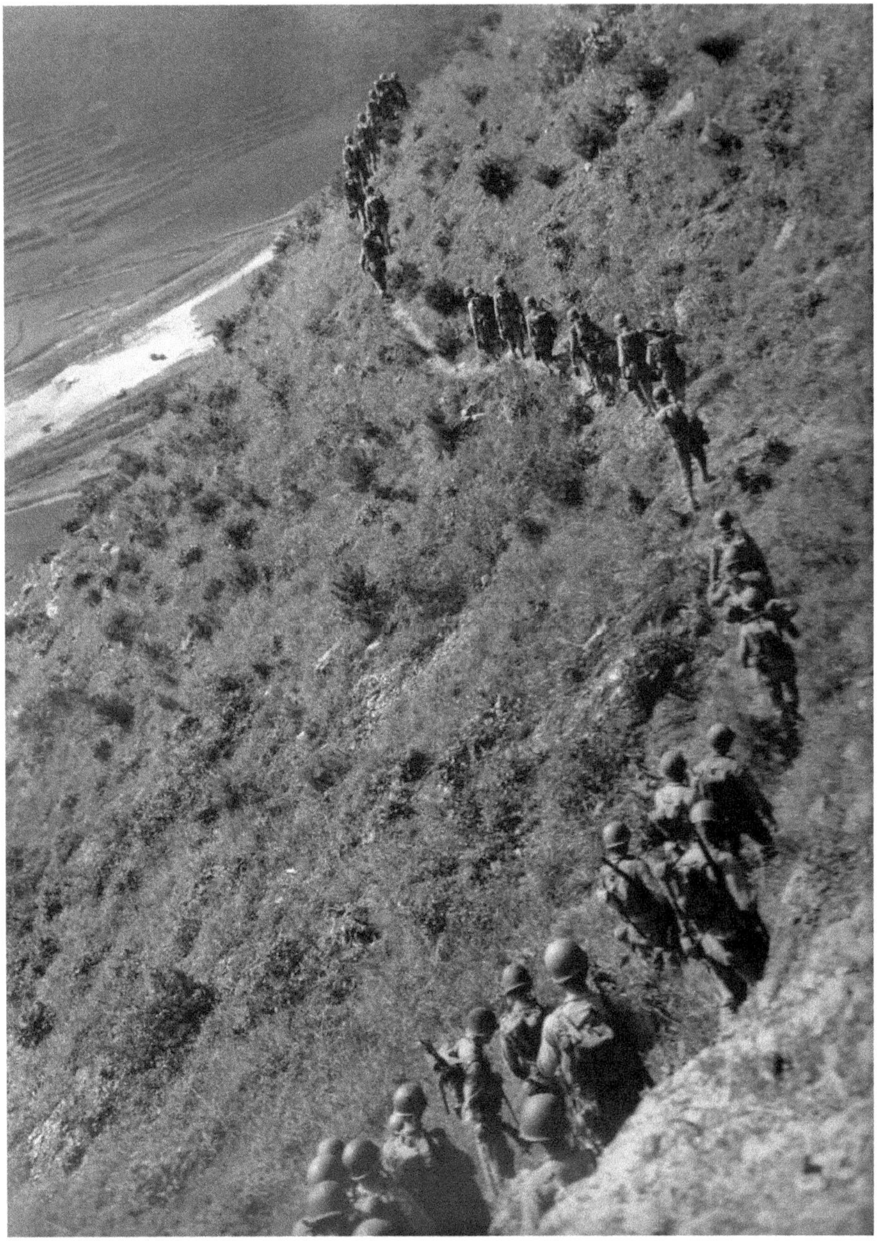

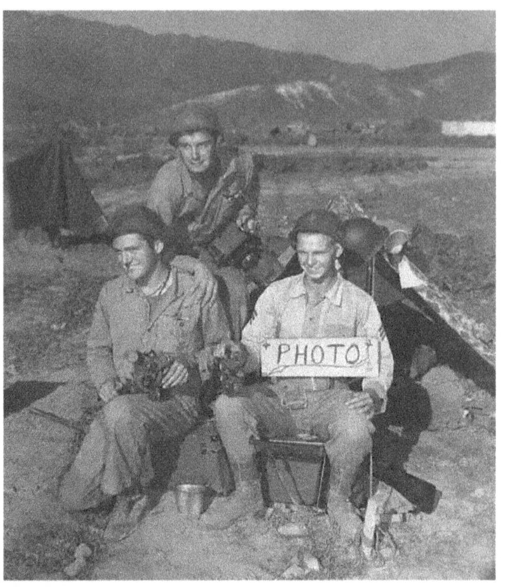

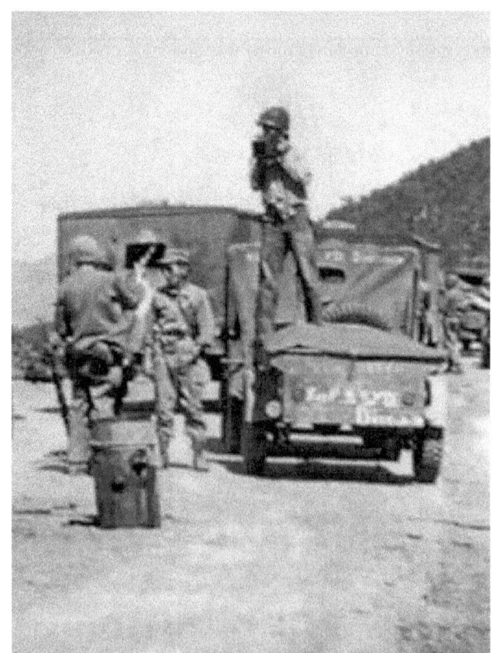

Opposite page: Newly deployed troops of the 1st Provisional Marine Brigade move out over rugged terrain to engage enemy forces in the Pusan Perimeter. *(Photo by Sgt. Frank C. Kerr, USMC)* **Top right:** The first three Marines to capture the Korean War on film. L-R: Combat cameraman Cpl. John Flynn, combat photographer Sgt. Frank Kerr, combat cameraman Cpl. Jake McKay. *(National Archives Photo, USMC)* **Bottom right:** Sgt. Kerr stands atop a trailer to frame a shot with his camera. *(National Archives Photo, USMC)* **Below:** Marines advance under heavy small arms and machinegun fire during action in the Pusan Perimeter, August 1950. *(Photo by Sgt. Frank C. Kerr, USMC)*

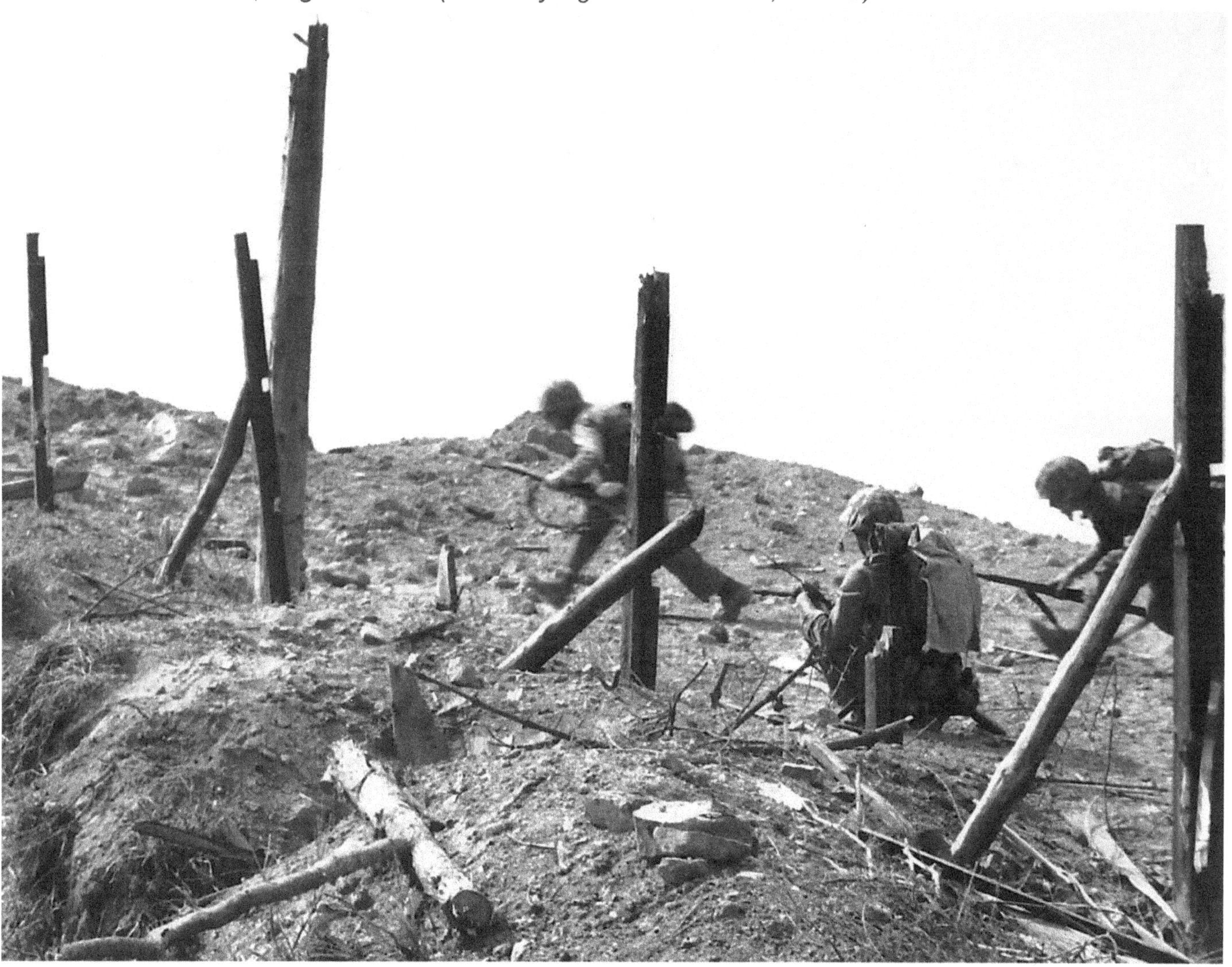

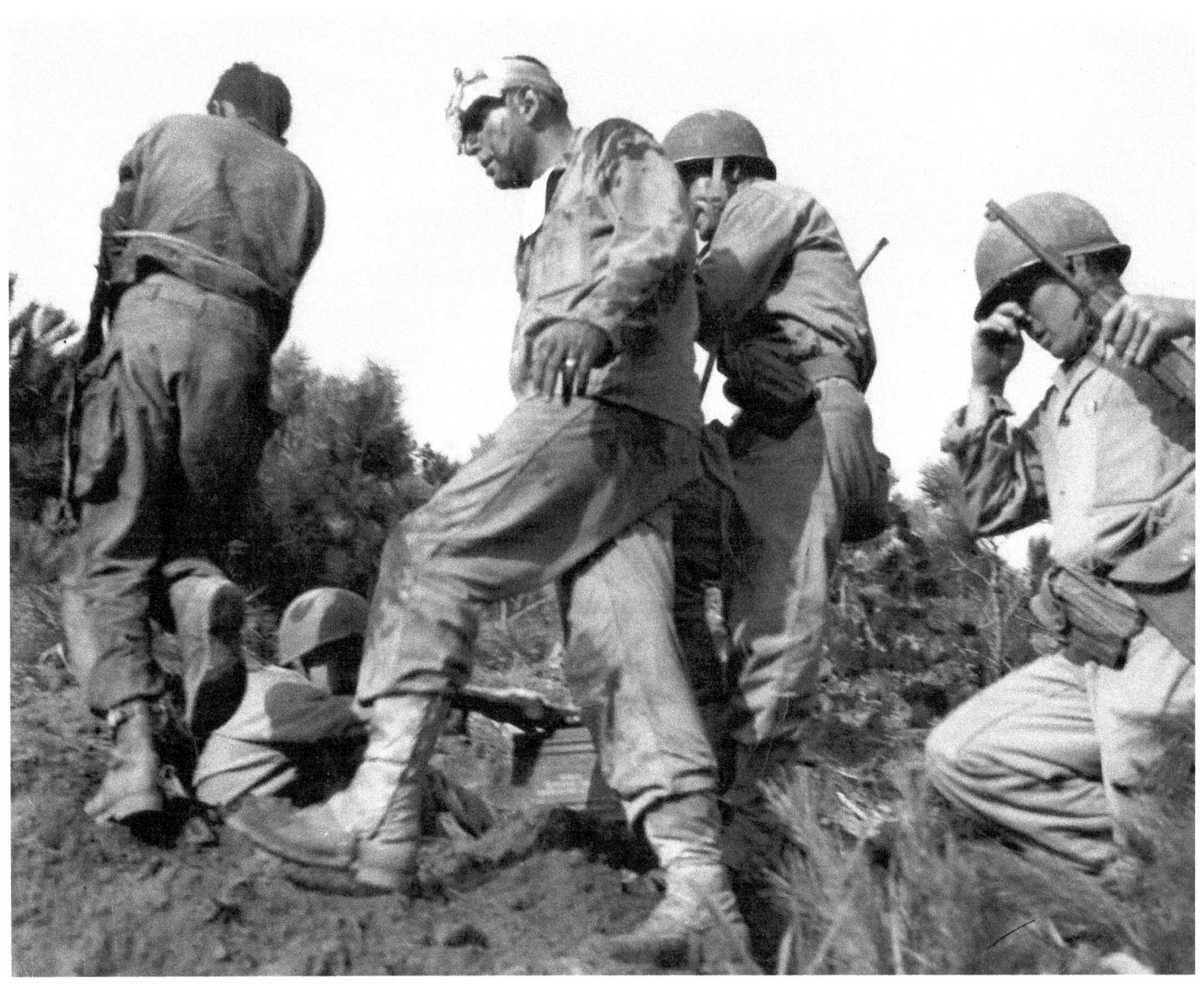

Marine wounded are led to a first aid station during fighting in the Pusan Perimeter. *Opposite page:* Marine patrol meets no opposition while cresting a hill in August, 1950. *Bottom left:* North Korean prisoners are marched from the front lines after being stripped to insure they carry no concealed weapons. Rear-echelon commanders later put a stop to this practice. *Bottom right:* PFC Harold Bates and PFC Richard Martin take a break following action in the Pusan Perimeter. *(Photos by Sgt. Frank C. Kerr, USMC)*

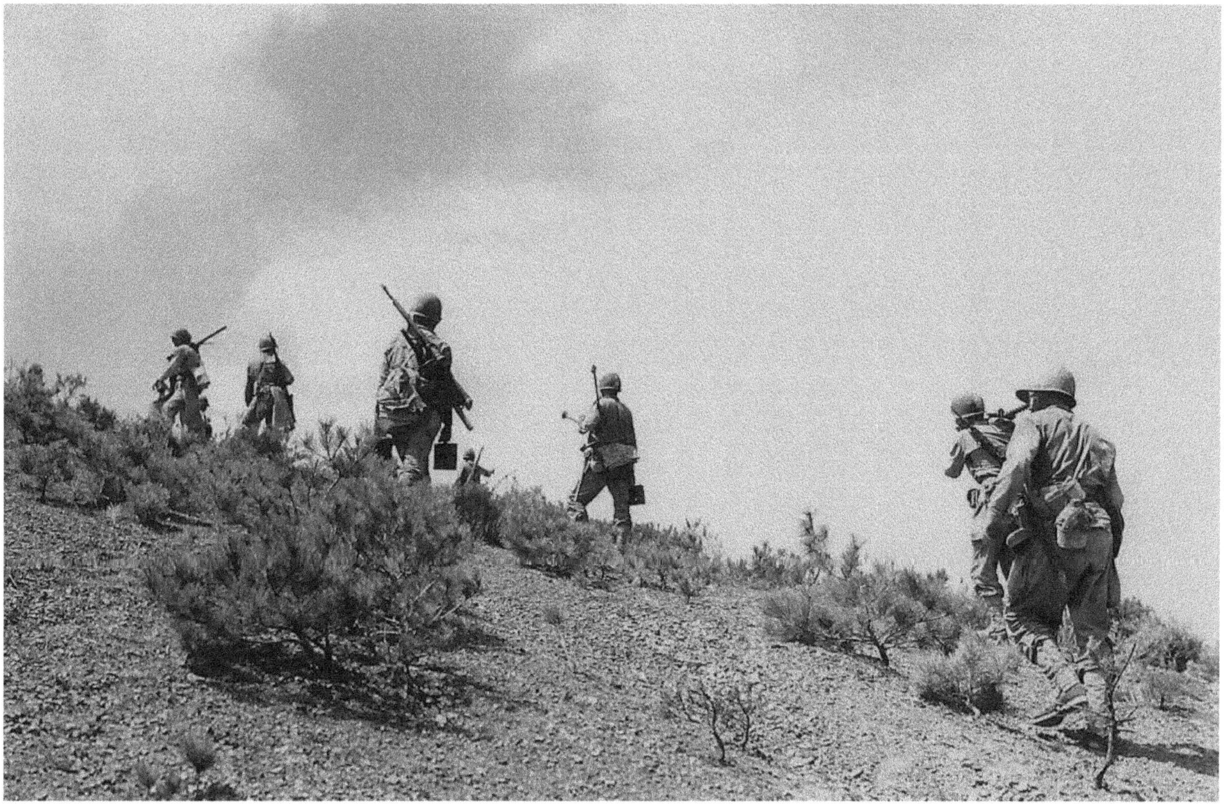

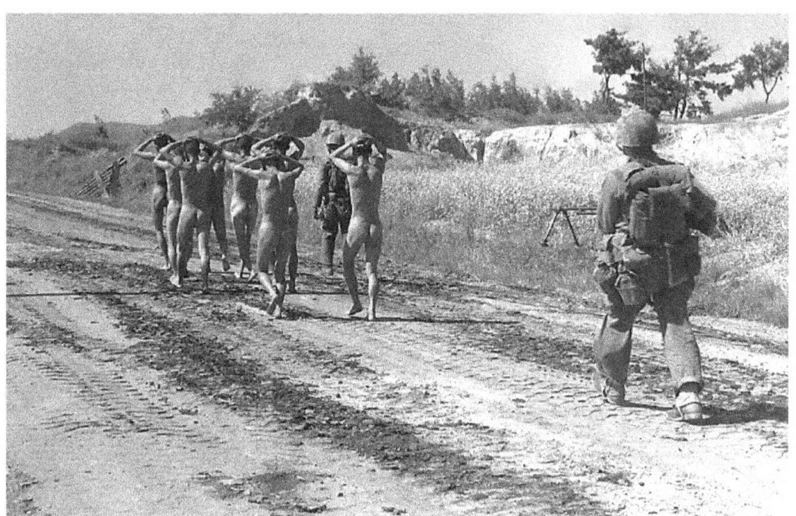

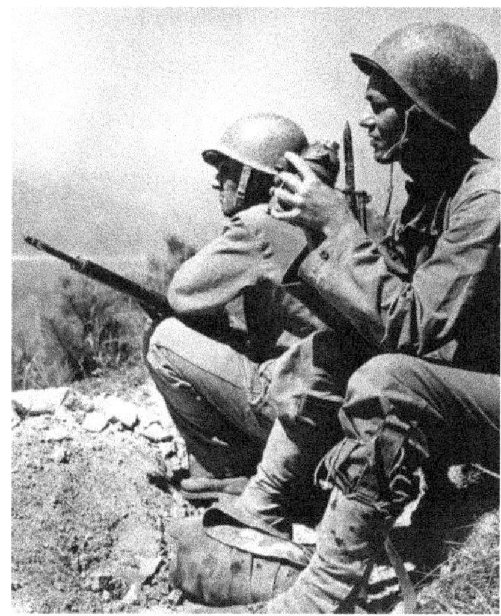

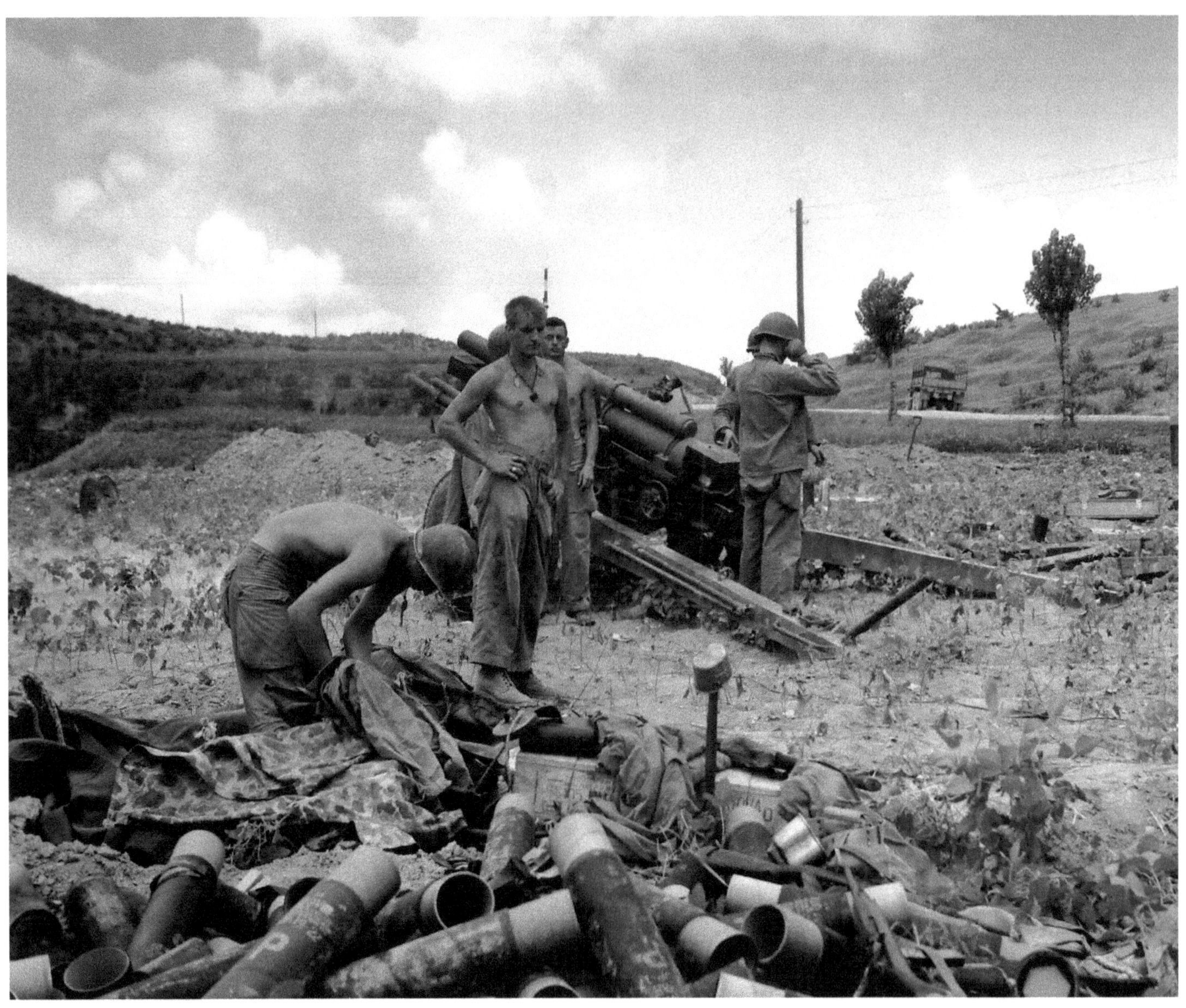

August, 1950. Marine artillery softens up communist positions prior to the 1st Provisional Marine Brigade's Naktong River offensive ***Opposite page:*** Marines advancing toward South Korea's Naktong River move past a burning North Korean T-34 tank, giving it a wide berth as a safeguard against exploding ammunition. *(Photos by Sgt. Frank C. Kerr, USMC)*

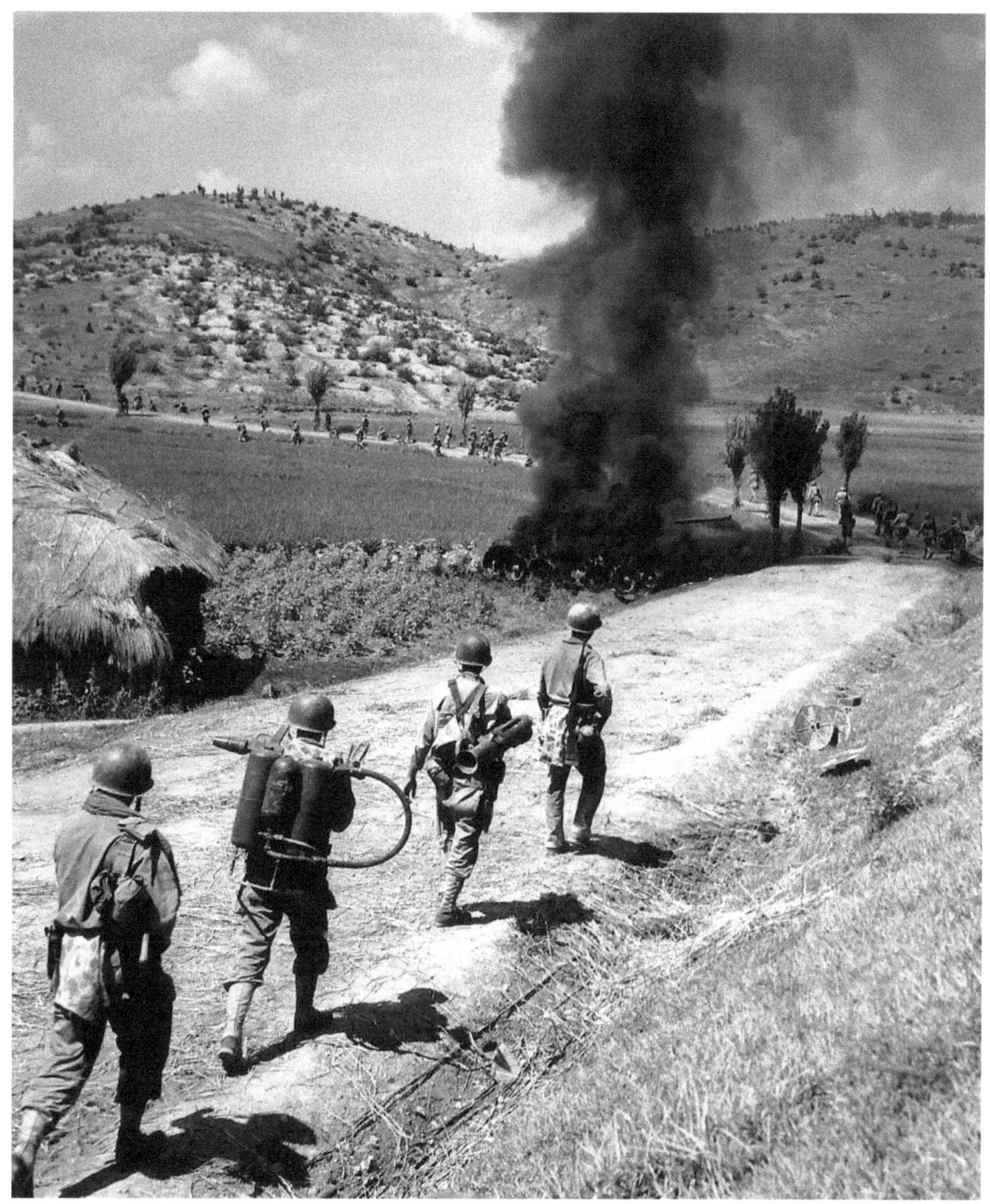

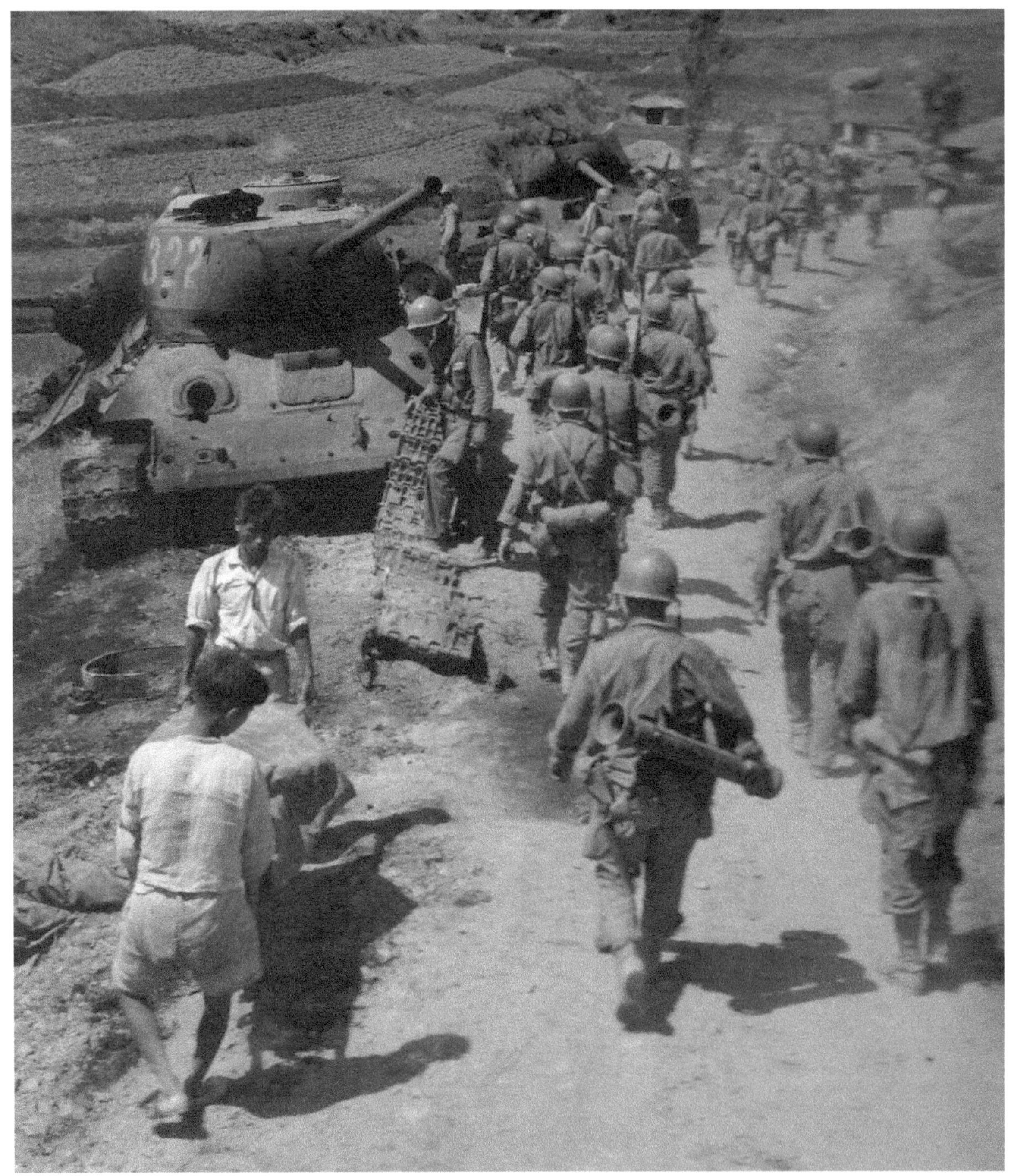

Opposite page: During their advance toward the Naktong, US Marines pass three North Korean tanks knocked out in a battle with American M26 Pershing tanks. In foreground, South Korean civilians remove U.S. Marine dead. *Below*: Leathernecks pause to examine the wreck of one of the Soviet built T-34s. *(Photos by Sgt. Frank C. Kerr, USMC)*

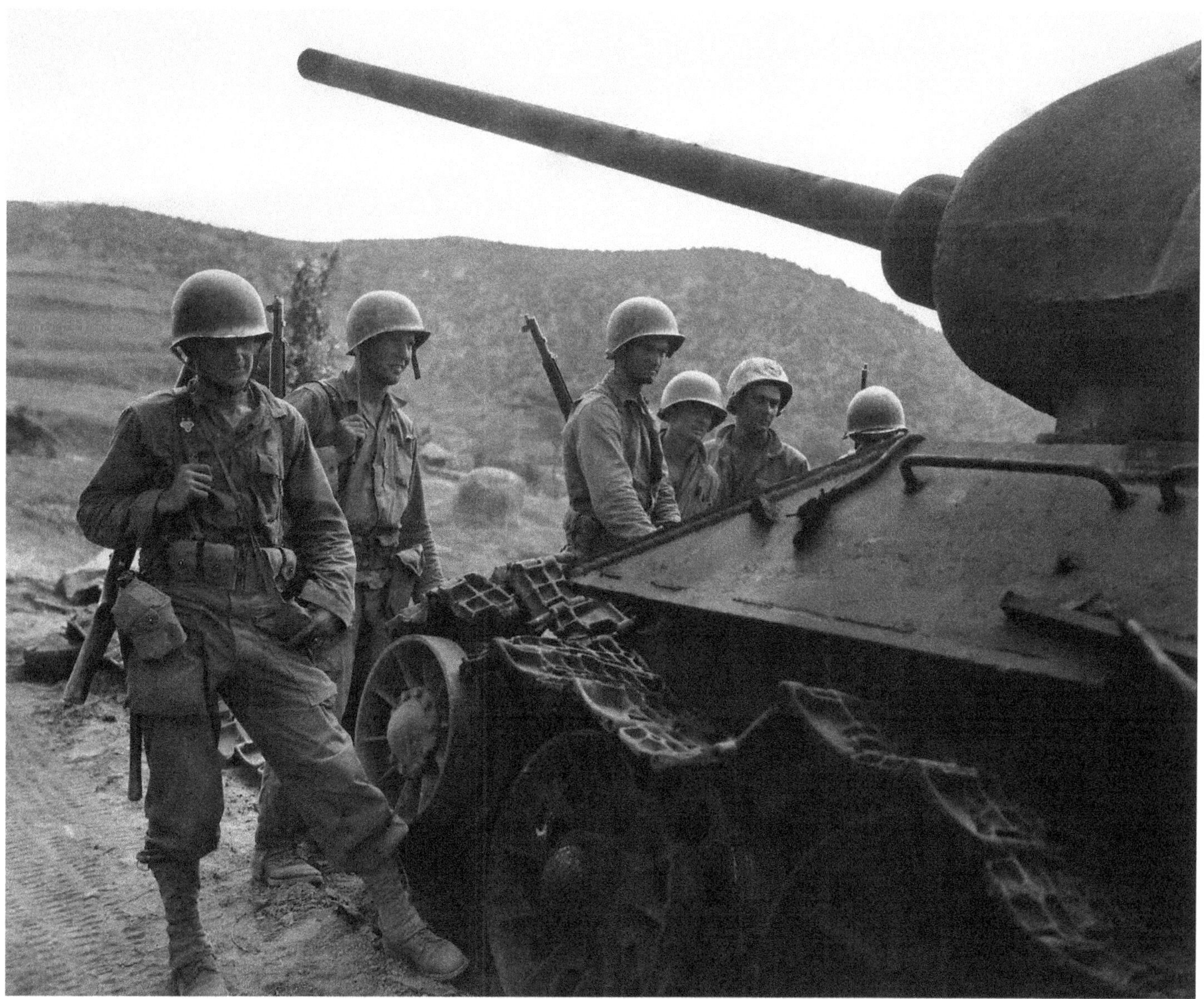

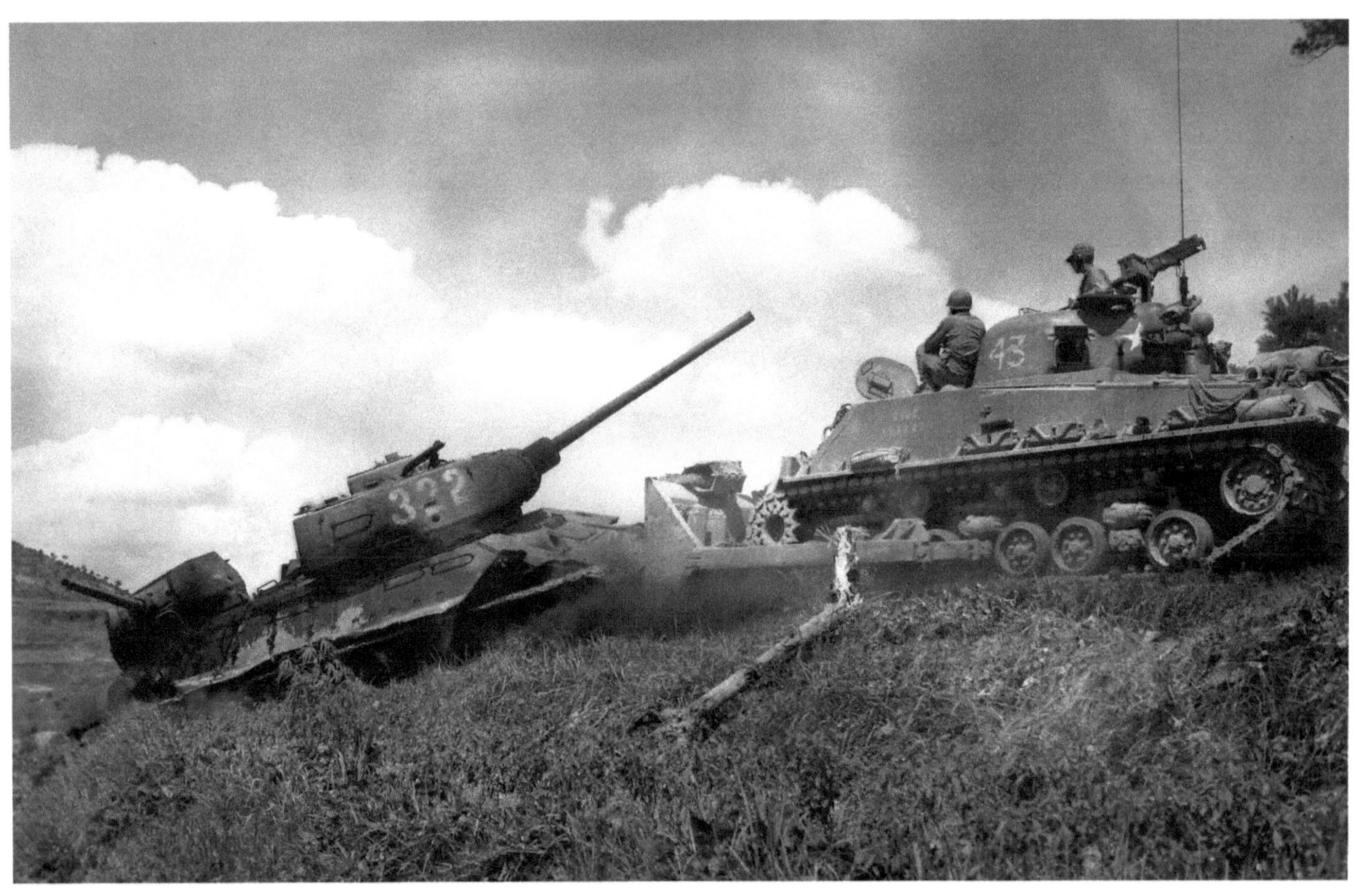

A Marine bulldozer tank pushes a destroyed T-34 off the road to make way for advancing troops. *Opposite page:* Hot and tired men of the 1st Provisional Marine Brigade relax on a hilltop overlooking the Naktong River in South Korea. August 19th, 1950. *(Photo by Sgt. Frank C. Kerr, USMC)*

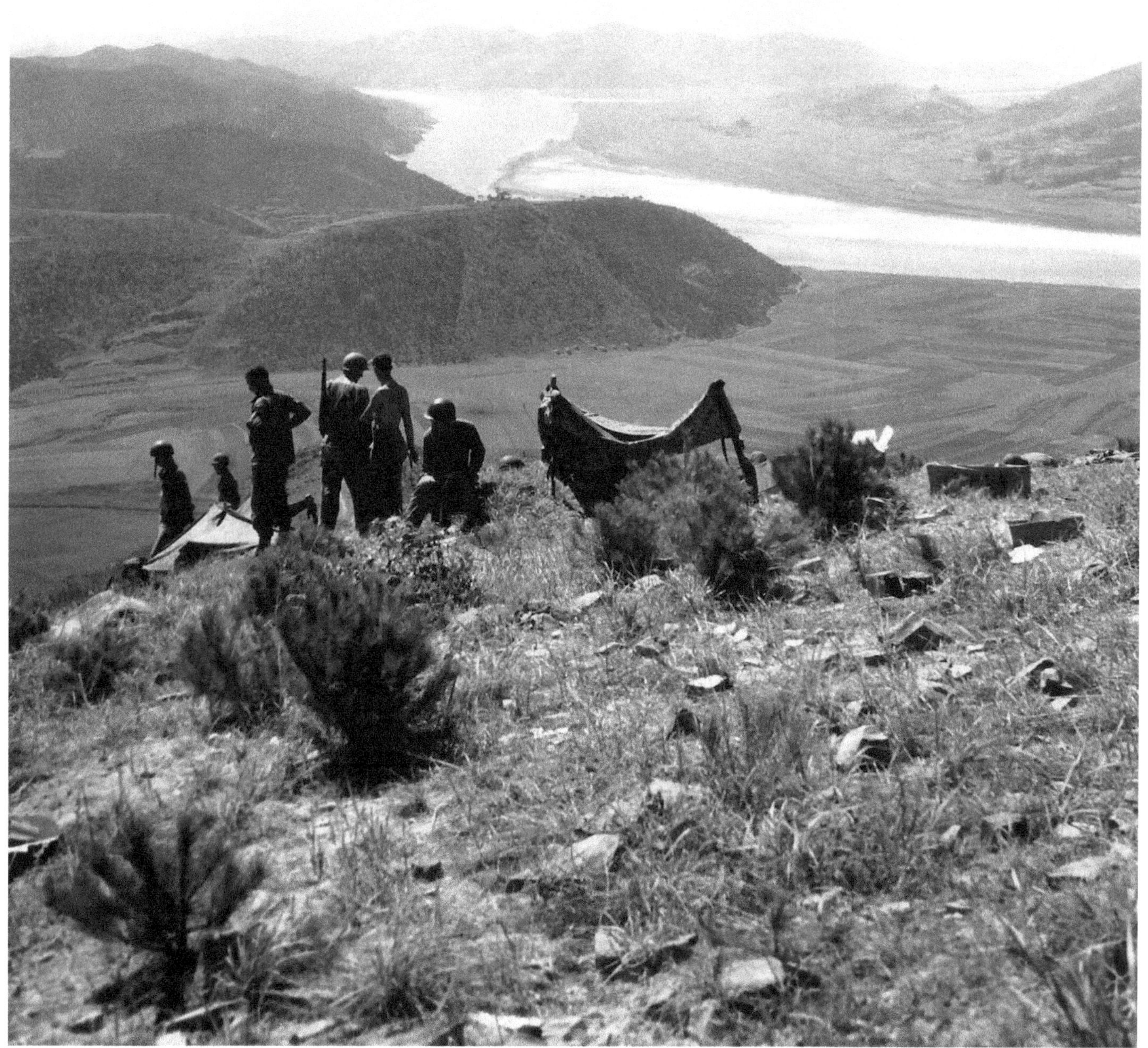

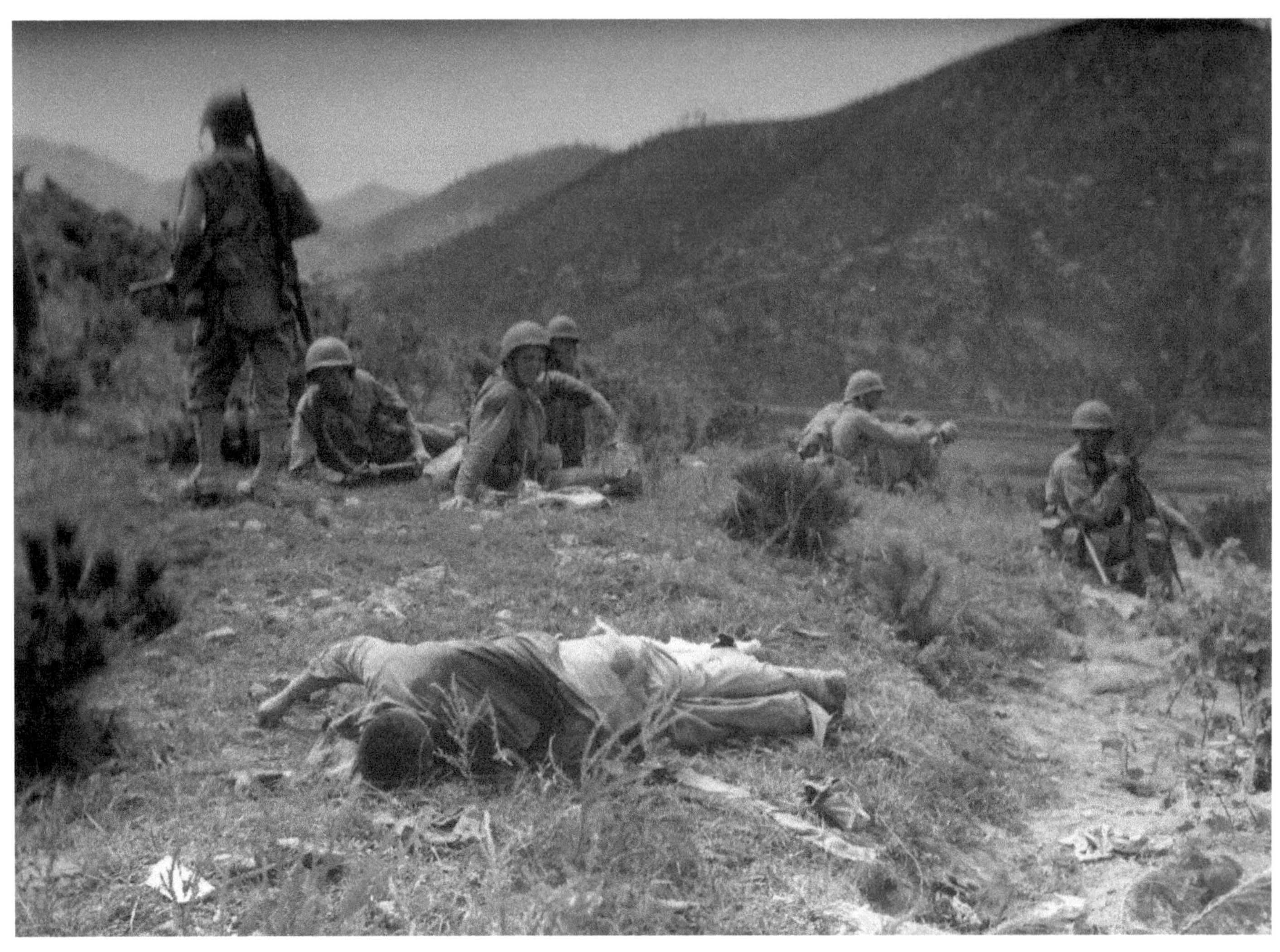

Leathernecks of the 1st Provisional Marine Brigade pause for rest near the body of a North Korean soldier killed in action at the Naktong. *(Photo by Sgt. Frank C. Kerr, USMC)*

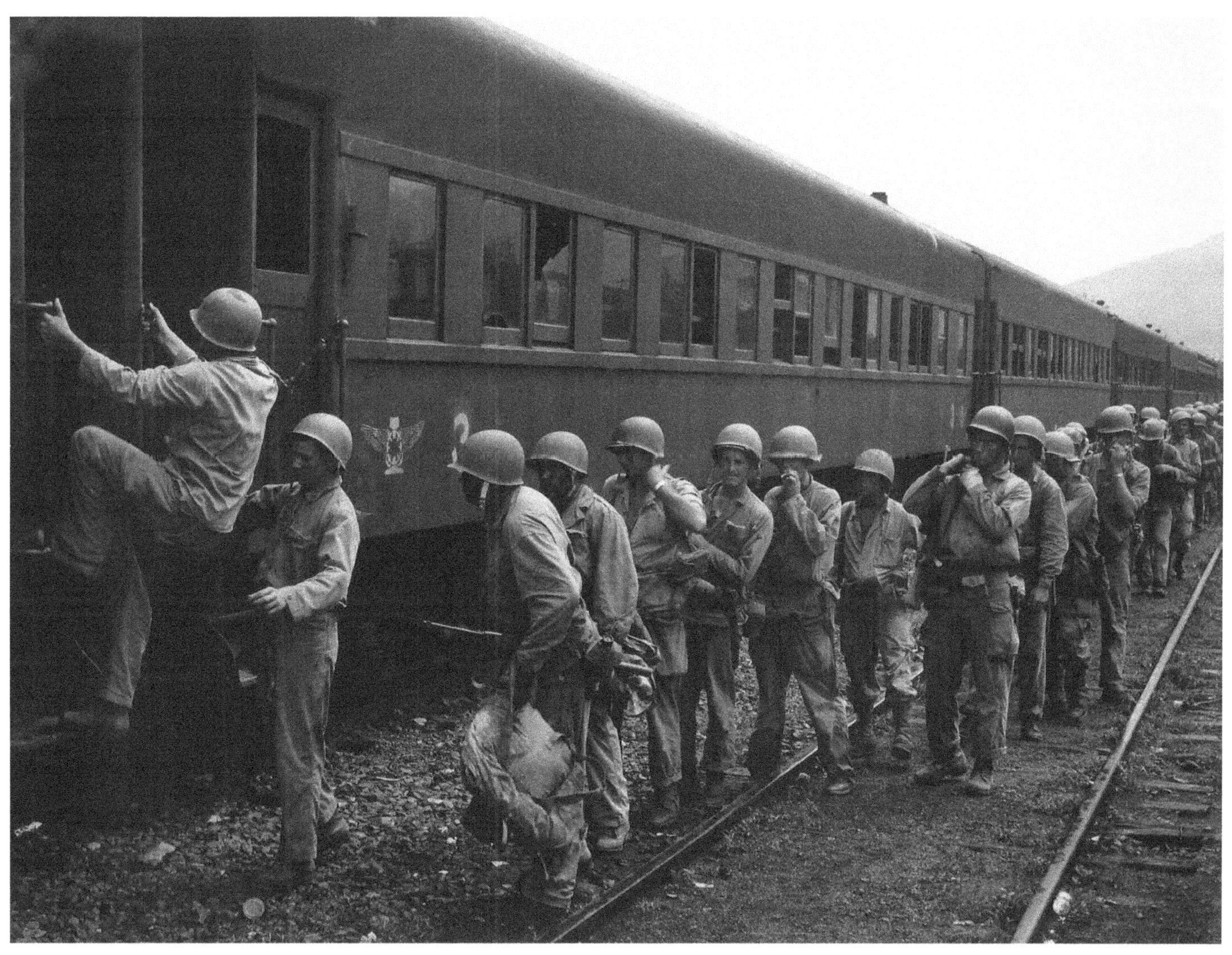

Tired, bearded and hungry, these Marine veterans of combat in the Pusan Perimeter climb aboard a train taking them to their next battlefront. *(Photo by Sgt. Frank C. Kerr, USMC)*

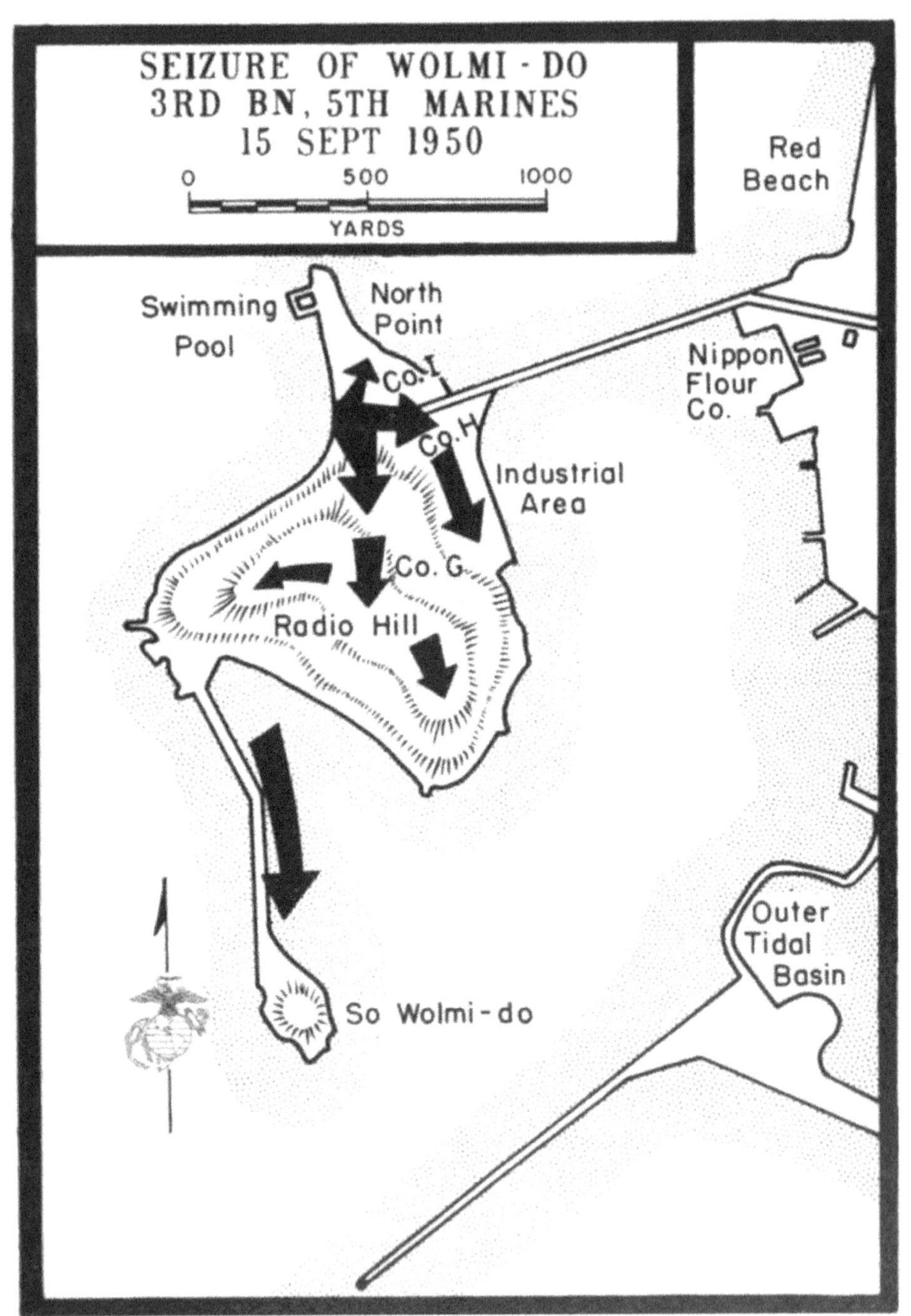
SEIZURE OF WOLMI-DO
3RD BN, 5TH MARINES
15 SEPT 1950
0   500   1000
YARDS
Swimming
Pool
North
Point
Co. I
Co. H
Industrial
Area
Co. G
Radio Hill
So Wolmi-do
Red
Beach
Nippon
Flour
Co.
Outer
Tidal
Basin

WOLMI-DO ISLAND

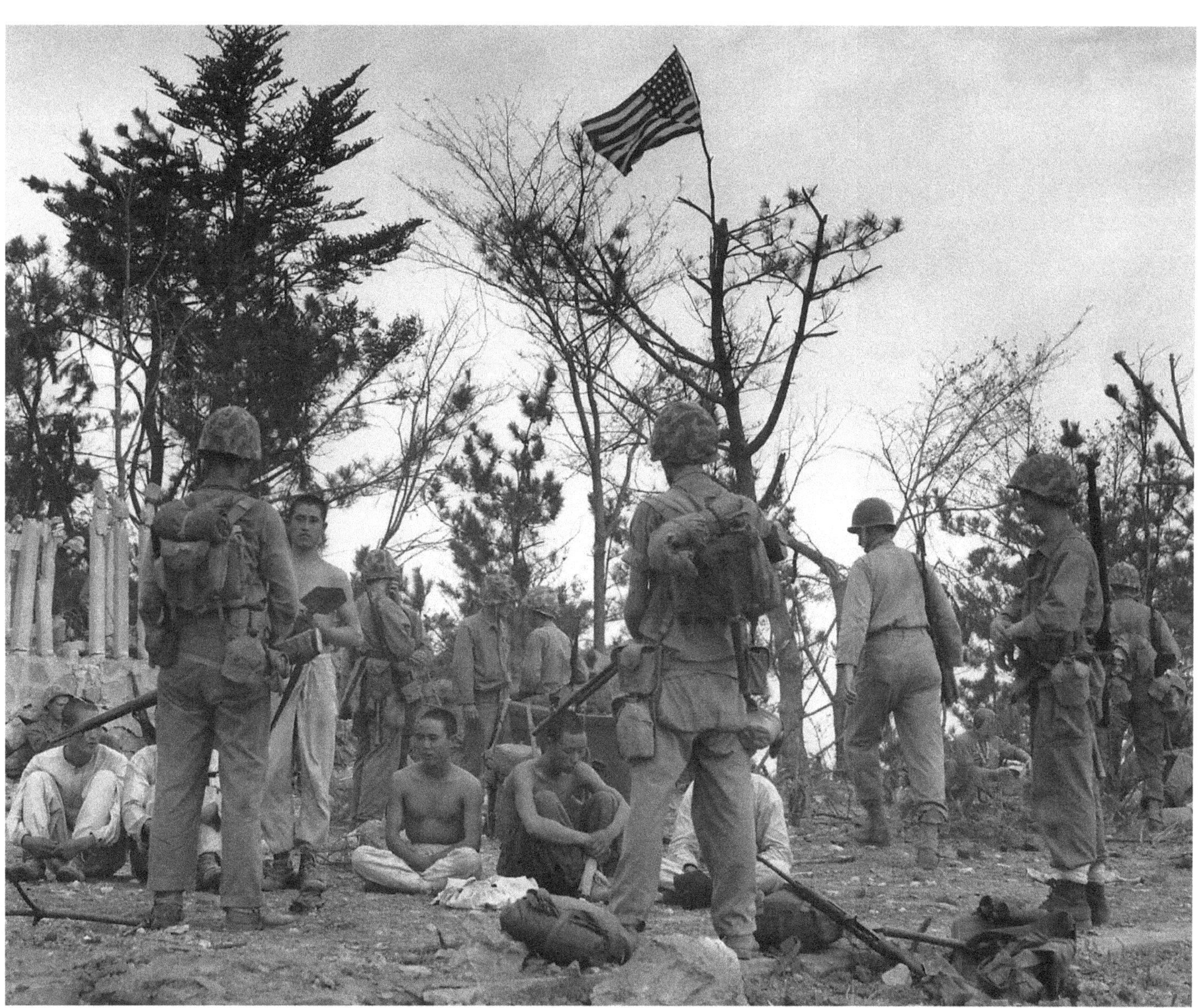

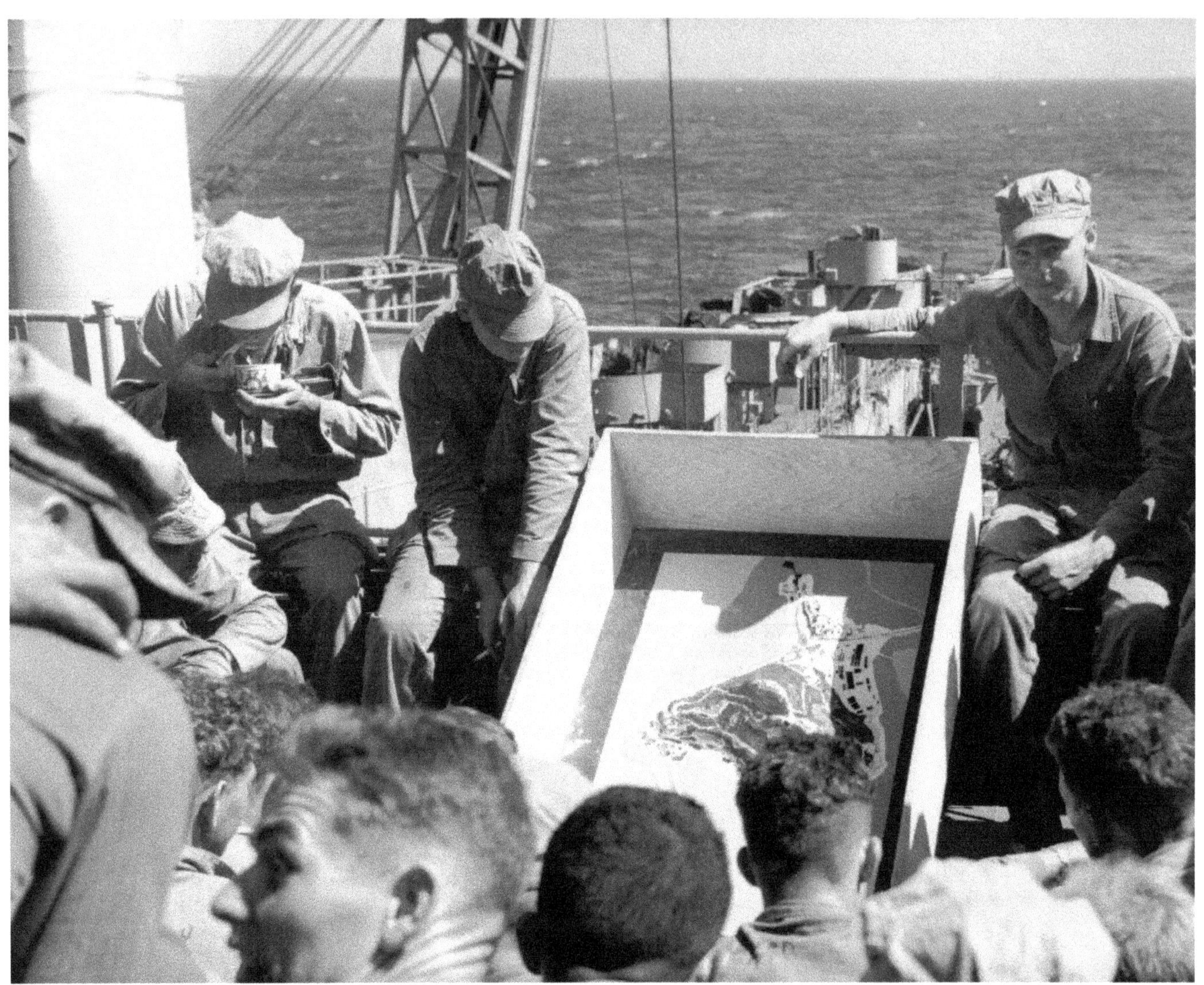

Aboard ship prior to the Inchon invasion, a briefing officer uses a scale model to familiarize Marines of the 3rd Battalion, 5th Marine Regiment with their first objective; the island of Wolmi-do, gateway to Inchon. ***Opposite page top:*** D-Day at Inchon, September 15, 1950. Shortly after dawn, Wolmi-do Island is aflame following a relentless naval bombardment. ***Bottom:*** "Green Beach" on Wolmi-do, where troops of the 1st Marine Division went ashore. In the background, warships of the invasion fleet provide fire support from Inchon Harbor. *(Photos by Sgt. Frank C. Kerr, USMC)*

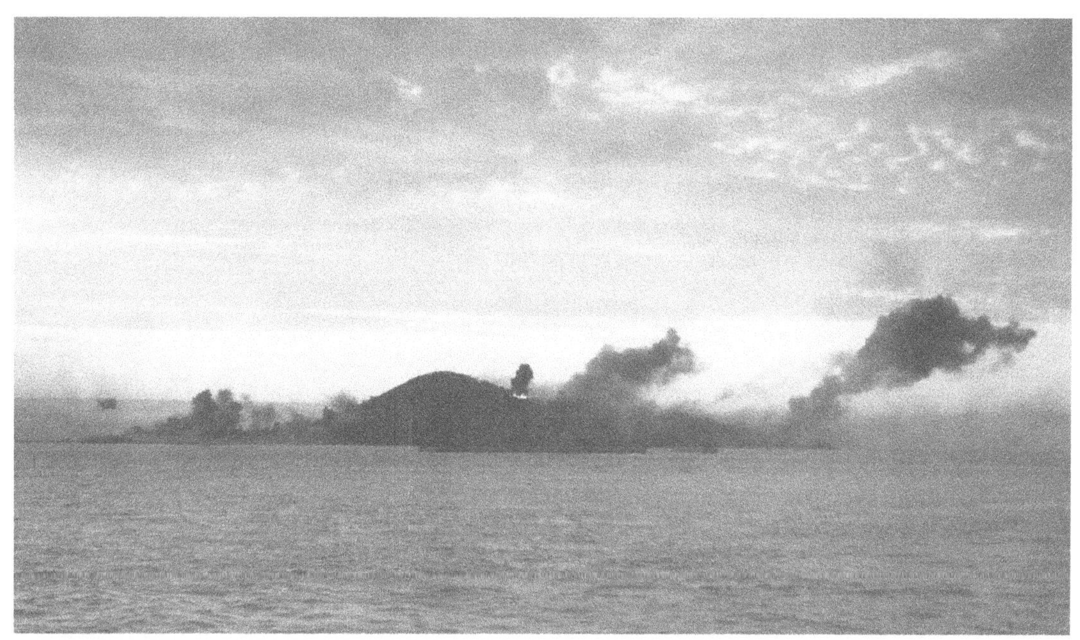

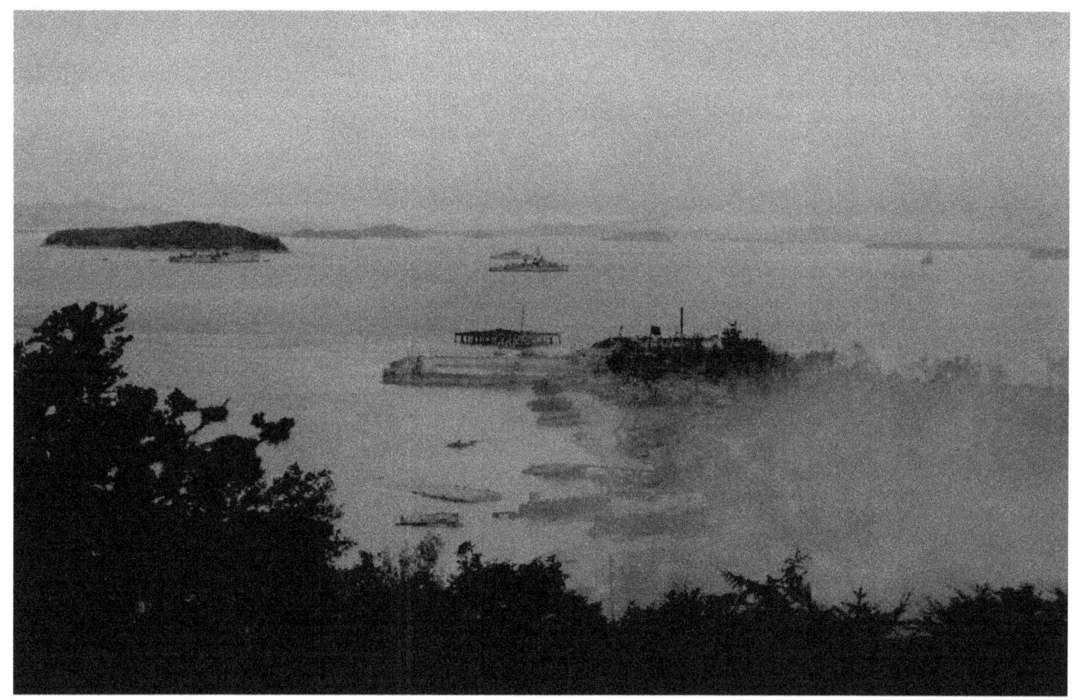

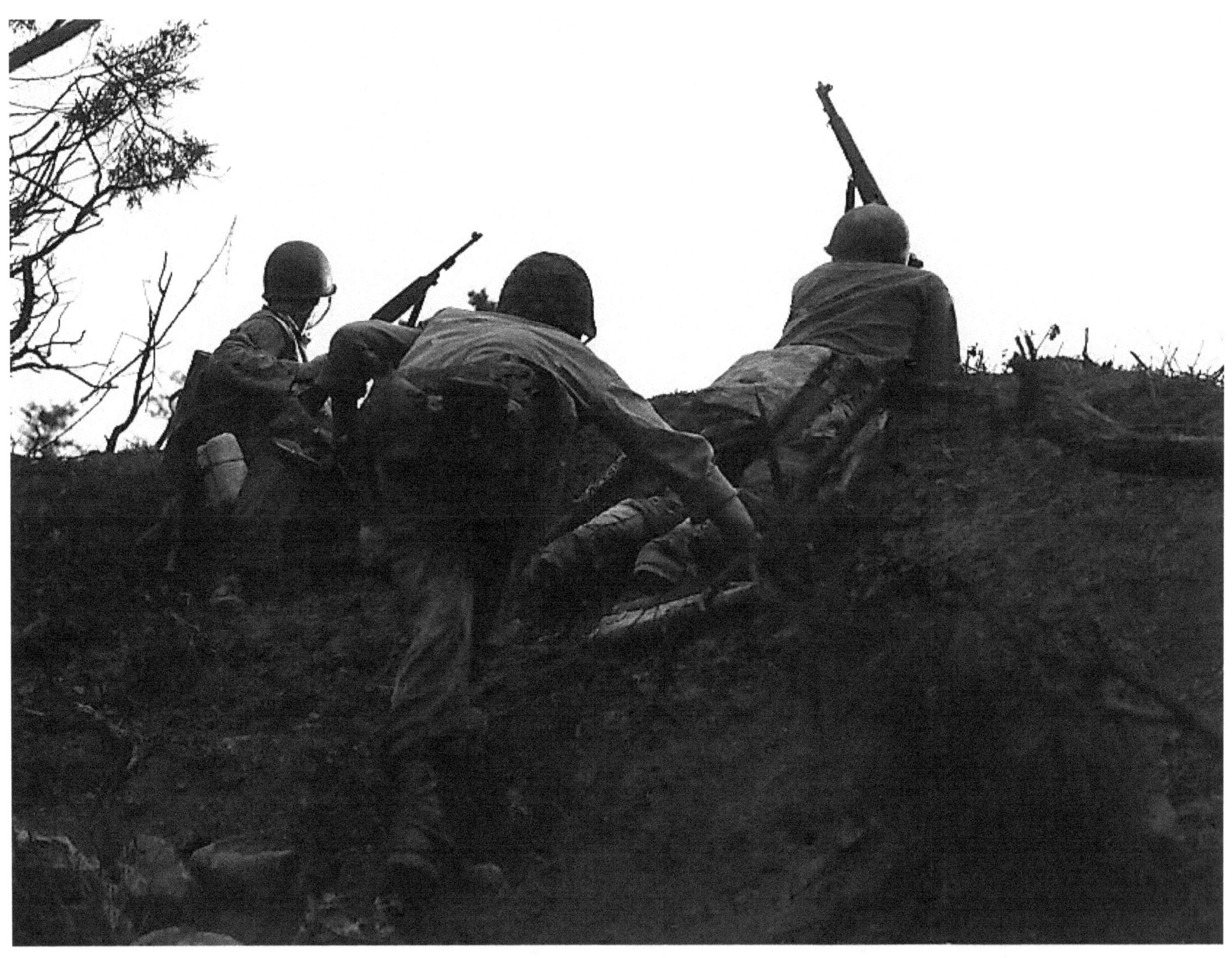

A fire team from the 3rd Battalion, 5th Marine regiment moves to knock out an enemy position during fierce fighting on Wolmi-do Island, September 15, 1950. *(Photo by Sgt. Frank C. Kerr, USMC)*

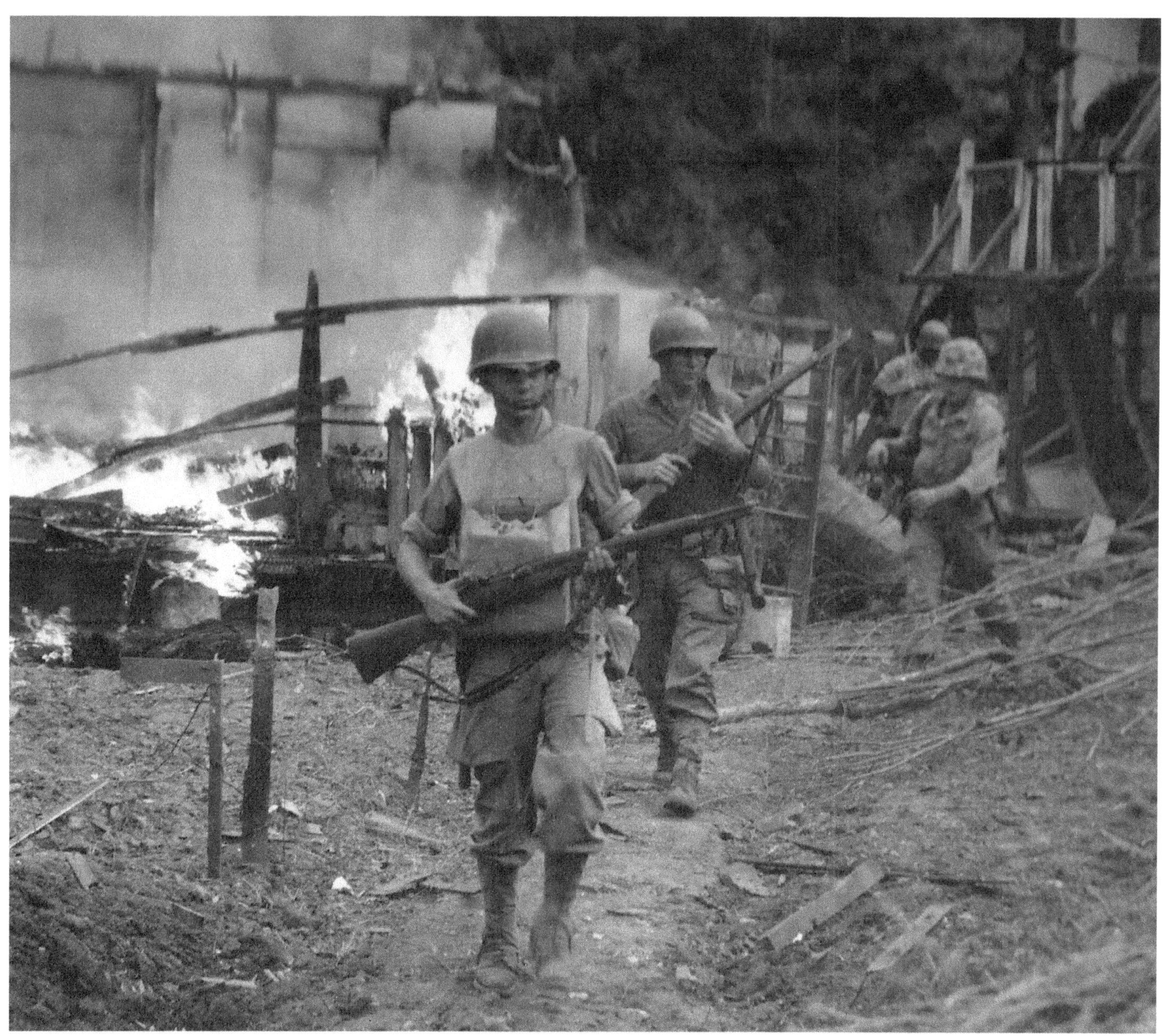

A Leatherneck patrol passes destroyed buildings on Wolmi-do. Note the standard issue canvas leggings worn by the lead Marine which would bleach and yellow over time. North Korean POW's told interrogators the "yellow legs" were the adversary their troops feared most. *(Photo by Sgt. Frank C. Kerr, USMC)*

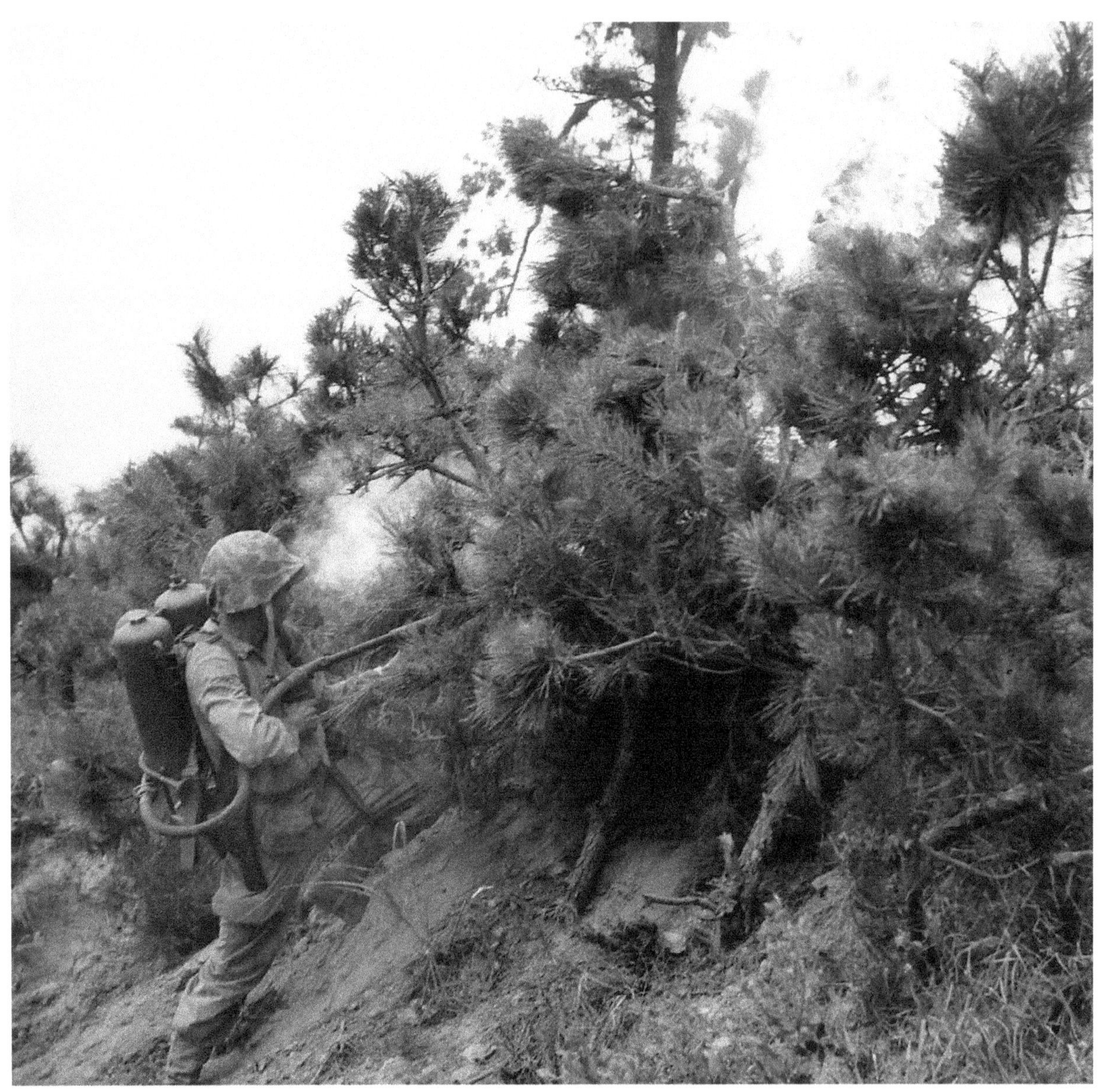

A Marine flamethrower goes to work on an enemy position at Wolmi-do. ***Opposite page top***: Marine infantry stand by while their bazooka man fires a round into a North Korean dugout after its occupants refused to surrender. ***Bottom left:*** A Marine squad cautiously approaches the dugout entrance. ***Bottom right:*** Flushed from their hiding place, these badly hurt North Koreans await medical treatment. *(Photos by Sgt. Frank C. Kerr, USMC)*

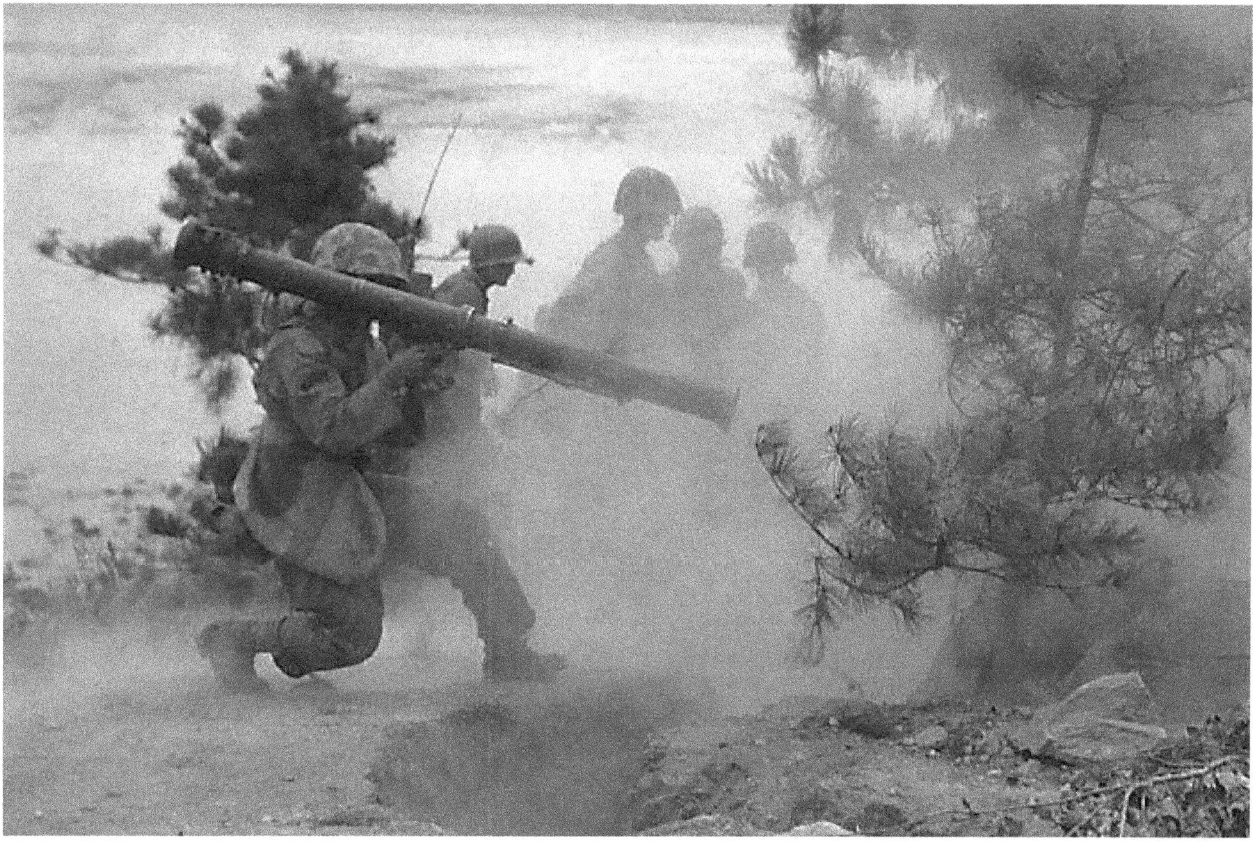

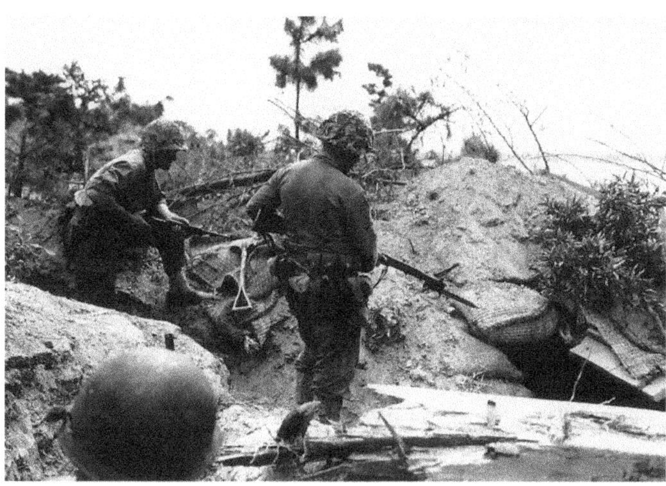

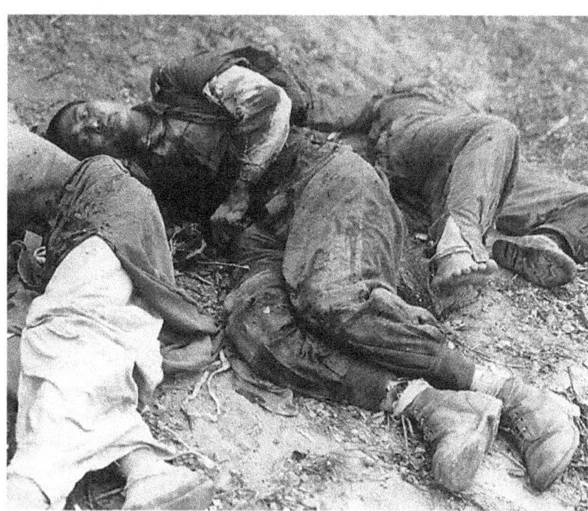

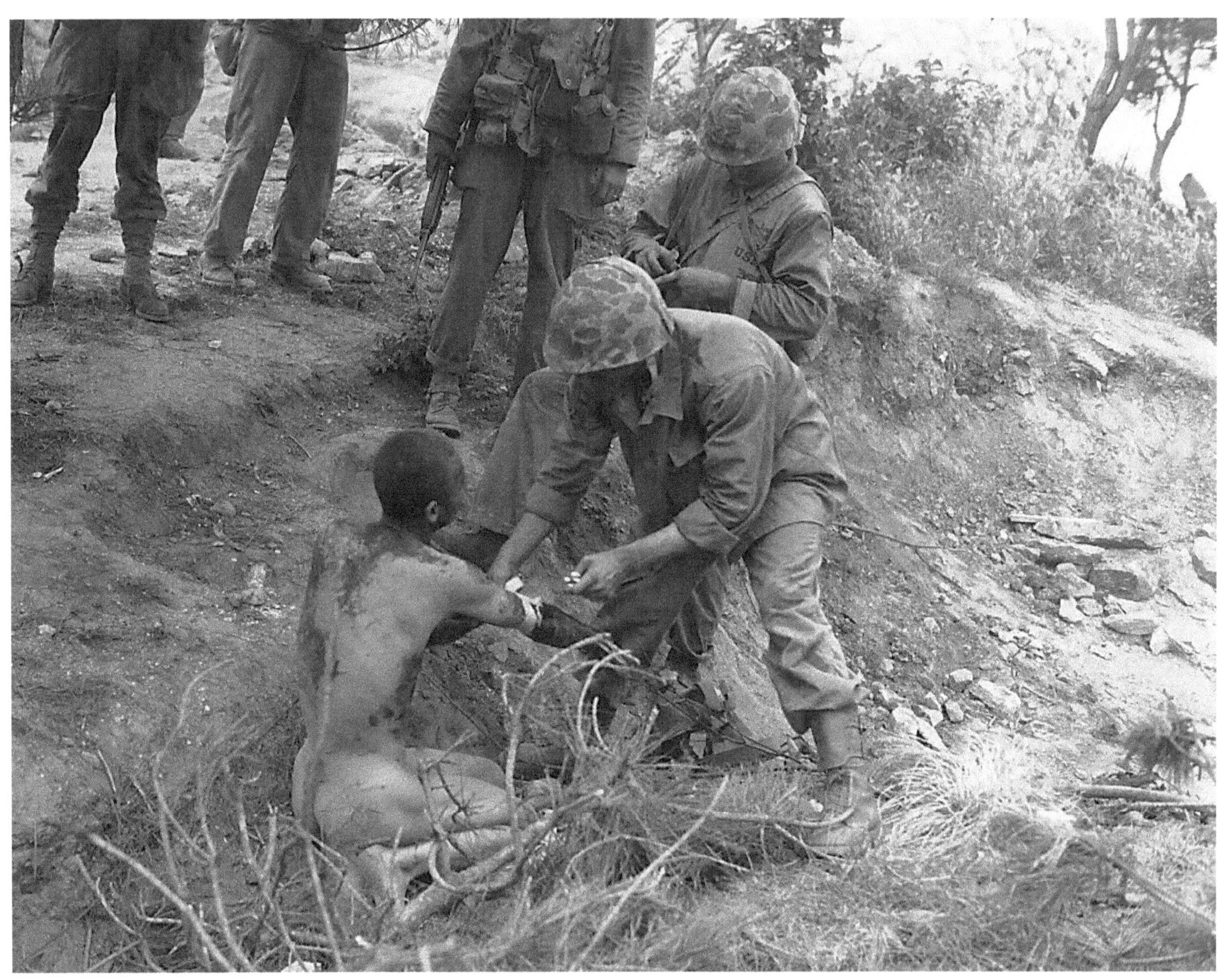

A wounded North Korean, stripped of his clothes following a search for concealed weapons, is administered first aid by a Navy hospital corpsman. Enemy combatants did not expect humane treatment from U.N. forces, but they were grateful for it. *(Photo by Sgt. Frank C. Kerr, USMC)*

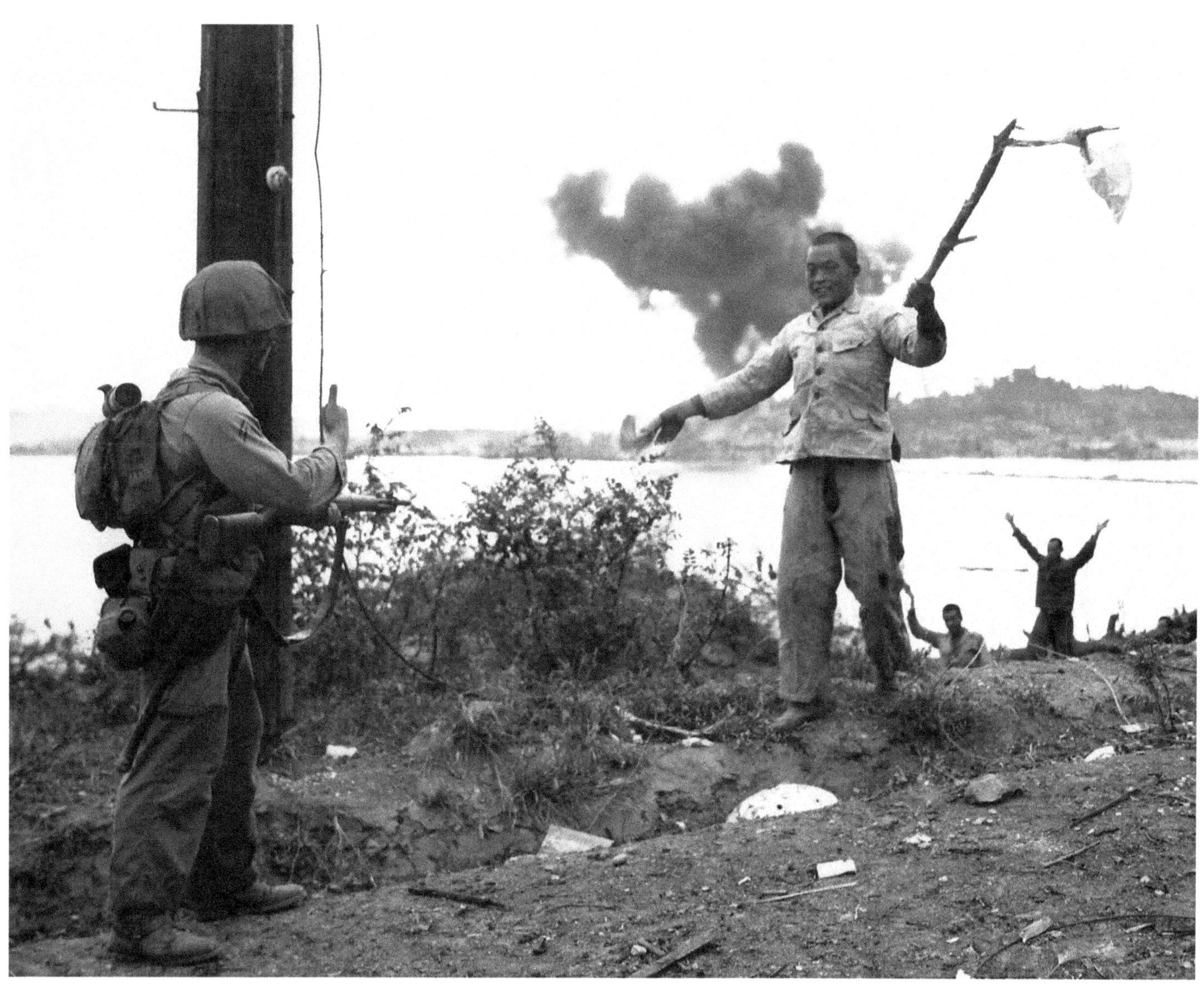

A surrendering North Korean soldier waves a white cloth as he leads his companions into the custody of U.S. Marines on Wolmi-do Island, September 15th 1950. *(Photo by Sgt. Frank C. Kerr, USMC)*

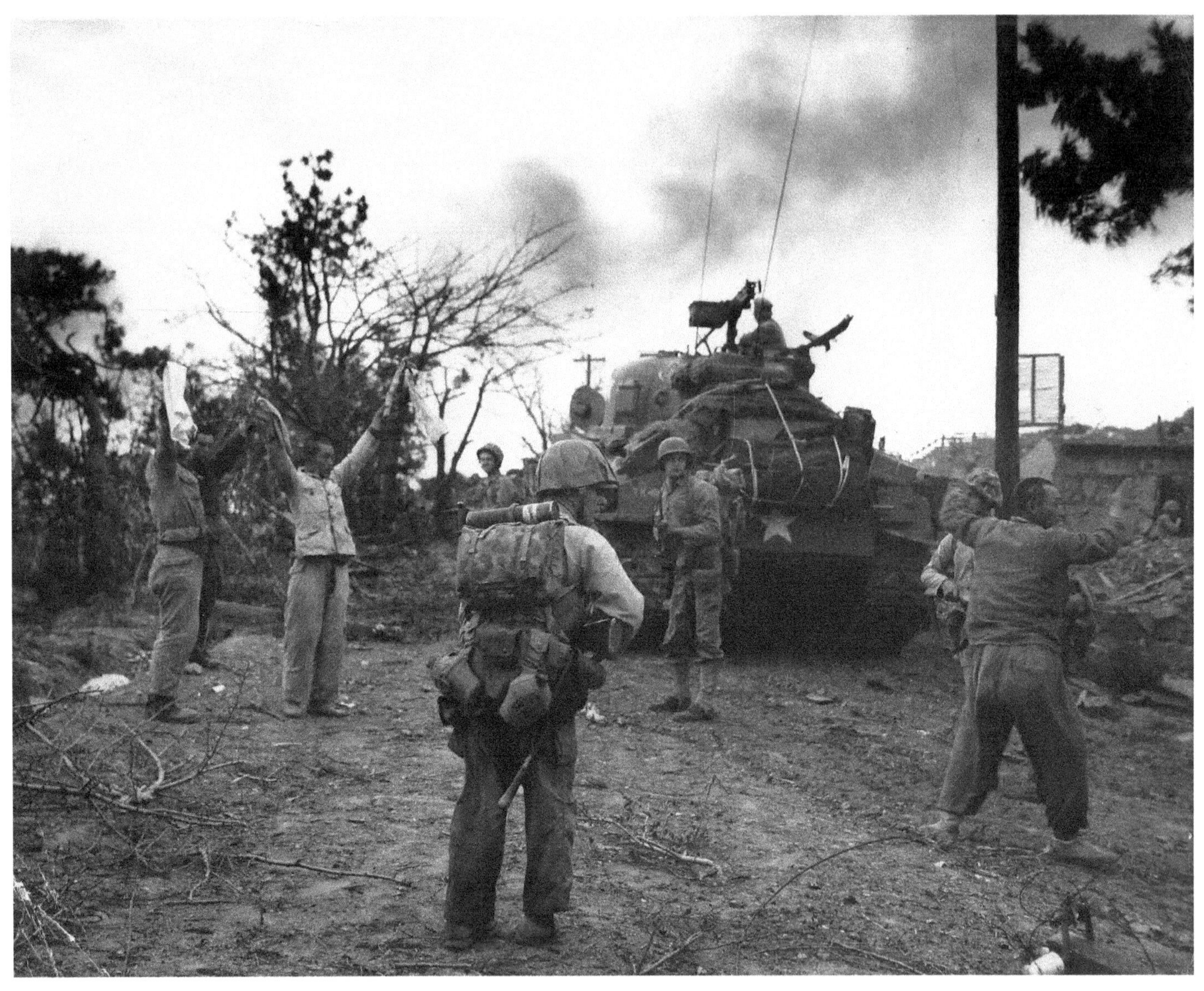

A tense moment between enemies as communist North Koreans begin surrendering to U.S. Marines for their own safety. *(Photo by Sgt. Frank C. Kerr, USMC)*

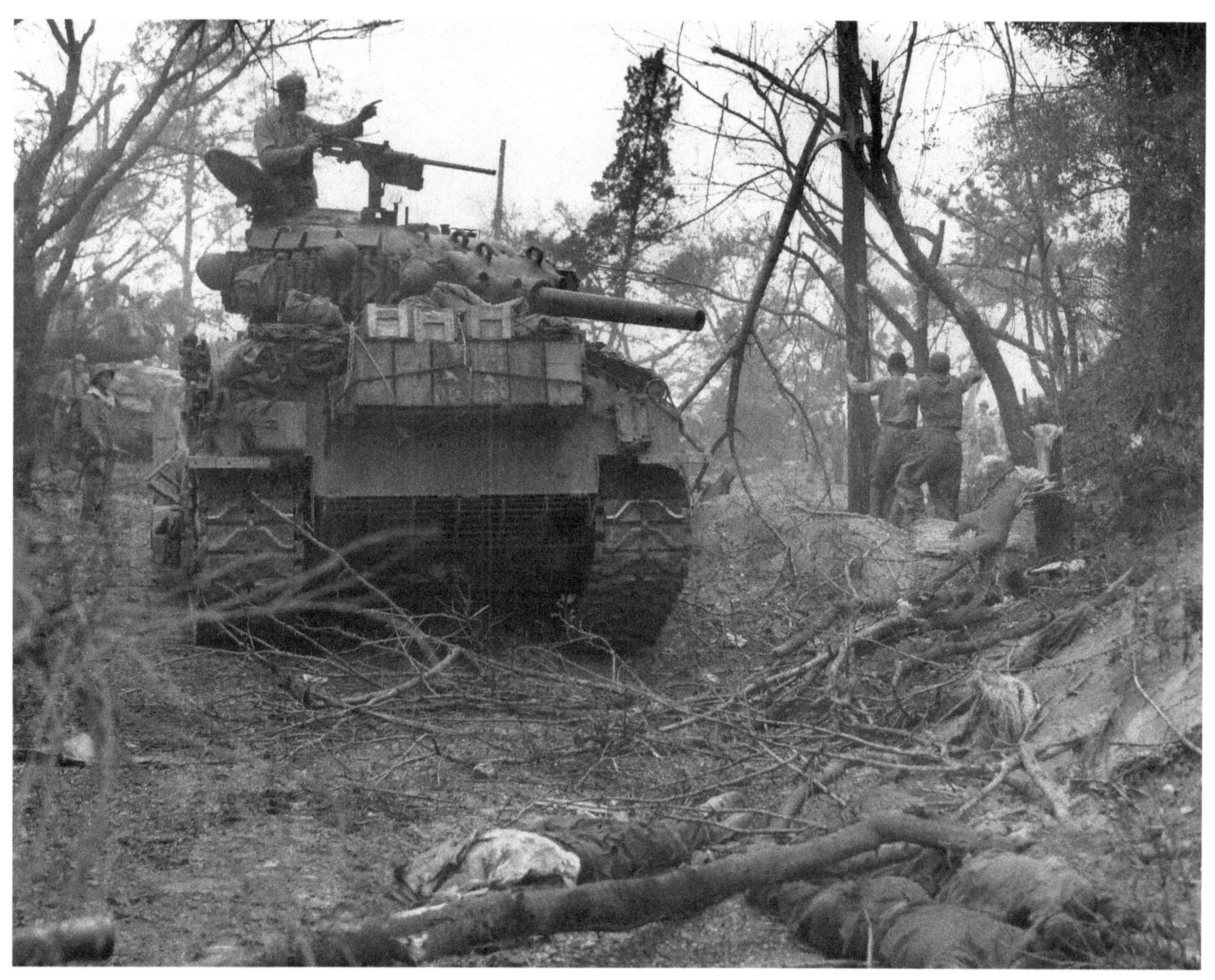

Marine infantry accept the surrender of enemy soldiers (right) on Wolmi-do as a tank commander points out the next target. *(Photo by Sgt. Frank C. Kerr, USMC)*

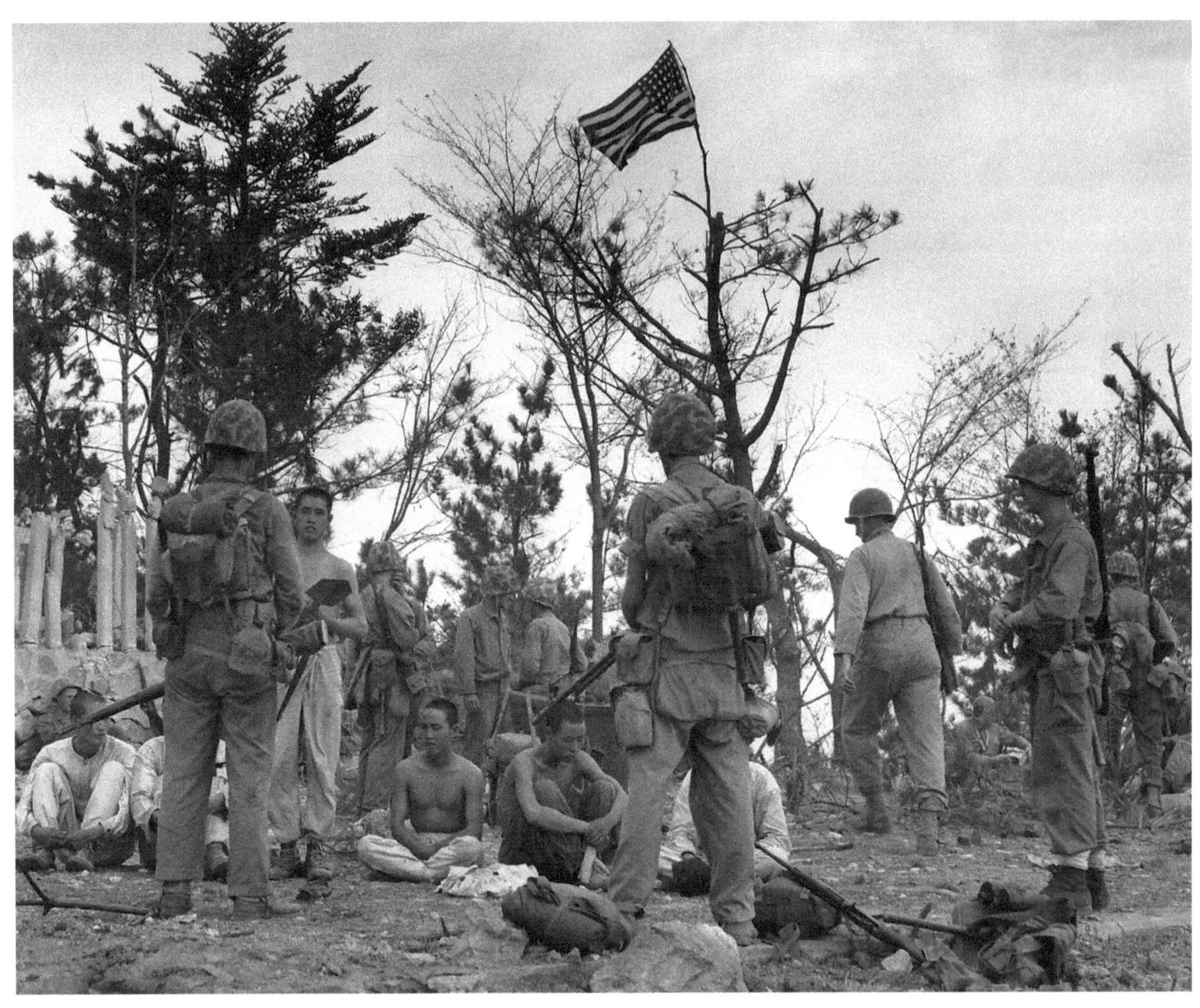

September 15th, 1950. U.S. Marines stand guard over their North Korean captives as the American flag flies proudly over newly won Wolmi-do Island. *(Photo by Sgt. Frank C. Kerr, USMC)*

34

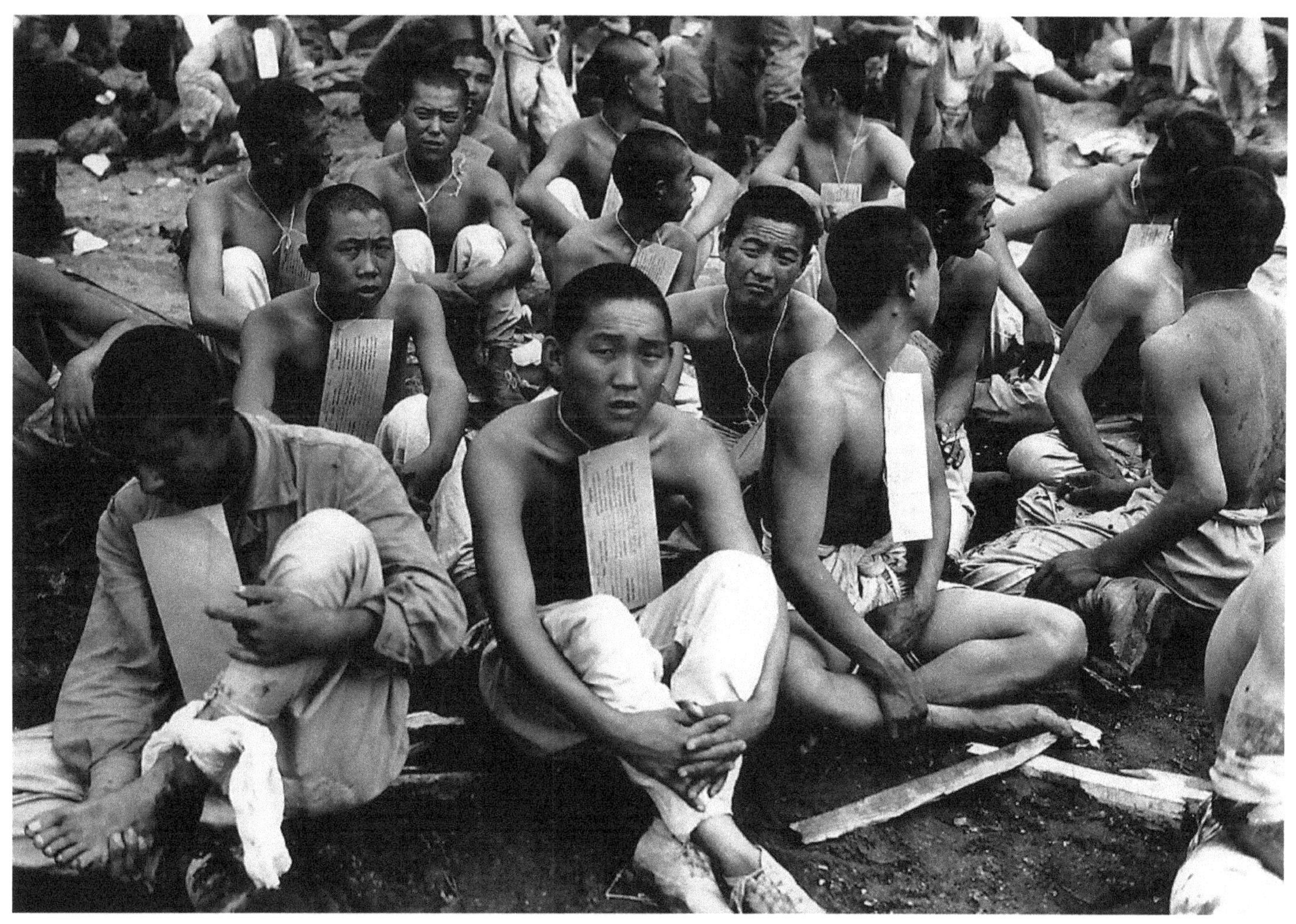

The war is over for these North Korean soldiers who await medical treatment at a concentration compound. Each prisoner has been "tagged" with their personal and medical information according to the rules of international warfare, then issued new clothing. *(Photo by Sgt. Frank C. Kerr, USMC)*

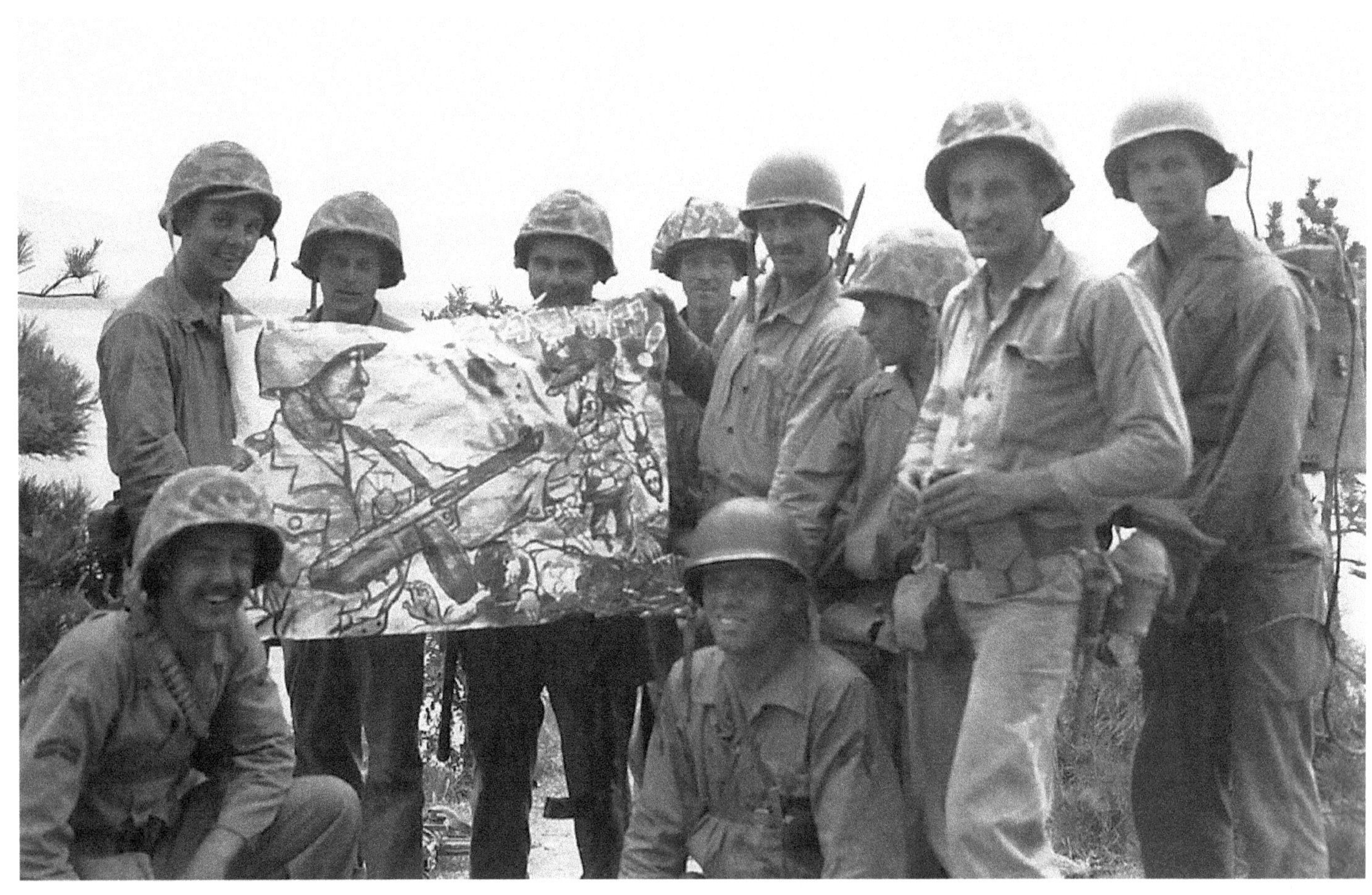

Mission accomplished. These smiling Marines on Wolmi-do display a captured North Korean battle flag depicting a communist giant grasping the "U.S. imperialist beast" as American bombs fall on Korean women and children. *(Photo by Sgt. Frank C. Kerr, USMC)*

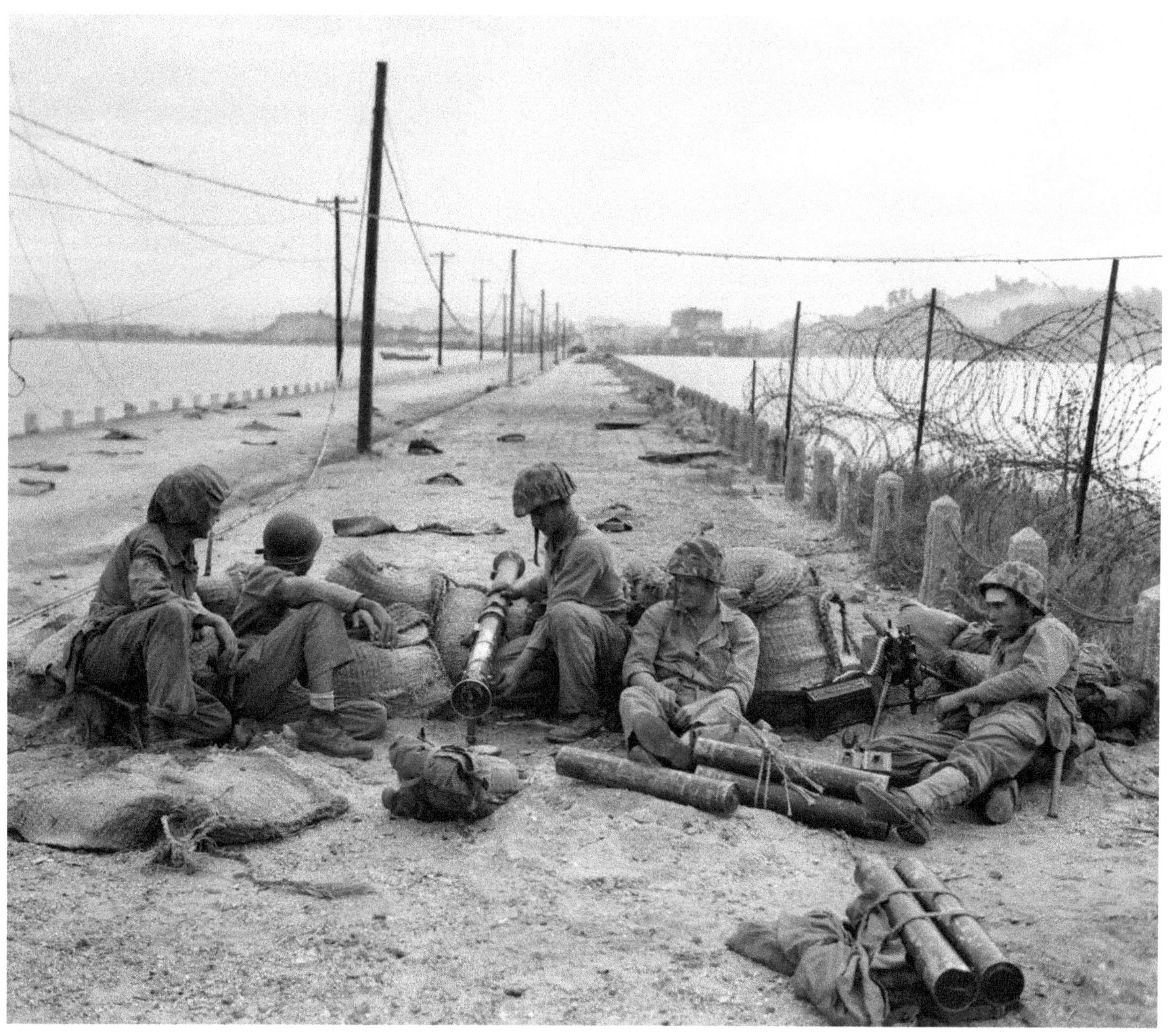

With Wolmi-do Island secured, Leathernecks of the 3rd Battalion, 5th Marine Regiment, armed with a bazooka and machinegun, man a security post on the causeway between the island and the North Korean mainland. *(Photo by Sgt. Frank C. Kerr, USMC)*

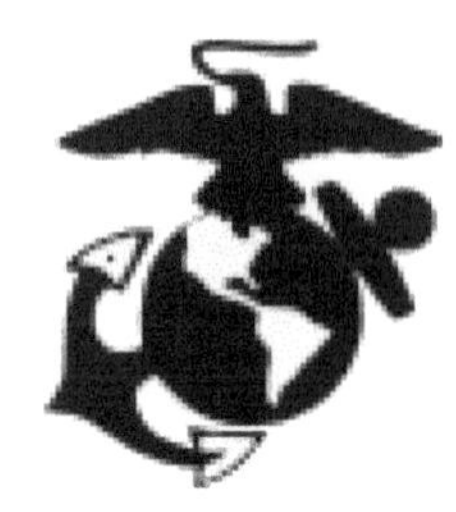

30 Sept 1950, Kimpo Airfield, Korea

Dear Mom,

...the situation sure has changed since we landed here two months ago. When we were fighting down south the war was really in a bad way, but now we're kicking hell out of the North Koreans and they know it. I hope the commies in the rest of the world learn a lesson from this war and stay on their own side of the fence from now on.

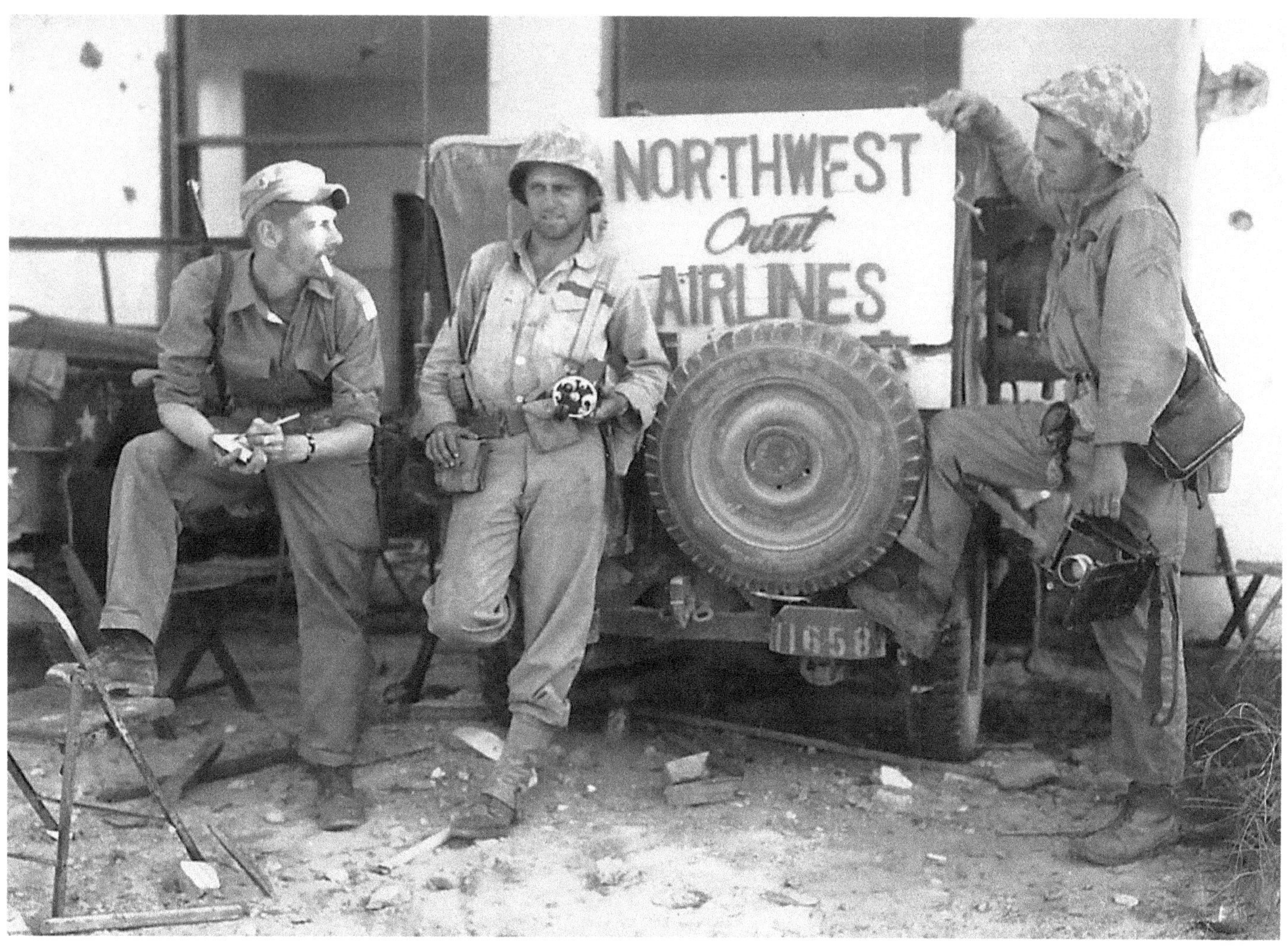

The author (right) at Kimpo Airfield, South Korea following the Inchon invasion. With him are L-R, combat cameramen Cpl. Mel Compton and PFC Berman.

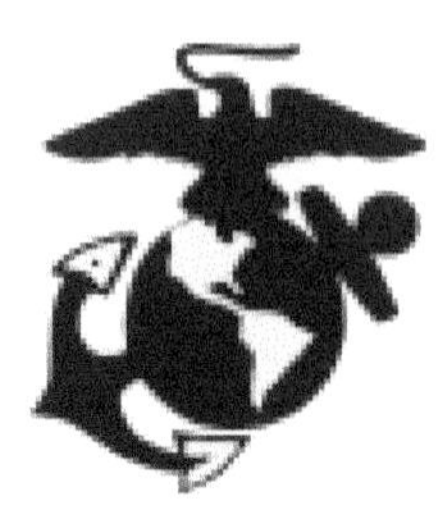

14 Oct. 1950, U.S.S. George Clymer, Inchon, Korea

Dear Mom,

… There's not too many of the old faces around anymore, the original members of the Brigade are few and far between. Take for instance the company that I started out with. When we came aboard ship there were only 17 of the original men left. Mateo has been wounded twice since we came over. He's killed more commies than an Army private ever saw, but he's had enough now and he's scared to go back in… I know I made a promise that I wasn't going to say anything to you about the war, mom, but I feel like the people back home just don't understand what the heck is going on. They take it for granted that we're winning the war, but I don't think they realize what goes on in winning a war.

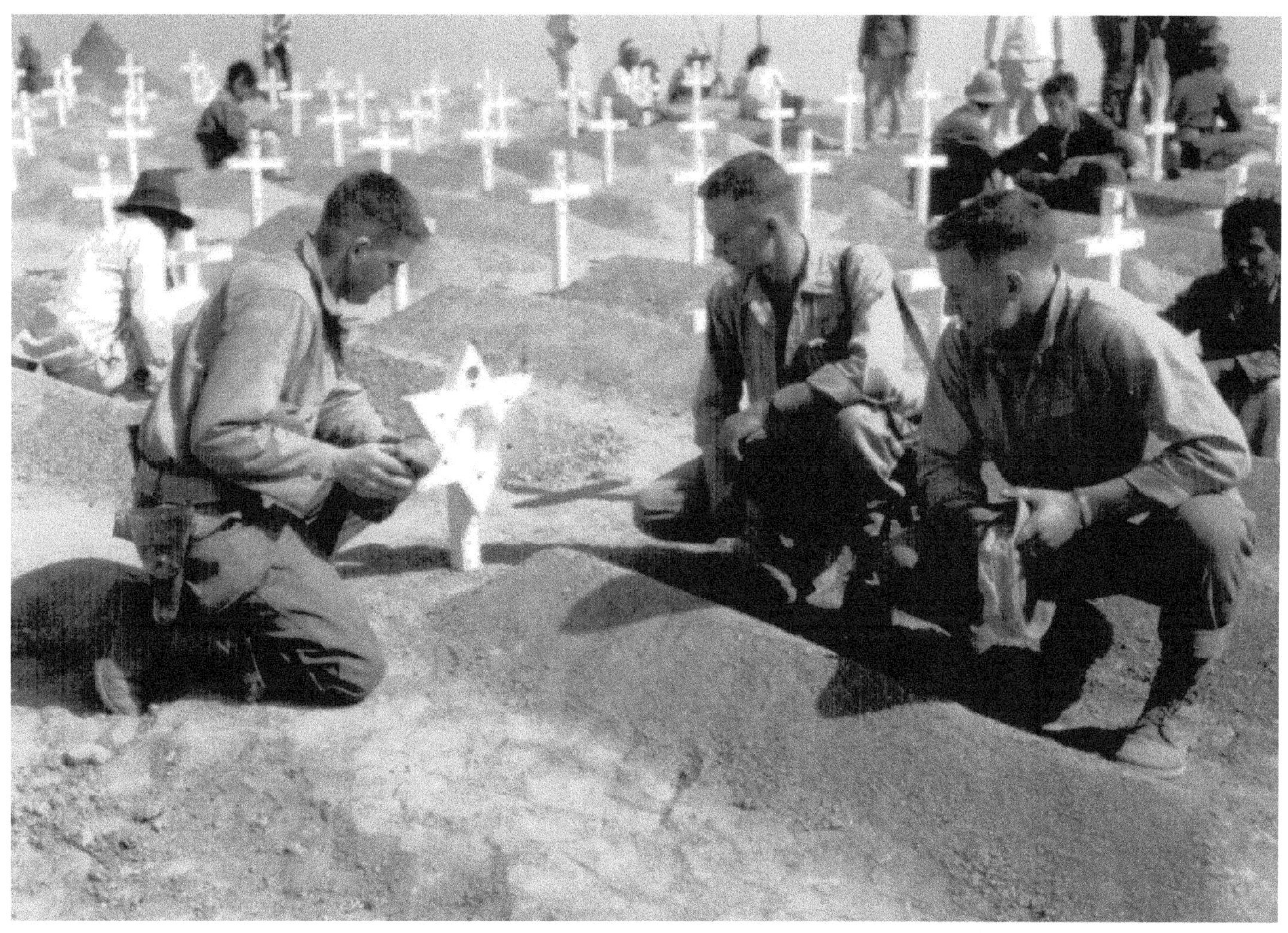

The author (left) kneels at the grave of Alvin Neustadt, a friend and fellow combat photographer who was killed in action with the 7th Marines. Opposite are (L-R) combat photographer Sgt. William Keating and combat cameraman PFC Walter Six. *(Photo by Cpl. William T. Wolfe, USMC)*

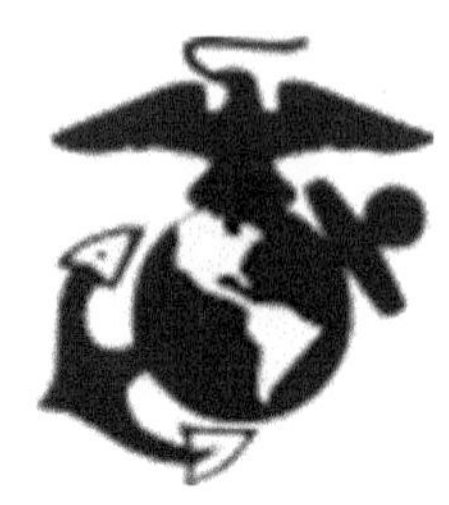

21 Nov 1950, Chosin Reservoir, North Korea

Dear Mom;

... Since the regiment I'm with landed at Wonsan we haven't run into much, however we did take a lot of prisoners including one Chinese soldier. About a week ago we moved over road for about 80 miles and now we're at the southern tip of the Chosin Reservoir. They say that in a couple of days we're going to pass through the 7th Regiment and take up the assault and maybe drive to the border. The general opinion is that we won't meet much trouble, of course I'll be able to say better about a month from now.

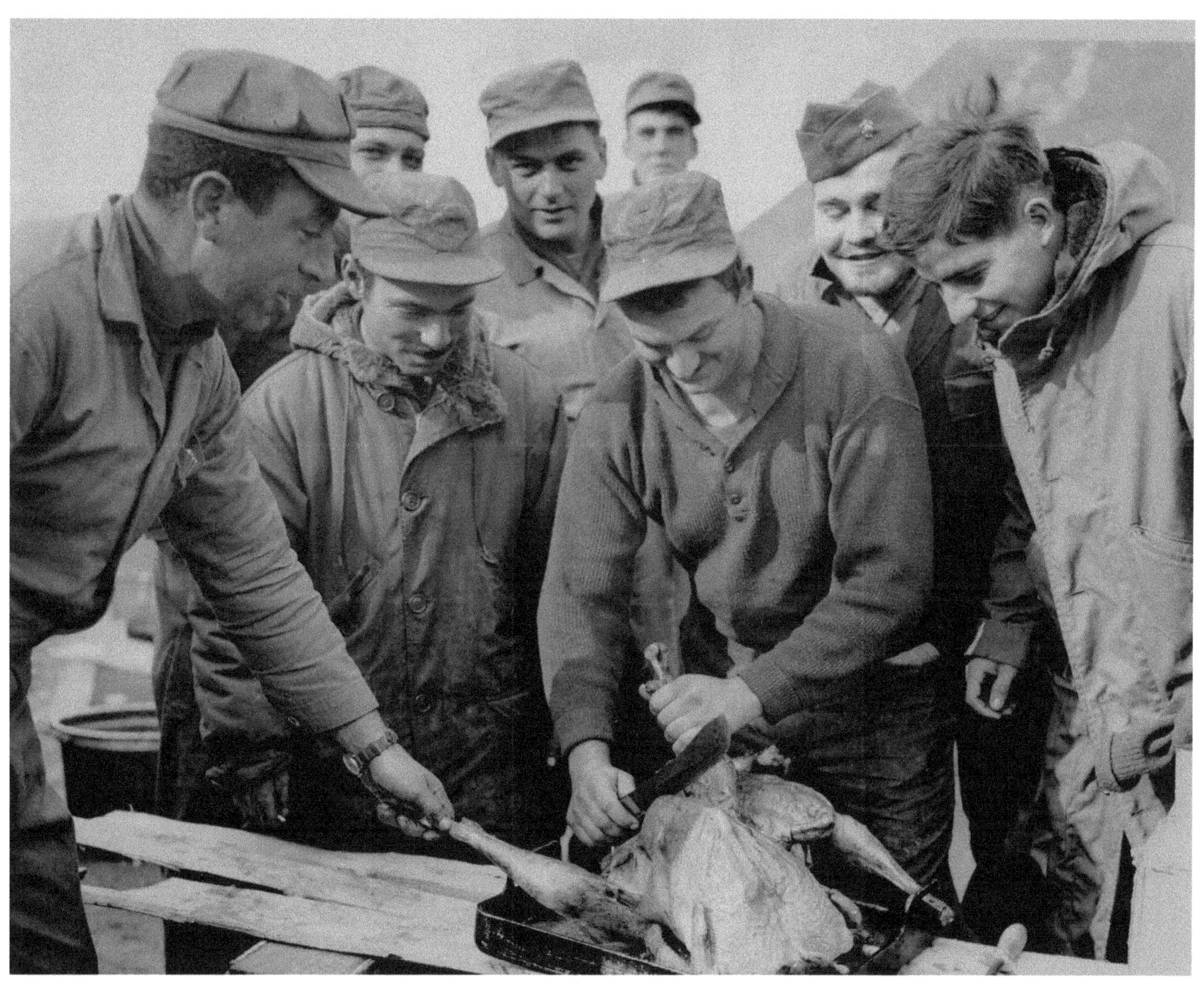

Thanksgiving at the Chosin Reservoir. Men of the 5th Marines carve turkey on November 23rd, 1950, four days before the Chinese Army launched its massive offensive to trap and destroy the U.S. 1st Marine Division at Chosin. *(Photo by Sgt. Frank C. Kerr, USMC)*

"Retreat Hell! We're just attacking in another direction."
Oliver P. Smith, Commanding General, 1st Marine Division

BATTLE OF THE CHOSIN RESERVOIR

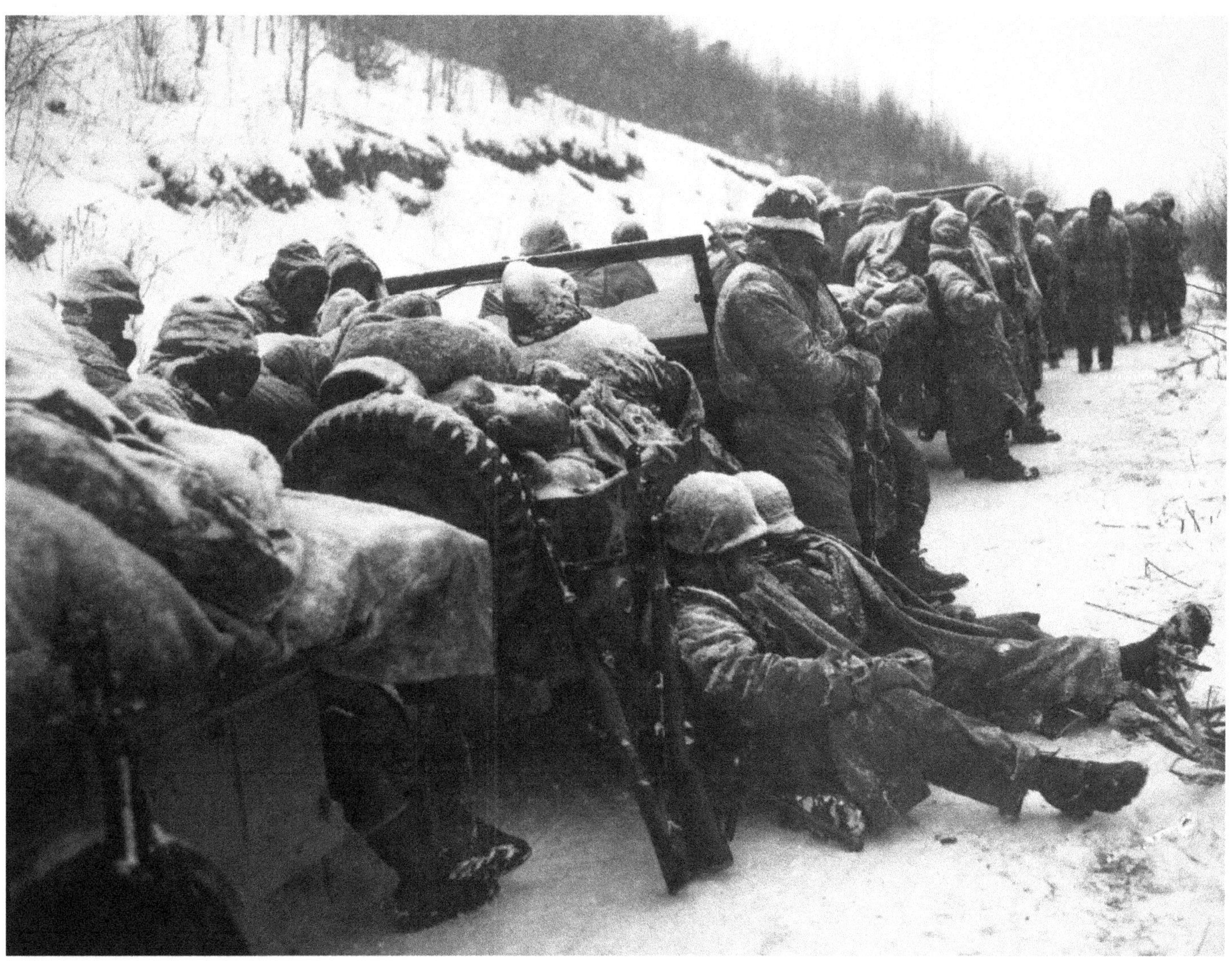

Bogged Down. Considered one of the iconic images of the Korean War, these snow-dusted, battle-weary troops of the 1st Marine Division wait for the column to roll again during their epic breakout from the Chosin Reservoir in December, 1950. *(Photo by Sgt. Frank C. Kerr, USMC)*

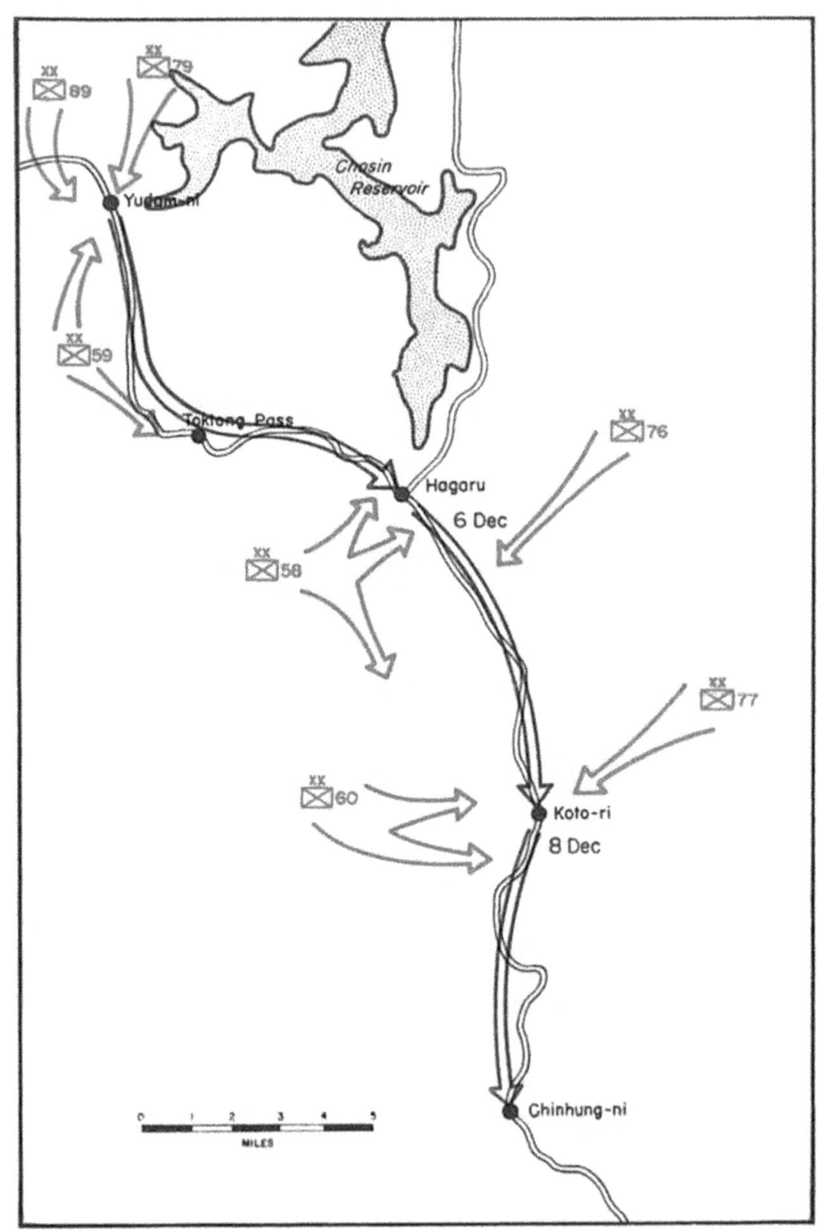

1st Marine Division's route of withdrawal from the Chosin Reservoir, indicating Chinese Army points of attack. November 27-December 11, 1950.

YUDAM-NI

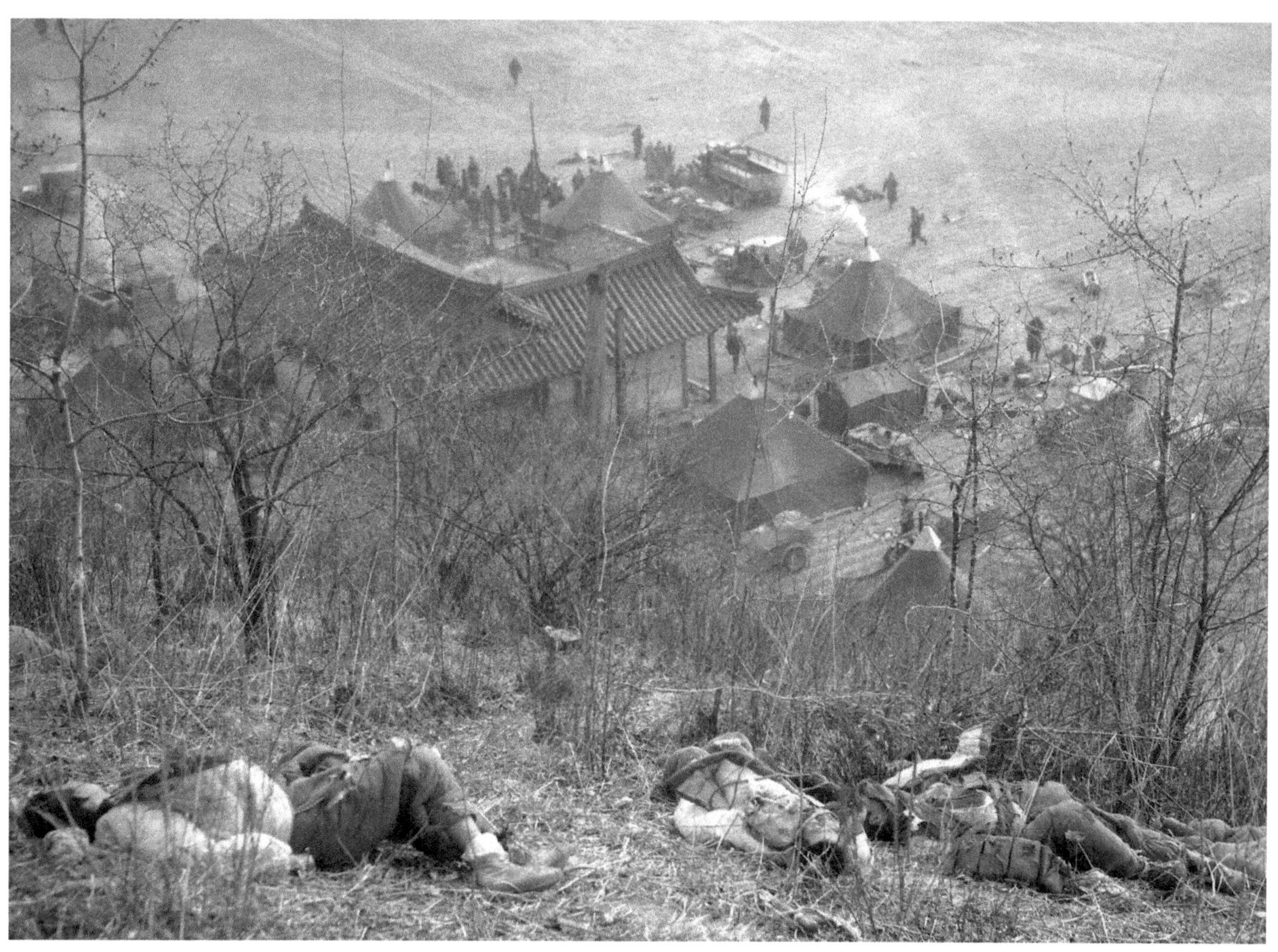

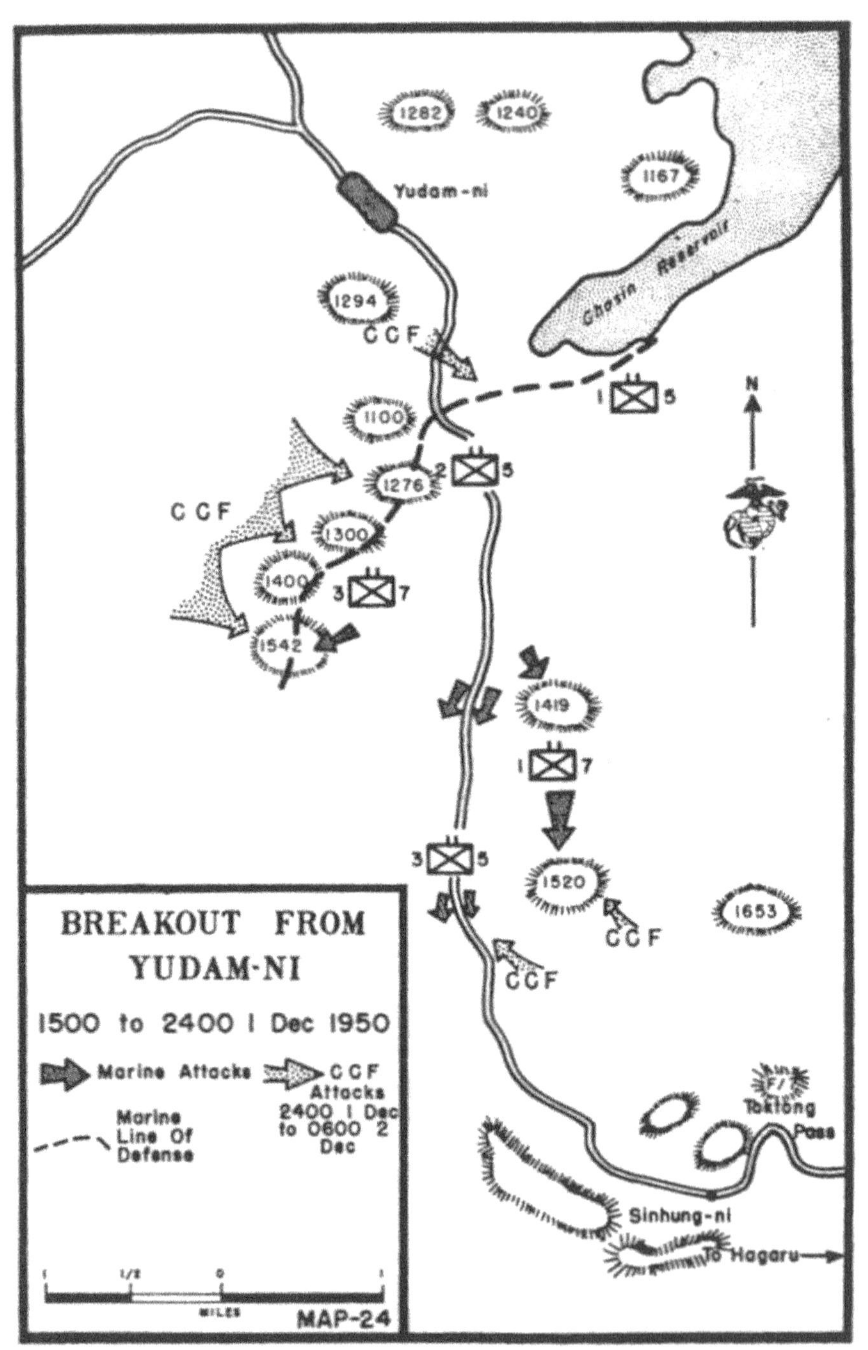

1282
1240
1167
Yudam-ni
Chosin Reservoir
1294
CCF
1 5
1100
2 5
1276
CCF
1300
1400
3 7
1542
N
1419
1 7
3 5
1520
CCF
CCF
1653
CCF
King
F/
Toktong
Pass
Sinhung-ni
To Hagaru
BREAKOUT FROM
YUDAM-NI
1500 to 2400 I Dec 1950
Marine Attacks
CCF
Attacks
2400 I Dec
to 0600 2
Dec
Marine
Line Of
Defense
1/2
0
1
MILES
MAP-24

Tucked behind mountain ridges and rocky foothills on the northwestern fork of the Chosin Reservoir lies the remote North Korean village of Yudam-ni. Like every man who marched with the 1st Marine Division in late November 1950, I arrived there with hopes of seeing the communists driven from the Korean peninsula, putting an end to the war, and getting back to the states before Christmas. Miles behind us, along the same perilous route we had come, allied troops were digging in and establishing supply depots at Hagaru-ri and Koto-ri. To the north, behind a veil of rugged mountains, lay our ultimate destination; the Yalu River on the border of communist China, where the retreating North Korean Army had taken refuge. What our Commander-in-Chief, General Douglas MacArthur, failed to realize—or decided to ignore—was how the Chinese would respond to allied troops knocking at their door.

We would soon find out.

As I entered Yudam-ni's perimeter with the 3rd Battalion, 5th Marine Regiment, fires were burning on one of the surrounding hills, the result of a napalm strike earlier that afternoon. Inside the encampment, men of the 7th Marines, who had arrived just ahead of us, huddled for warmth against the biting Manchurian cold. Although most were quiet, alone with their thoughts, there was also an undercurrent of tension in camp, with hard fighting still ahead and a nagging suspicion that Red China was drawing our forces into a trap.

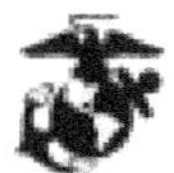

As night fell on the 27th of November and the temperature began to plummet, I ducked into an abandoned schoolhouse to escape the cold and get some sleep, only to discover scores of other Marines had beaten me to it. I cleared some space, removed my heavy boots and climbed into a sleeping bag with my clothes on. But just as I was drifting off, a frantic voice bellowed from the schoolhouse door, "Get the hell up, the Chinese are attacking!"

Like every Marine in that room, I was immediately back in my boots and grabbing my weapon. When shit hit the fan—like it was that night at Yudam-ni—I served the Corps as a rifleman first and photographer second, so it was my trusty M1 I took with me into the fight, not my camera. Back in the Pusan Perimeter our military issue carbine had a nasty habit of jamming at all the wrong times, and the damn thing flat-out refused to budge in the cold of Chosin, so I had traded it for the bolt-action M1. That rifle only fired one round at a time, but at least it worked in a pinch.

The battle was growing in intensity as I broke from the schoolhouse and headed for cover. Small arms and machine gun fire echoed from the foothills and tracer bullets streaked through the dark, making bizarre patterns against the night sky. As the Chinese pressed closer to the camp's perimeter, a panicked South Korean interpreter took shelter behind me, frantically waving a loaded .45 pistol near the back of my head. A quick-thinking gunnery sergeant saw what was happening, snatched the gun away, then handed it back to him without the clip. Meanwhile, as the fight drew nearer, alarming reports began coming in from our units battling in the hills. The 2nd Battalion radioed that the enemy had overrun their positions and was headed our way. We hastily organized a firing line to meet them, but a Marine infantry company formed in front of us and counterattacked, driving the communists back into the hills.

Following a pattern that would repeat over the coming days, the Chinese broke off their assault before dawn, leaving behind a scene of heartbreak and desolation. Our first aid stations were jammed with injured men and still they kept coming; some walking, others carried, many on stretchers. As I moved among them with my camera, a wounded Marine asked with a grin, "How 'bout a picture Sarge?" before another called out, "You should have been with us last night, Sarge." I'm no coward, but I was grateful I hadn't been in the hills with those infantrymen that night. They shared hair-raising stories of ferocious combat; how they had fought until they ran out of bullets, grenades and men. How they had clubbed the enemy with rifle butts and entrenching tools, and finally with their fists when all else failed.

In one corner of the aid station I came upon a dazed, red-eyed platoon sergeant with a shattered arm and ice-encrusted beard, cursing the Chinese, and himself, through bitter tears. His platoon had been decimated during the fight, and in his crushing grief the sergeant was blaming himself for the loss of his men. Two wounded survivors of the battle were doing their best to comfort him, but the man was inconsolable. At that moment my every instinct as a photographer screamed, *take the picture*! To this day I'm certain it would have made one of the great photographs of the Korean War. Instead, I turned away and moved on. I just didn't have the heart to take it.

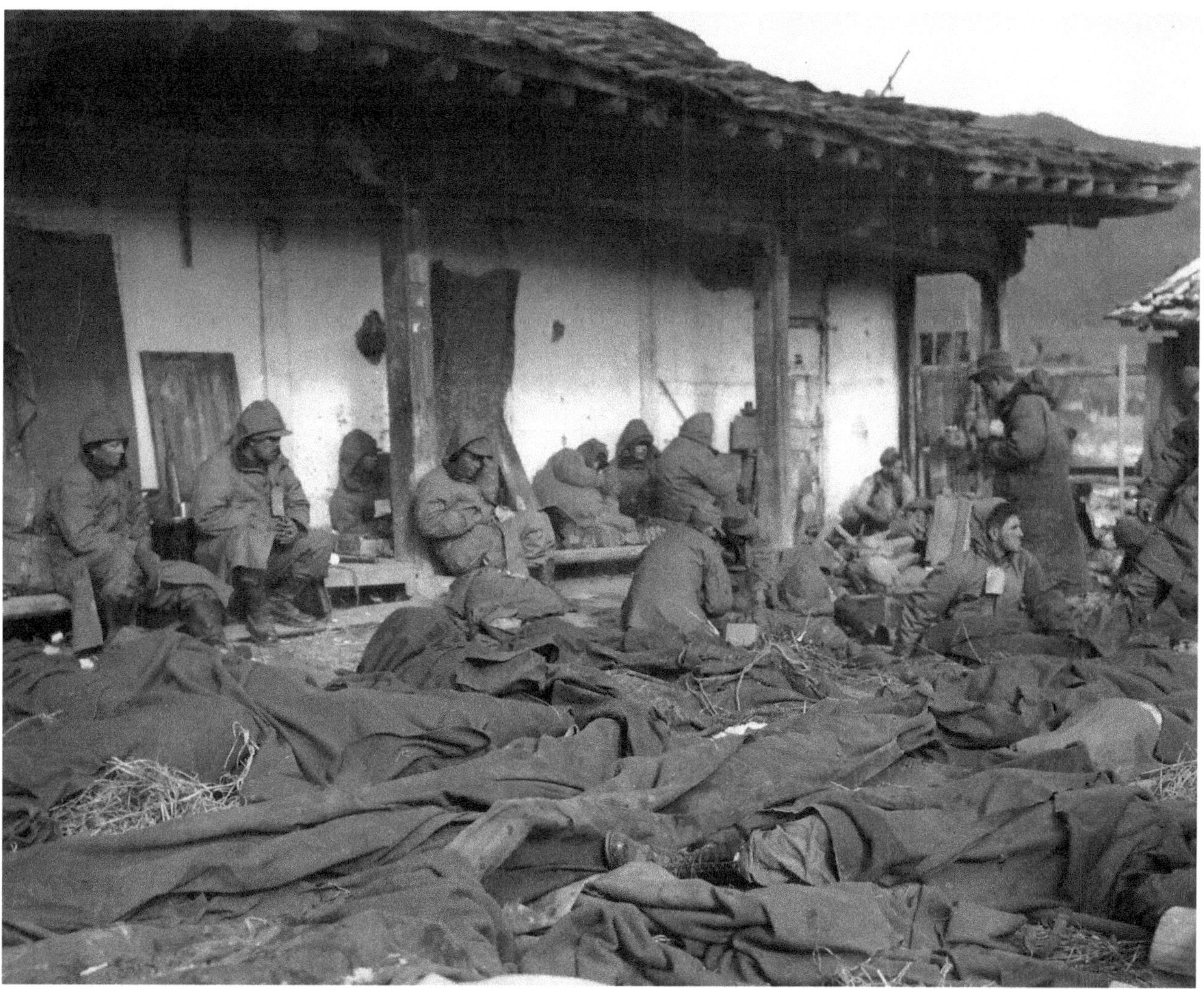

U.S. Marine casualties are assembled at Yudam-ni for medical aid and evacuation to hospitals behind the fighting fronts. November 28th, 1950. *(Photo by Sgt. Frank C. Kerr, USMC)*

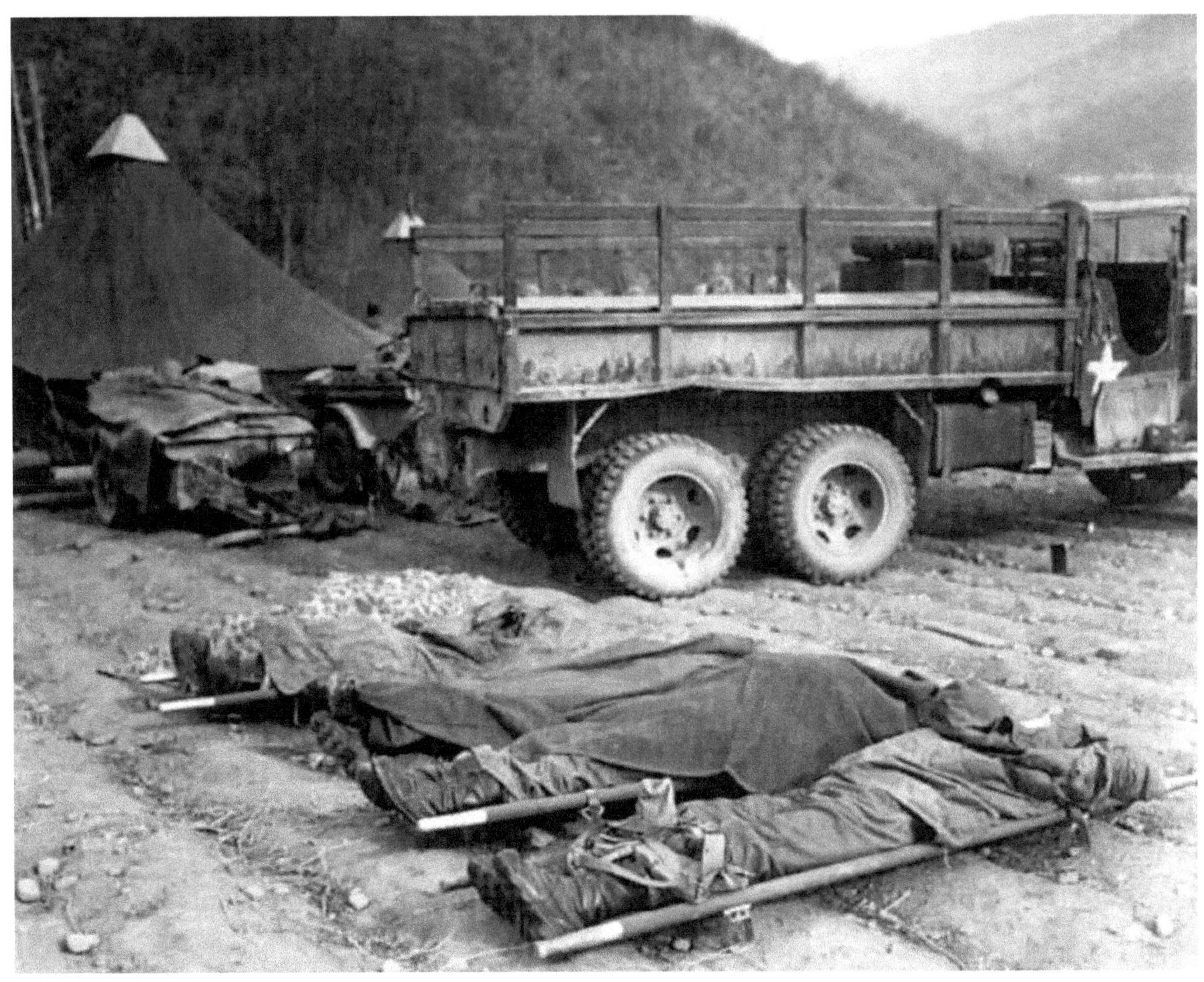

Marine dead await loading onto the truck that will take them for burial at Yudam-ni. Standard practice at the Chosin Reservoir was to carry troops who died fighting in the hills down to the road for retrieval by the regiment's Graves Registration Detachment. *(Photo by Sgt. Frank C. Kerr, USMC)*

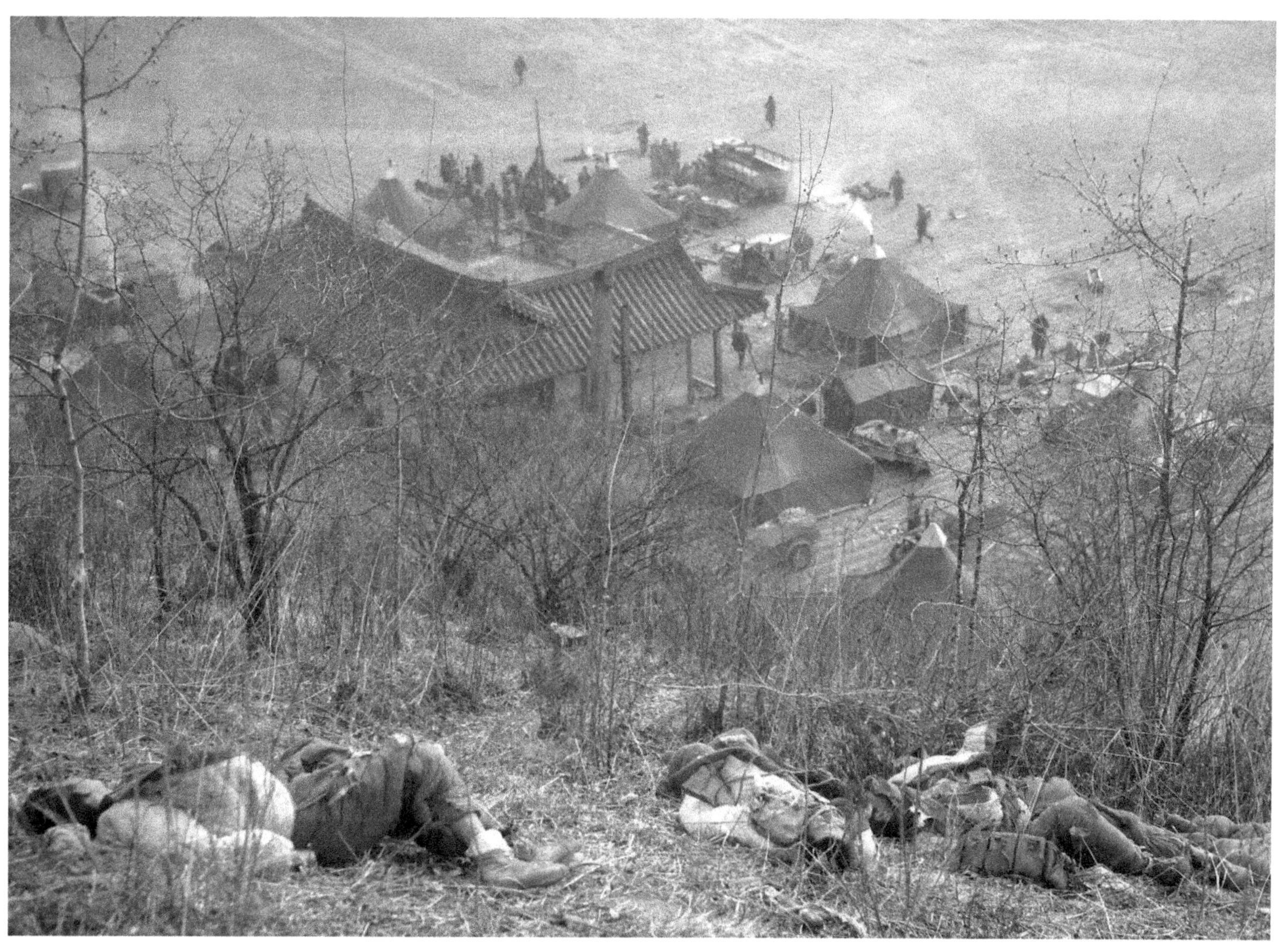

Following a night of savage fighting, these Chinese soldiers lay frozen in death on the hills overlooking the Marine camp at Yudam-ni. *(Photo by Sgt. Frank C. Kerr, USMC)*

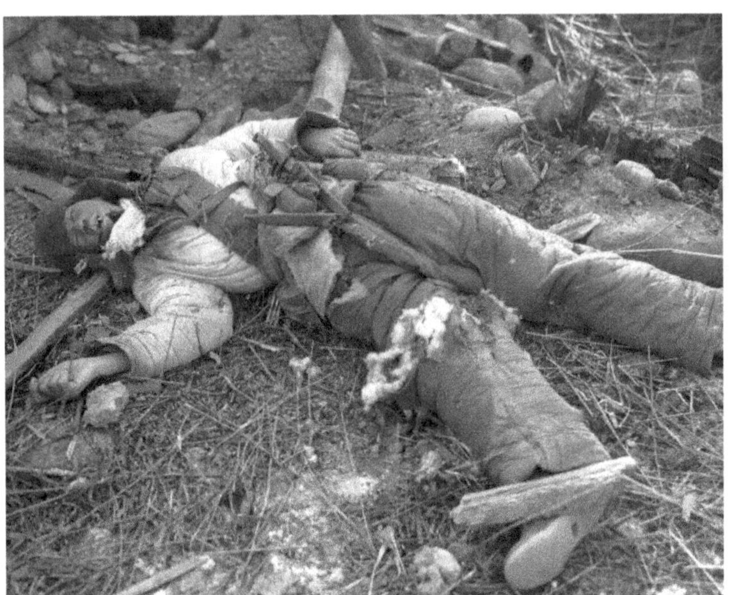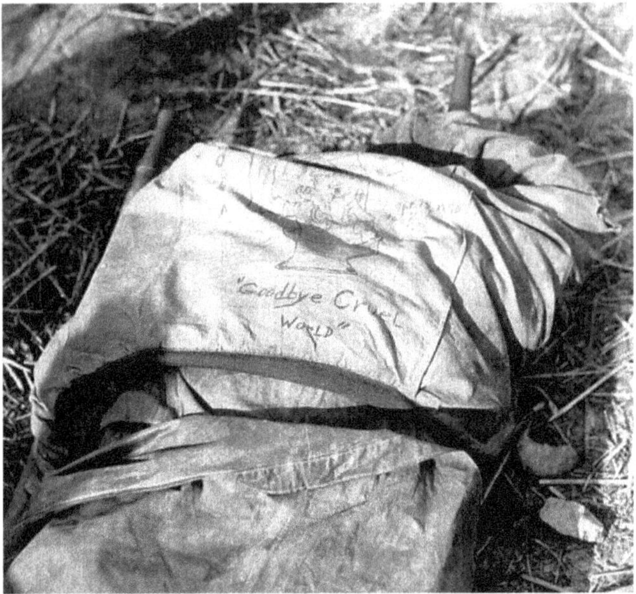

Left: A Chinese soldier killed in combat at Yudam-ni. **Right:** Days before this Marine infantryman died at Chosin, he had scrawled a prescient message on the back of his jacket. The message reads, "Goodbye Cruel World". *(Photos by Sgt. Frank C. Kerr, USMC)*

To understand the precariousness of our situation at Yudam-ni, all one had to do was take a good look around. We were encircled, completely cut off from U.N. forces to the south, and it wasn't hard to spot enemy soldiers maneuvering for position on the high ground overlooking the village. Every Marine infantryman had been called in from the hills to strengthen the camp's perimeter, and whenever the Chinese pressed too close, our artillery and mortar crews would unleash a barrage of shells that sent them scurrying back to their own lines.

Our biggest advantage at the reservoir was ownership of the skies. Like angry bees, Marine Corsairs swarmed the valley during daylight, and the pilots had little trouble finding targets for their cannons and napalm bombs. As I stood next to the tactical air controller's jeep listening to their radio chatter, one would think those flyboys were the only Americans left in Korea and the Chinese occupied the rest. "Looks like a bunch in that draw to your left," one would report, before the next would cut in, "Think I see one of their CPs on top of the hill. Permission to go after them," followed by the controller's prompt reply, "Permission granted. Give 'em hell." Once their bombs and ammunition were expended, the pilots would buzz the TACP on their return to base, signing off with, "Thanks for the target. See you later. Good luck."

As daylight faded and our troops began bracing for another night attack, several Chinese prisoners were brought in and interrogated. They claimed no assault was planned for that evening, but our commanders were taking no chances. Every able-bodied man at Yudam-ni was expected to arm himself, regardless of rank or position. Even our wounded were asking for weapons. I joined two Marines in their machine gun nest on the perimeter, helping fill sandbags and gathering extra grenades and ammunition before settling in for a tense night keeping watch.

Other than the occasional crack of a bullet fired from some itchy fingered Leatherneck, the only sound heard after midnight was a bored Marine with a dark sense of humor crooning *There's no Tomorrow*, sung to the classic tune *'O sole mio*.

There's no tomorrow

When love is new.

Now is forever

When love is true.

So kiss me and hold me tight.

There's no tomorrow

There's just tonight.

Given our circumstances, my foxhole companions and I were unamused by his song choice and loudly told him so—with a few expletives thrown in for good measure. But the singing

Marine simply ignored us, and from the darkness somewhere down the line he continued serenading the troops—and probably a good many Chinese as well.

As the night grew longer and the air turned colder, my eyes began playing tricks on me. Shapes moved in the dark where there were none, and trees transformed into enemy soldiers then back into trees again. By the small hours of the morning my brain was numb and so were my extremities as the temperature kept plunging—by some accounts as much as thirty-five below zero. I stomped my feet to keep the blood moving and thought of anything warm; hot coffee, the beaches of Southern California—even those miserably hot August days in the Pusan Perimeter. But mind over matter was no defense against such weather. Ask any man who lived through the Chosin campaign and he'll tell you that once the Manchurian cold got inside you, it was there to stay.

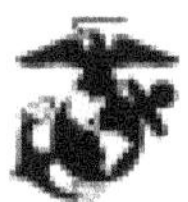

The feared assault never happened that night, but with China fully committed to war, the military situation in Korea had been turned on its head. The 1st Marine Division was encircled at Yudam-ni, Hagaru-ri and Koto-ri by a massive force of over one hundred thousand enemy soldiers, and it didn't take a genius to realize that General MacArthur's grand plan to drive the communists from the Korean peninsula before Christmas was now just a pipe dream. Instead of celebrating the holidays at home, we would be punching our way out of a communist trap—marching fourteen hard miles along a single-lane dirt road, through rugged terrain, arctic-like cold, and enemy lines to reach the nearest supply depot at Hagaru on the southernmost tip of the reservoir.

While the brass was busy drawing up plans to withdraw from Chosin, the enemy was making our lives miserable with constant mortar barrages that drove us into overcrowded bunkers filled with sleepy-eyed Marines. One night, as those damnable tubes were thumping and shells were falling, we were joined in the bunker by a young Navy Corpsman who was bellyaching about the weather, the Chinese Army, and the stinking company he was keeping. He had joined the Navy fresh out of high school with plans to sail on ships and see the world, but here he was in some miserable place, sharing a filthy bunker with a bunch of unwashed gravel-crunchers. Truth is, Marines think the world of Navy Corpsmen and we kidded our grumpy young friend that he'd never had it so good—and wasn't it a fine thing to travel all the way to exotic North Korea for an up-close look at Chinamen?

As unpredictable and lethal as those falling mortar shells could be, even more troubling were the snipers who roamed the hills above Yudam-ni, picking men off from the high ground. Occasionally a Marine patrol would go out hunting them, but every time one of those snipers was silenced, another would crawl up to take his place. Back at Pusan, a World War Two veteran told me to ditch the flashgun on my Graflex camera, concerned its shiny reflector would attract North Korean sharpshooters. I'd seen more than a few Marines felled by that hidden enemy since then, but it never felt personal until one of those sneaky bastards put me in his crosshairs at Yudam-ni. I was crossing a frozen rice paddy, minding my own business, when a bullet struck the ground a few feet in front of me. For a brief moment I thought it might be a stray round, until the next one hit even closer. That was my cue, and I took off running with bullets kicking at my heels. There are a few undeniable truths one learns in war, not the least of which is; it's no fun when someone is trying to kill you.

If mortars and snipers weren't worrisome enough, there were always the air drops that delivered supplies and ammunition by parachute to our encircled force. Of course it was a welcome sight when that lifeline from the sky appeared over the camp, but it could also be nerve-wracking as hell. Those heavy crates sometimes broke loose from their tethers and came plummeting to earth like bombshells, smashing through huts, into vehicles and anything else beneath them. Whenever cargo planes were droning overhead it was all eyes to the sky, waiting for them to lift their noses and spill their loads. After that it was every man for himself. Strange, but no matter how much you zigged and zagged, it seemed one of those damn crates was always headed straight for you. Up until that point in the war I had managed to avoid getting killed by bullets, mortar shells and artillery rounds. I sure as hell didn't want mom getting a telegram informing her that Sergeant Kerr had been clobbered by a load of C-rations.

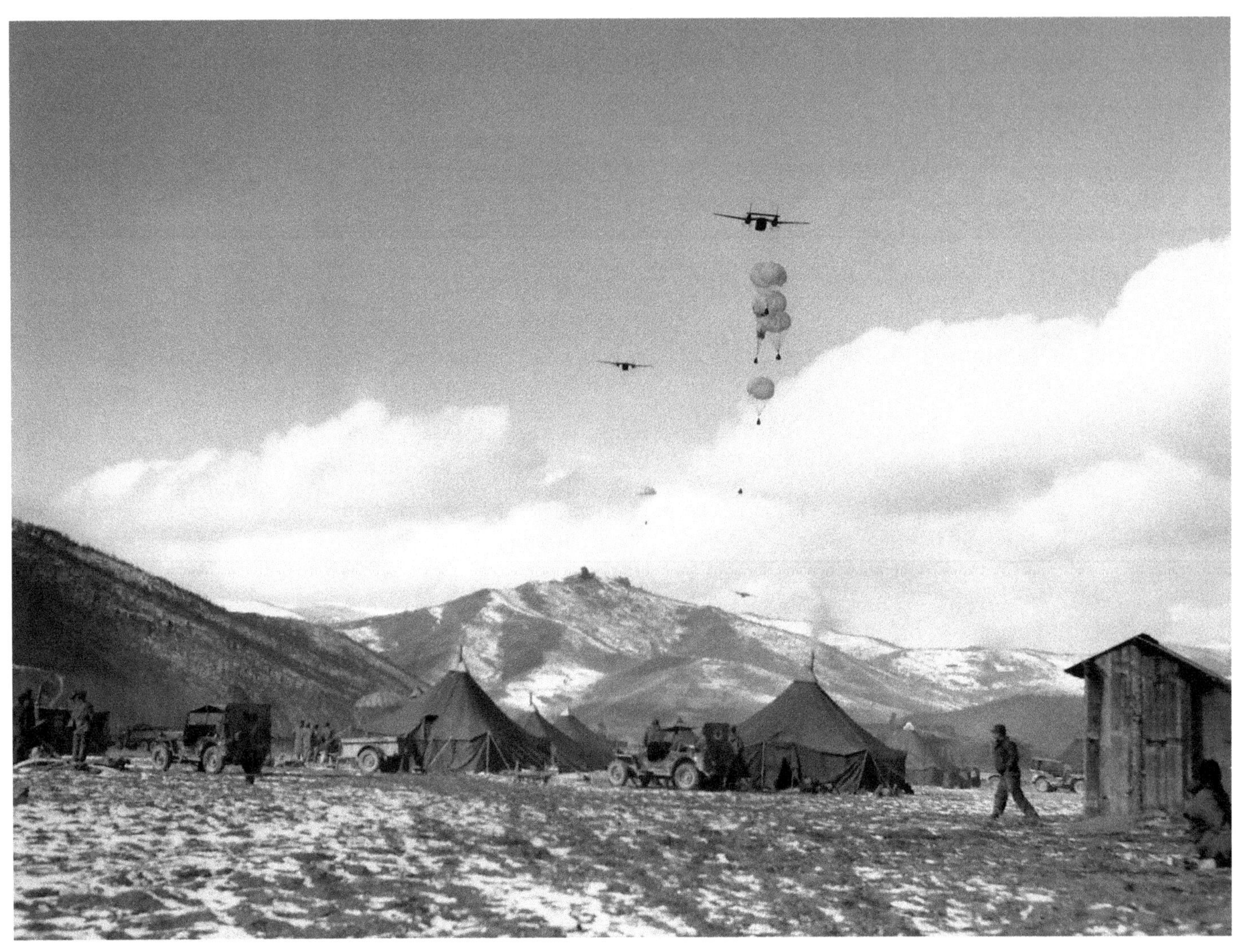

Allied aircraft drop supplies by parachute for Marines encircled by Chinese forces at Yudam-ni, November, 1950. *(Photo by Sgt. Frank C. Kerr, USMC)*

On November 30th, another bitterly cold day at the reservoir, preparations were well underway for abandoning Yudam-ni, which our fed up and frostbitten troops were now calling "You-damn-me". As ordered, we burned our excess gear, needing all our strength to carry ammunition and food on the difficult march ahead. In addition to my camera and rifle, I packed two extra bandoliers of ammunition, a couple of hand grenades, my sleeping bag, an extra pair of socks, and a .45 caliber pistol, which I shoved in my pocket for use as a last resort. Then I pulled on dry clothes and burned all the rest. Nothing was to be left for the Chinese.

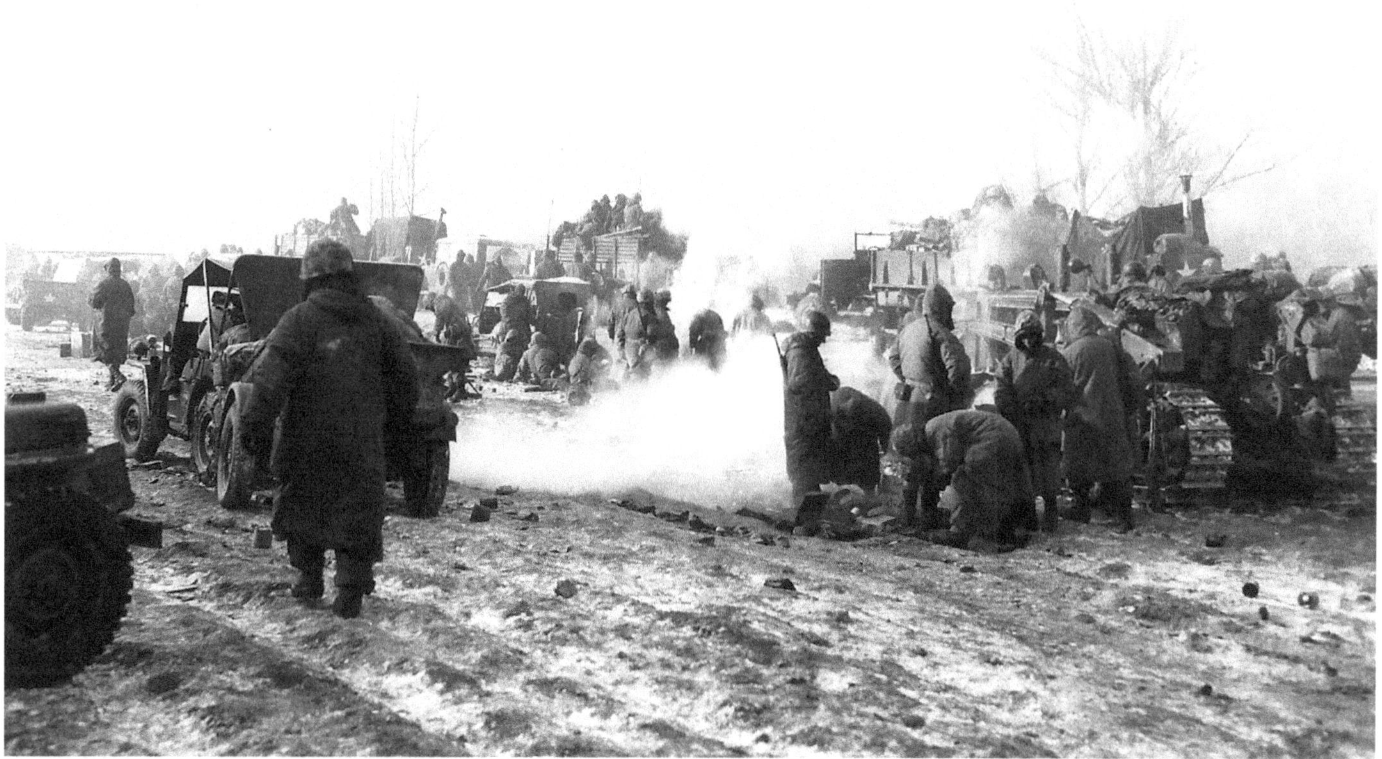

This page and next. After fighting off three Chinese divisions, men of the 5th and 7th Marine Regiments burn their surplus gear and prepare to withdraw from Yudam-ni and the Chosin Reservoir on November 30th, 1950. *(Photos by Sgt. Frank C. Kerr, USMC)*

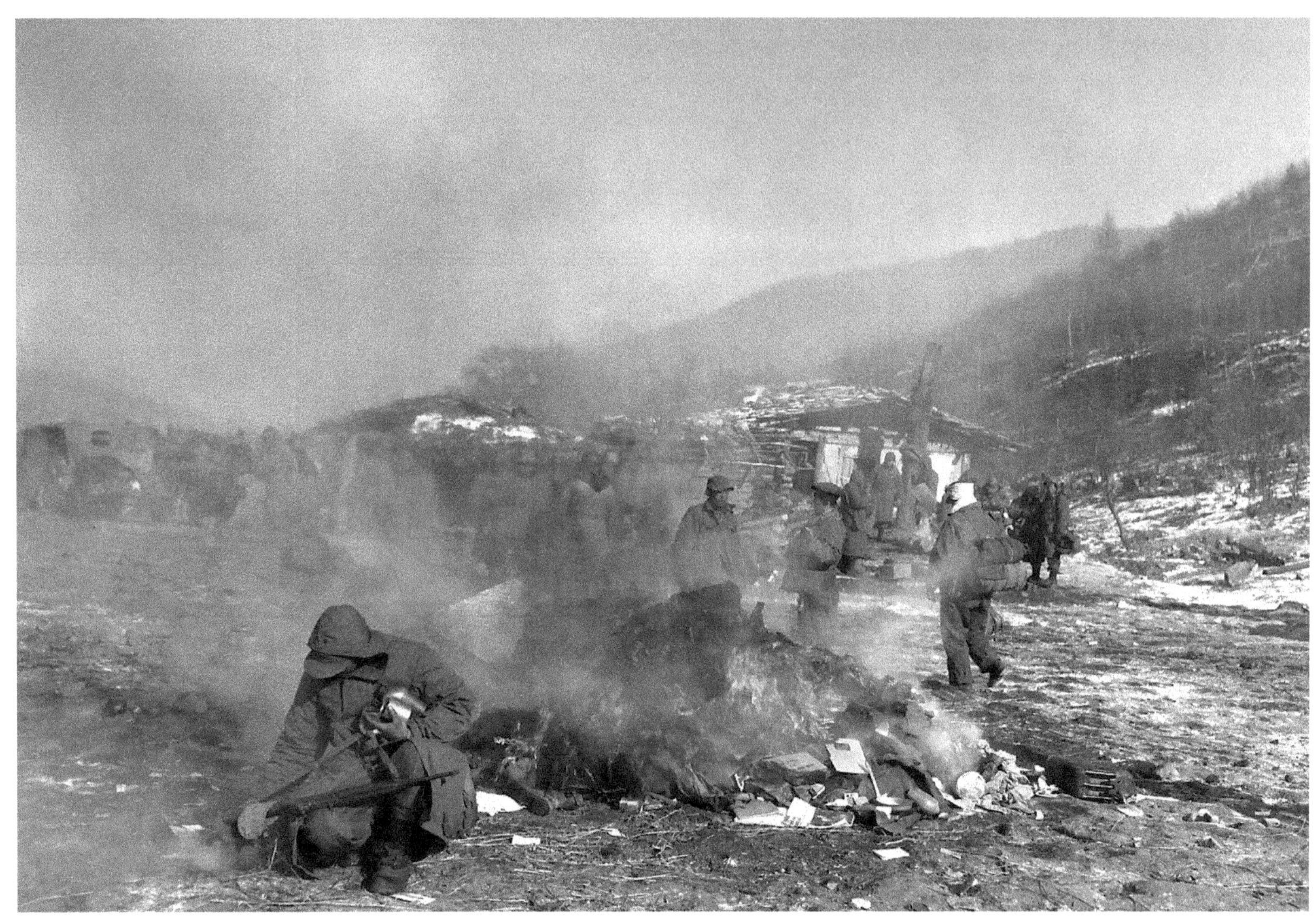

Strange as this might sound, the bigger concern among most Marines in camp was not the Chinese Army, but how the world, and those who served, would view our withdrawal from Chosin. It is a point of great pride that U.S. Marines never turn from a fight, and by pulling up stakes and heading south, the men worried they were tarnishing the Corps' long and proud heritage. It hardly mattered that more Chinese would be in front of us than behind, or that the division's commanding officer, General Oliver P. Smith, insisted we were merely "attacking in a different direction". On a rational level perhaps that made sense, but it sure didn't make the boys feel any better. Sitting around a Coleman burner, eating rations on our last day at Yudam-ni, one grizzled Leatherneck snarled, "If I get out of here and anyone says we retreated, I'll let him have it."

For my parting meal I chose a can of frozen spaghetti, removed the lid and placed it over the burner. As the spaghetti thawed, what I failed to consider were the immutable laws of thermodynamics—namely that heat produces steam, which creates pressure, which can fire a frozen lump of pasta from a tin can like a mortar shell. The blast knocked the helmet off my head and dropped me flat on my back, prompting a good deal of much needed laughter and one smartass Marine to remark, "I suppose you'll want a Purple Heart for that."

As we grabbed our gear and prepared to go our separate ways, another man broke out a roll of Life Savers candy and offered it to the group. When there were no takers, he went quiet for a moment then repeated emphatically, "These are *Life Savers*." He passed the roll again and this time every Marine took one, including yours truly. I've never considered myself the superstitious type, but when faced with your own mortality it doesn't hurt to err on the side of caution.

Watching the 1st Marine Division begin its epic withdrawal from the Chosin Reservoir on December 1st, 1950 still moves me in ways I can't explain. Weeks earlier I had witnessed the spectacular pre-invasion bombardment of Inchon, but what I saw that morning at Yudam-ni struck a different kind of emotional chord. Beneath a thick haze of smoke from burning clothes and equipment, a seemingly endless column of men and military vehicles began the long trek south. Sick and injured Marines were piled onto trucks and jeeps, while alongside them trudged the walking wounded—men with bandaged heads, bullet-shattered arms and frostbitten hands incapable of working a rifle. They would ask, "Do you think we'll make it?" And always our reply, "Hell yes, we'll make it."

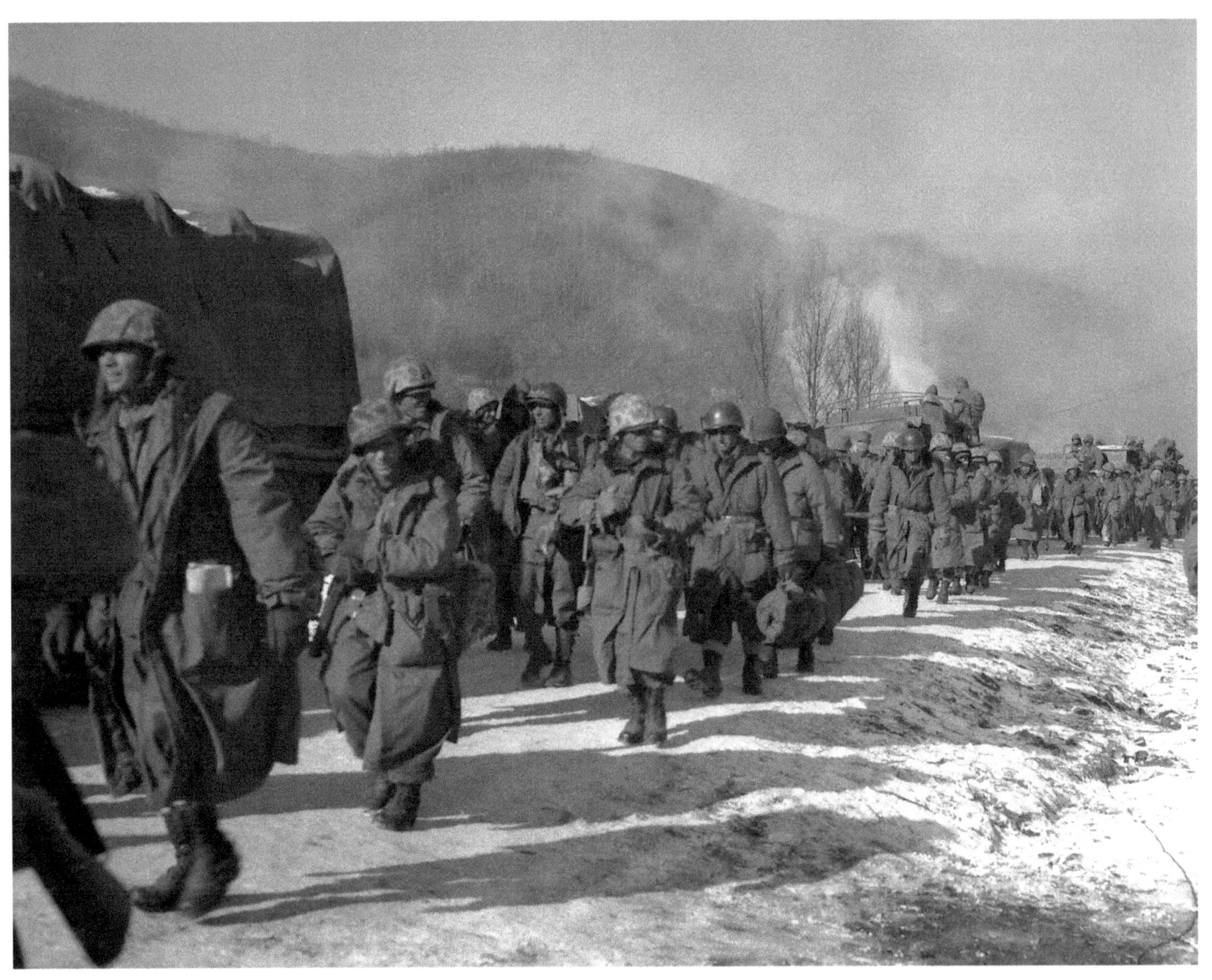

Yudam-ni, December 1st, 1950.   Taking their wounded and their equipment, the 5th and 7th Marines begin their epic breakout from the Chosin Reservoir, moving fourteen miles through enemy lines and bitter cold to the next allied supply base at Hagaru-ri. *(Photo by Sgt. Frank C. Kerr, USMC)*

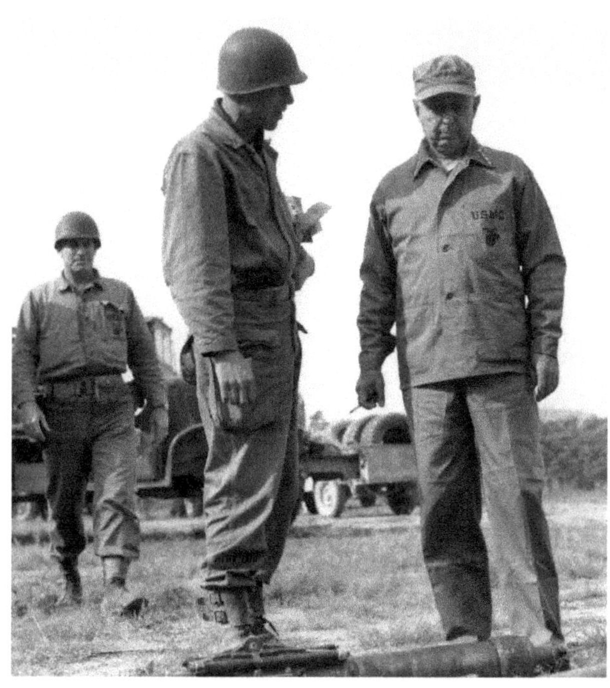

Lieutenant Colonel Ray Murray (right) commander of the 5th Marine Regiment.. (Photo by Sgt. Frank C. Kerr, USMC)

The division's only tank at Yudam-ni rumbled toward the head of the convoy as the 5th Marines' regimental commander, Lieutenant Colonel Ray Murray, strode the line shouting directions and offering encouragement. His marching orders were to keep the train moving, but progress was painfully slow. It seemed another enemy roadblock was always around the next bend, and our vehicles were constantly breaking down, their batteries drained and motor oil turned to sludge by subzero temperatures Sometime in the late afternoon, as a biting Manchurian wind whistled through the mountains, one truck lost control, swerved off the narrow, ice-covered road and rolled over the bank, crushing and trapping the men inside. As the convoy came to a halt, exhausted Marines jammed their rifles, bayonet first, into the frozen earth and leaned against them to rest. Occasionally they fell asleep standing up, which seems impossible until you've witnessed a man utterly worn out by the rigors of combat, constant marching, and bone-numbing cold.

In fits and starts, the column continued its snail's pace toward Hagaru-ri while our troops cleared enemy roadblocks, trudged through windblown drifts, along rocky chasms and past hillsides scorched by napalm and littered with the charred bodies of Chinese dead. In our haste to escape the reservoir, we marched through the night, moving quietly in the mountain dark save for the clank of rifles against canteens and the crunch of our boots in snow. Even the wounded stayed silent, gritting their teeth against the pain and trusting their fellow Marines to get them through. When there was important news to share, it traveled word of mouth, spreading in hushed voices along the column. "Seventy-fives to the front," one man would whisper to the next, "and stay clear of the ditches, they're mined."

When the night attacks did come, we took cover and returned fire, knowing we probably weren't hitting a damn thing in that deep darkness. In my completely exhausted state, as I watched enemy grenades explode, often three at a time, I remember thinking what a wonderful picture it would make—like Roman candles on the 4th of July. Then some NCO would bark, "You Marines can't stay here forever! Let's go you sons of bitches, you're holding up the war!" And with that I'd be off and running in a semi-crouch, hoping some Chinaman's bullet wouldn't find me.

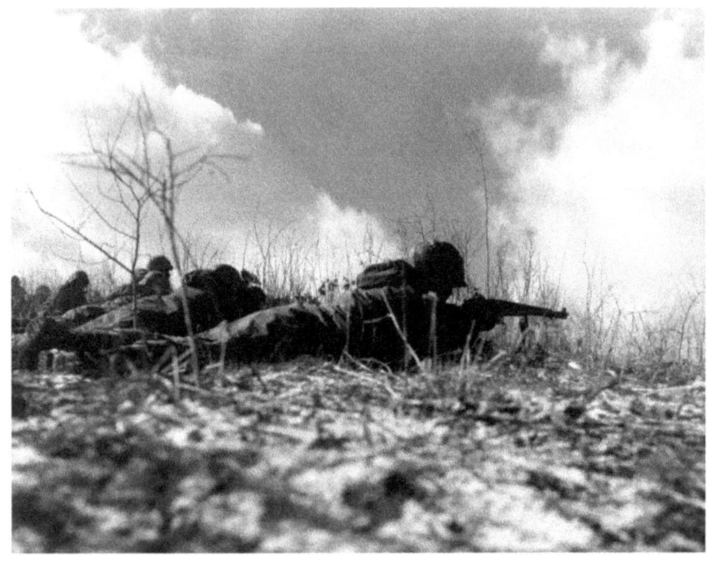

A Marine firing line forms during the 1st Marine Division's withdrawal from Yudam-ni. (Photo by Sgt. Frank C. Kerr, USMC)

As morning broke on December 3rd, and with a light snow falling over the North Korean high country, a large enemy patrol was spotted moving along a ridgeline just a few hundred yards distant. But those soldiers must have been as cold and tired as we were because neither side fired a shot. Shortly thereafter I ran into Corporal Walter Six, a combat cameraman from Sharonville, Ohio who had trained with me in the Reproduction and Photographic Service Section at Camp Pendleton. Together we walked the column, focusing our cameras on the snaking line of haggard, unshaven men. It was hard to believe these were the same Marines who had marched so confidently into North Korea just a few weeks before. Helmets were pierced and parkas torn by bullets and shrapnel, and the strain of combat was etched deep in every dead-eyed, wind-burned face. I swear, in seven days those boys had aged seven years.

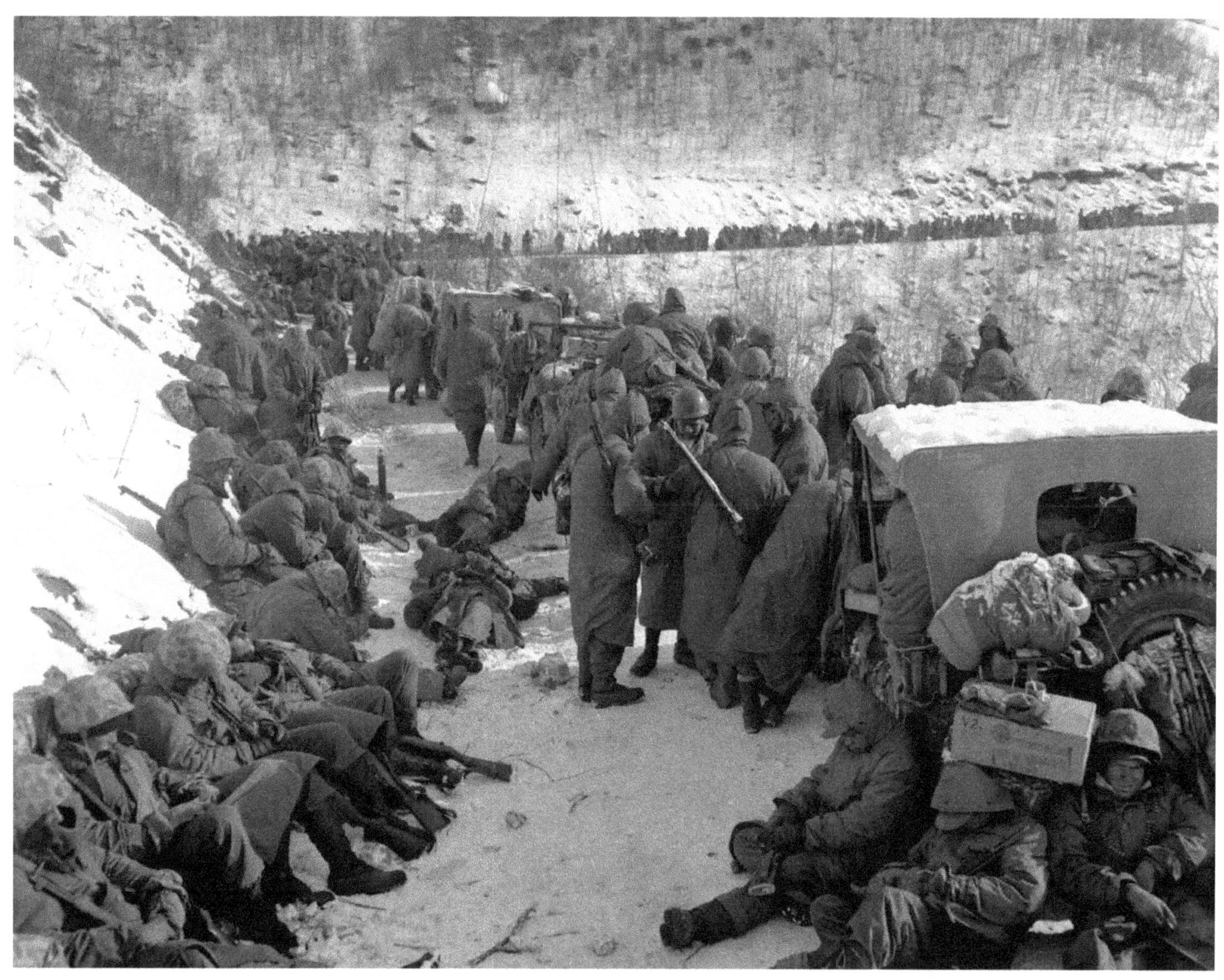

The Road Back. Marines of the 5th and 7th Regiments rest on the MSR (Main Supply Route) while lead units clear the ridges of enemy combatants. ***Following pages:*** Cold and exhausted Leathernecks withdraw from the Chosin Reservoir in December, 1950, pausing to rest only when the column was halted. The cold at Chosin was so intense that a man could lie down, fall asleep, and freeze to death. *(Photos by Sgt. Frank C. Kerr, USMC)*

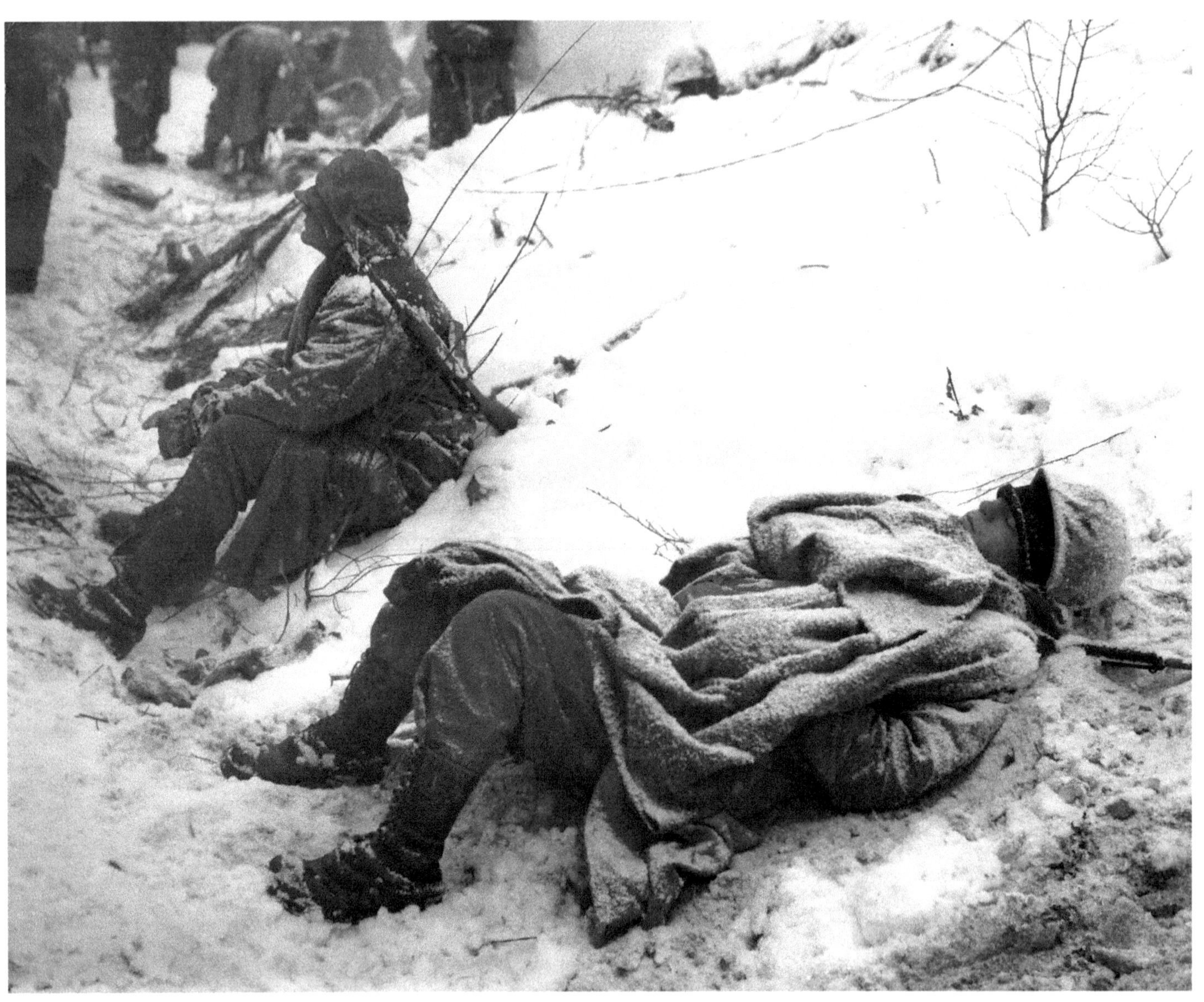

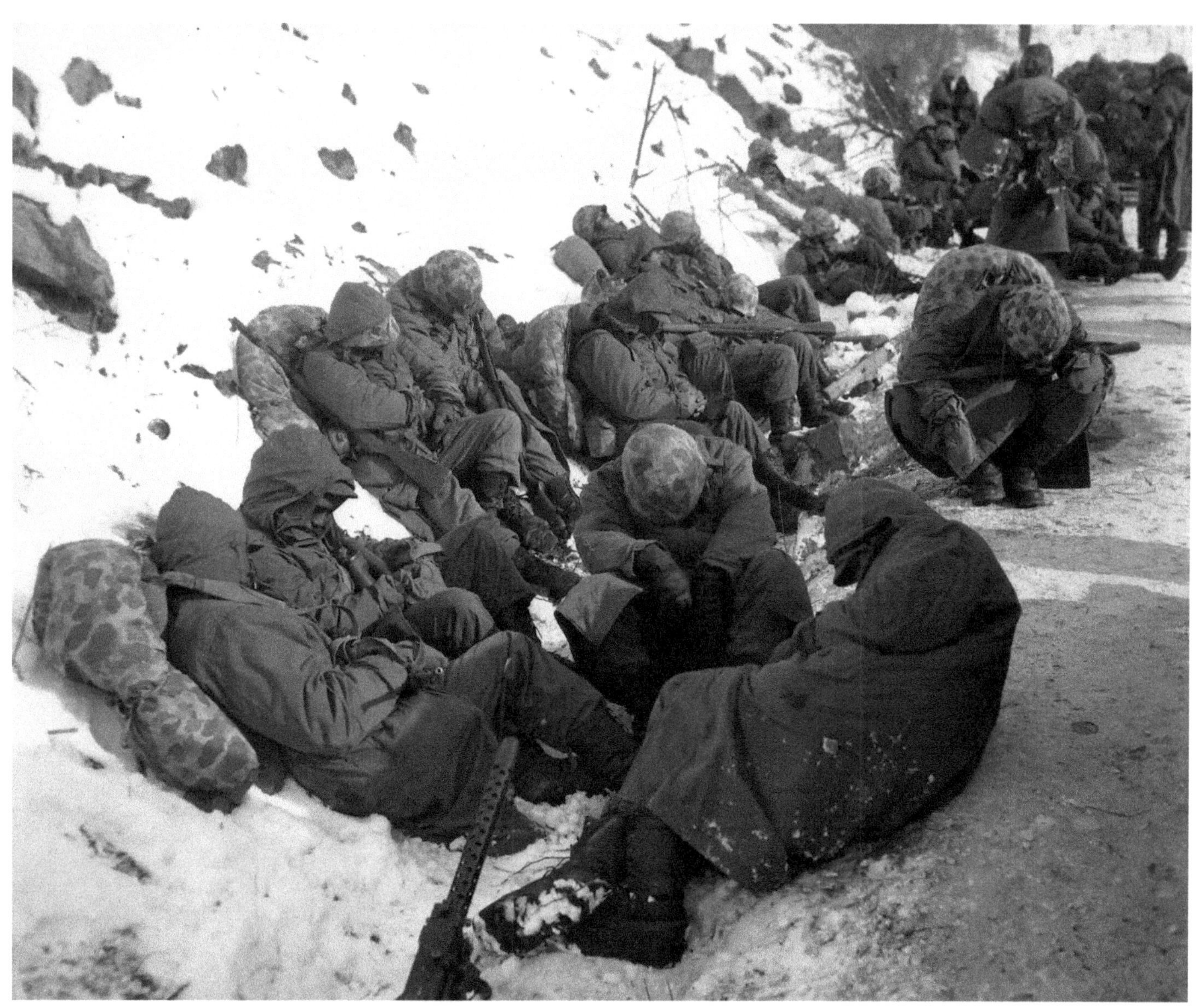

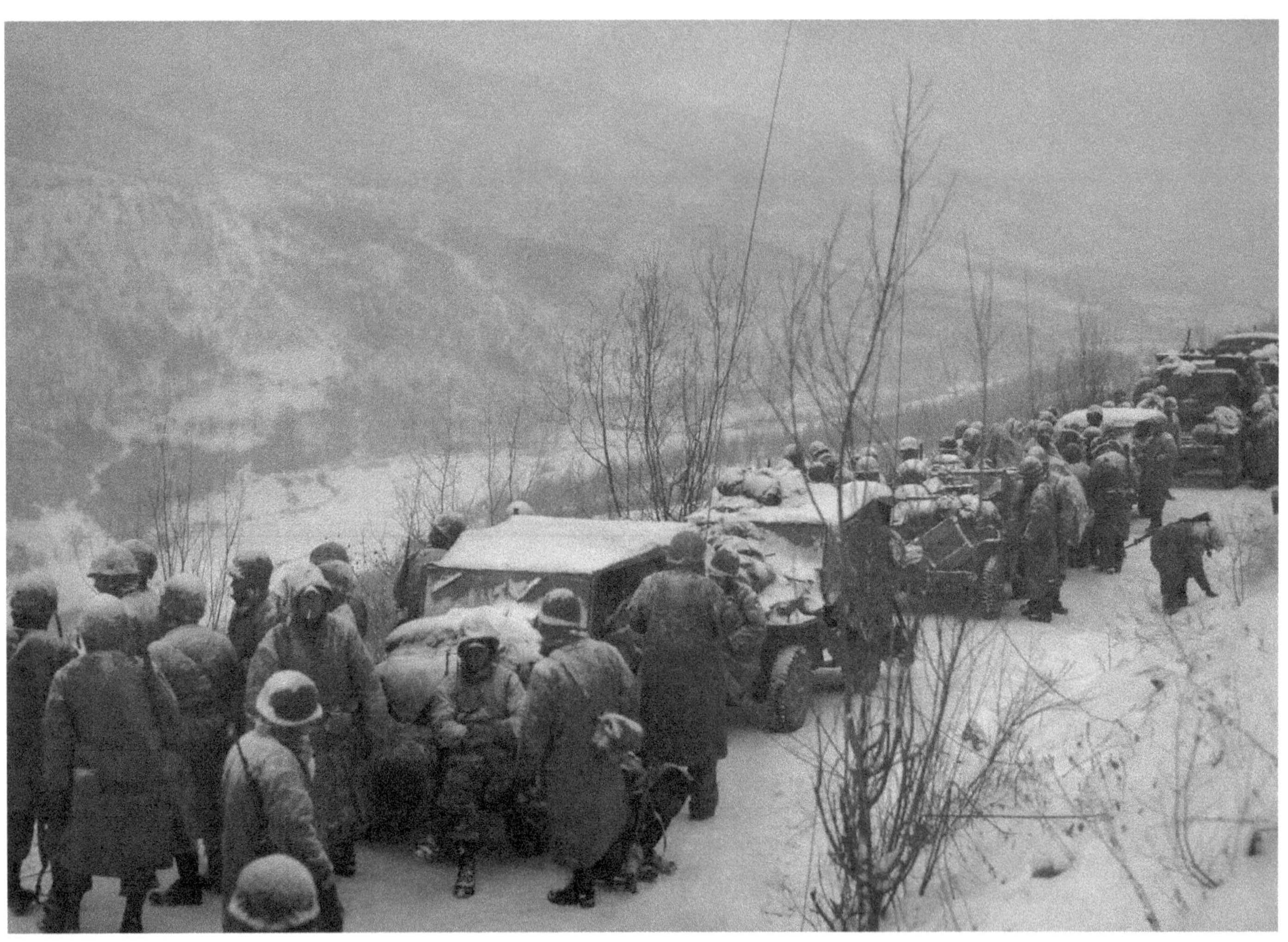

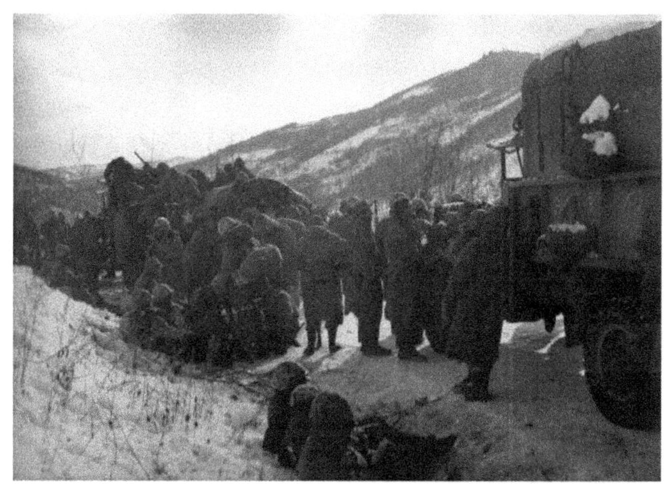

Leathernecks of the 7th Marines take a much-needed break on their way south from Chosin. *(Photo by Sgt. Frank C. Kerr, USMC)*

With dusk creeping over the reservoir, and with it the threat of another communist attack, our pace quickened toward the mountain pass that would lead us into Hagaru. On the way there we came upon a circled Marine artillery battery, its big guns pointing in all directions. As we were passing, one of our troops wryly observed, "Hey, look. We've got them surrounded."

The accelerated pace soon spread out the column, and my frostbitten feet were in such agony that I stopped trying to keep up and waited by the roadside for a vehicle that might have some extra room. A truck came along shortly, and I was about to climb aboard when, for some inexplicable reason, I let it pass and hitched a ride, instead, on a trailer towed by the truck that followed. The convoy continued on another hundred yards or so then came to an abrupt halt. Just ahead, the vehicle I had declined to board was over the bank and upside down, with bodies strewn across the slope. Was it gut intuition or blind luck that saved me from that fate? Maybe sometimes you need a little of both.

As we approached Hagaru, an MP warned our truck driver to speed through the stretch ahead. A Marine tank was burning by the roadside and the Chinese were picking men off as they passed through the firelight. Corporal Six climbed onto the trailer's fender and I held him

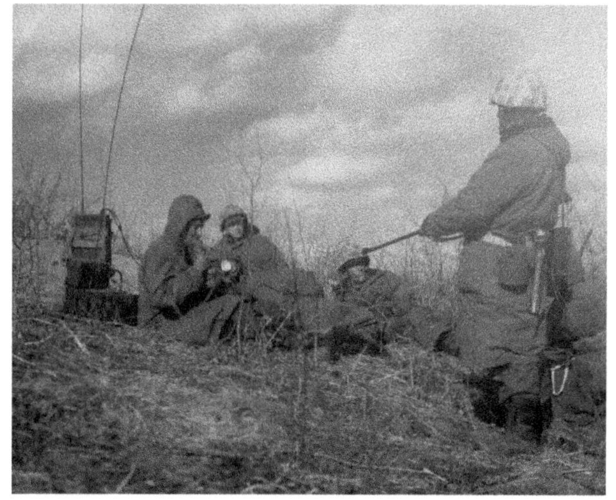

A radioman with the 7th Marines tries to contact Fox Company, cut off and under siege by the Chinese in hills overlooking the division's route of withdrawal. *(Photo by Sgt. Frank C. Kerr, USMC)*

as the truck rushed past that engulfed tank. When we reached the outskirts of town, and without orders being given, our weary troops set exhaustion aside, closed ranks and marched square-shouldered and proud through the camp's perimeter. It was a stirring sight to see, and more than a few battle-hardened men had tears in their eyes and lumps in their throats watching those "magnificent bastards" march into Hagaru that night.

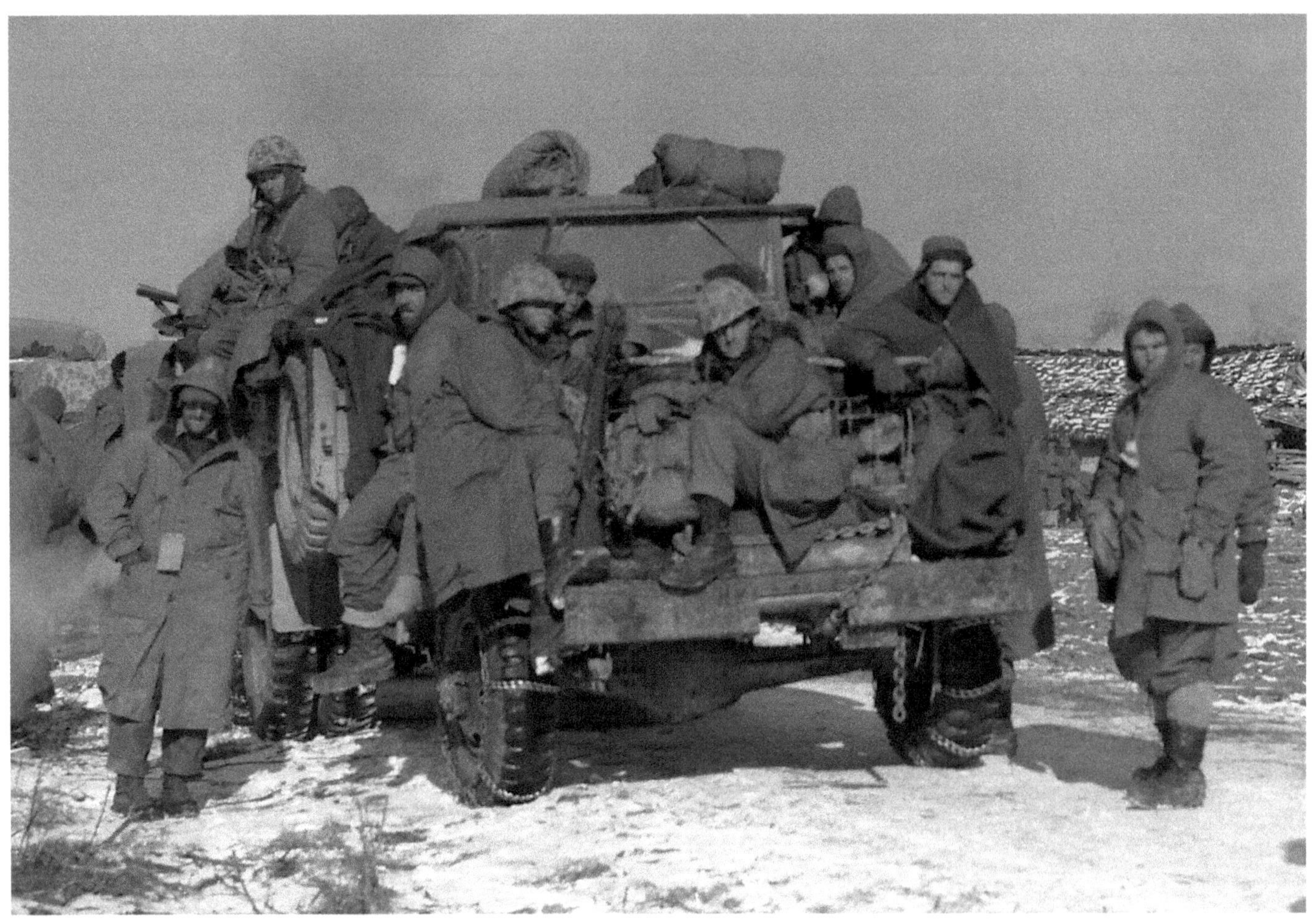

After a long and arduous trek from Yudam-ni, these U.S. Marines wait for the column to move again on the last stretch of road before Hagaru. *(Photo by Sgt. Frank C. Kerr, USMC)*

HAGARU-RI

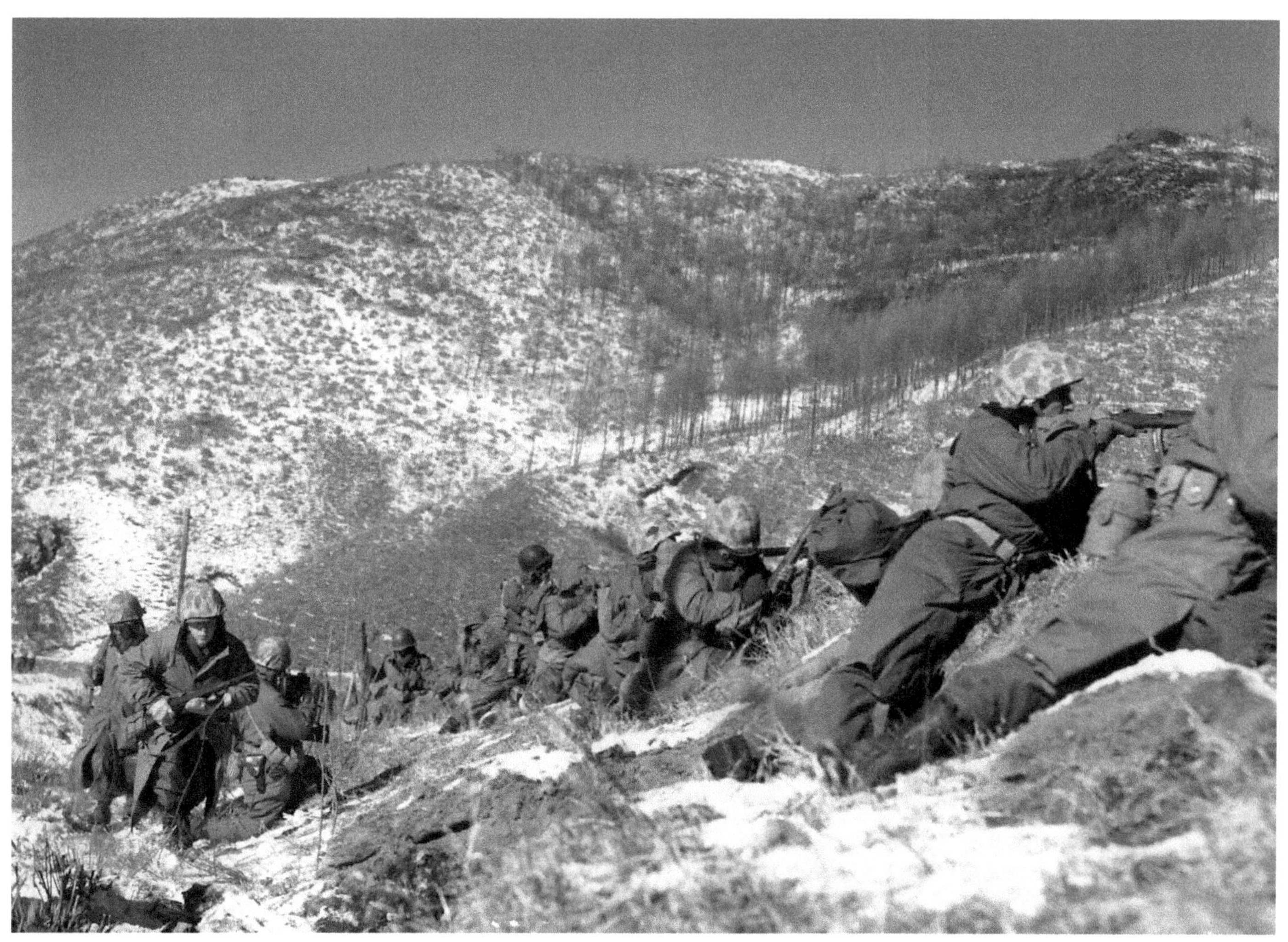

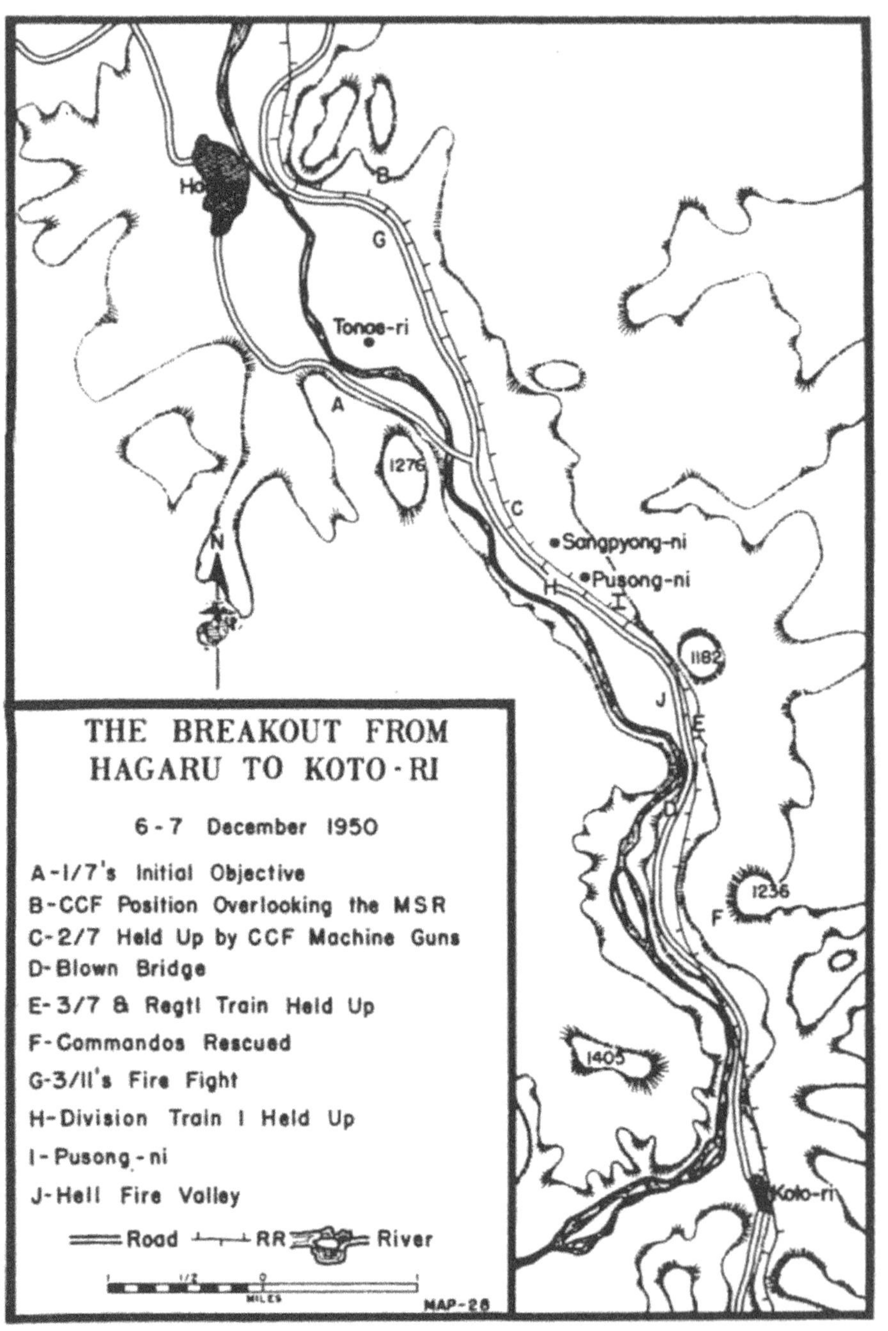

Ha
B
G
Tonae-ri
A
1276
N
C
Sangpyong-ni
Pusong-ni
H
I
1182
J
E
1236
F
1405
Koto-ri
THE BREAKOUT FROM
HAGARU TO KOTO-RI
6-7 December 1950
A-1/7's Initial Objective
B-CCF Position Overlooking the MSR
C-2/7 Held Up by CCF Machine Guns
D-Blown Bridge
E-3/7 & Regtl Train Held Up
F-Commandos Rescued
G-3/11's Fire Fight
H-Division Train I Held Up
I-Pusong-ni
J-Hell Fire Valley
Road   RR   River
1/2   0
MILES
MAP-28

Off the road and clear of the Chinese Army—at least for now—Walter Six and I found ourselves in a hut with hot coffee, plenty of rations, and a glowing stove that filled the room with glorious heat. It was there that I reconnected with my good friend and fellow still photographer, Corporal Peter McDonald, who sat us both near the stove, removed our boots, and rubbed our frostbitten feet until the blood was flowing again. After pouring coffee, Pete shared the latest news from the war—and none of it was good.

The Chinese had surrounded Hagaru and cut off Koto-ri, our next supply depot eleven miles further south. And if that wasn't enough of a gut-punch, the U.S. 8th Army was in full retreat from North Korea, while three Army battalions on the reservoir's east side had been overrun and chopped to pieces. Just a few weeks earlier those same G.I.'s had relieved our regiment and we had tossed the usual wisecracks at each other—as soldiers and Marines often do. Now a lot of those boys would never see home again.

It was astounding how quickly the war had turned. With its numerically superior army, China was out to exterminate the 1st Marine Division piecemeal, denying it the supplies and reinforcements necessary to reach its ultimate destination, the port city of Hungnam, where preparations were underway to evacuate our troops by ship. The situation looked bleak, but I still had a job to do.

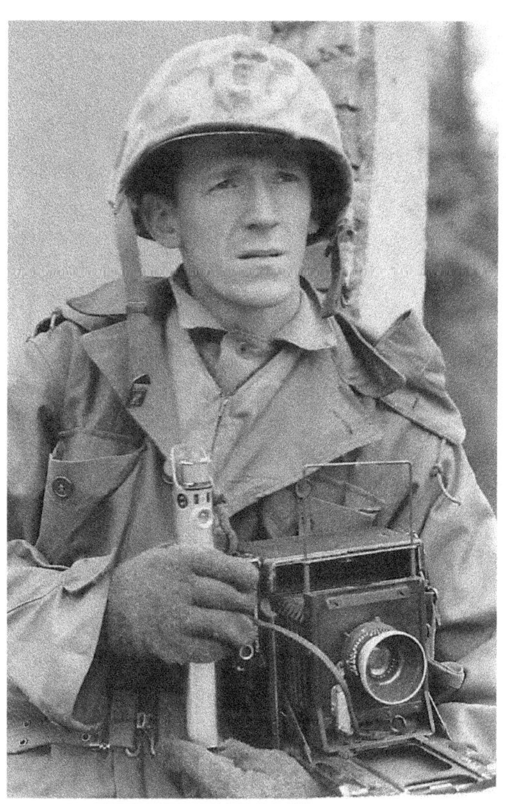

Cpl. Peter McDonald, USMC combat photographer. (National Archives photo)

To cover the next leg of the division's withdrawal, I had a fresh supply of film flown in on a C-47 transport, one of many aircraft using a makeshift runway that Marine combat engineers had hacked from the frozen earth to evacuate our wounded. After handing over my exposed film to the air crew, I noticed some of the wounded waiting in line for evacuation were stalling—falling back in the queue, hoping to stay in the fight alongside their fellow Marines. It was a sentiment I understood and shared. Though my feet were painfully frostbitten, nothing short of a Chinaman's bullet was going to stop me from marching out of the Chosin Reservoir with the 1st Marine Division.

With fresh film in my camera, I wandered through camp looking for photos to take and eventually came upon a group of Marines warming themselves by a fire. A few had set canteens close to the heat to melt the ice inside, while another was so fatigued, and his feet so numbed by frostbite, that he didn't realize his boot was burning until a sleepy-eyed Marine beside him said, "Hey pal. Your foot's on fire."

As the boot was snuffed out, a visibly shaken combat engineer joined the circle. The man had spent a hard week helping build the runway at Hagaru while under enemy fire and his nerves were shot. "We'll never make it out of here," he muttered anxiously. "They'll slaughter us." Without lifting his eyes, a bearded Marine growled back, "Shut the hell up."

Message delivered, that engineer never spoke another word.

If I was to die at Chosin, I figured I might as well die well-groomed, so on the eve of our withdrawal from Hagaru, I got myself a shave from a North Korean barber who, according to our interpreter, had once done the same for a communist general. I returned to the hut clean-shaven and was getting my gear in order when a familiar face walked through the door wearing a big-hearted grin beneath his heavy beard.

First Lieutenant Karle Seydel was a twenty-six year old platoon leader with a wife and two young kids living back in Seattle Washington, just on the other side of the Cascades from my family home in Yakima. The lieutenant had seen his fair share of combat, as bullet holes in his parka testified, and was cold and hungry that night, so I poured him a cup of hot soup. After a few sips he turned with a sly grin and said, "So, anything exciting happen to you lately, Sergeant Kerr?" I had to laugh. During our time in the Pusan Perimeter, Karle and I had spent an unpleasant afternoon pinned down in a thicket by a North Korean

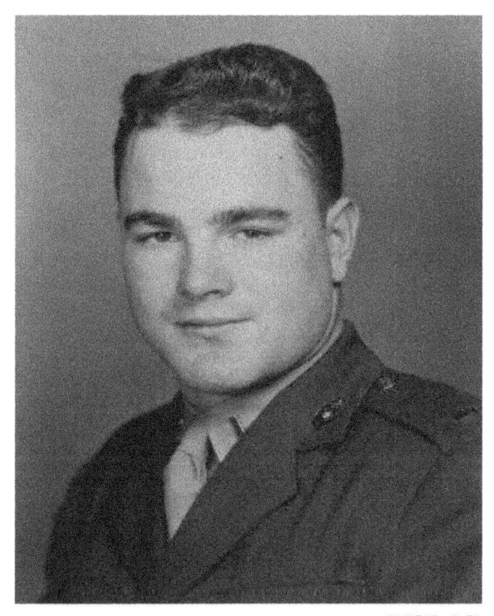

1st Lieutenant Karle Seydel, USMC

machine gun, so close we could smell the men trying to kill us. We survived thanks to a P-51 pilot who strafed the nest—and the thicket he didn't know we were in—until the machine gun was silenced. As we emerged four hours later without a scratch, the lieutenant shook his head in amazement and said, "It sure makes a Christian out of you, don't it?" The two of us had been friends ever since. That night we talked for hours of war and home until the time came for Karle to rejoin his platoon. I never saw him again. First Lieutenant Seydel was killed two days later defending his company's position during the savage fight for East Hill, a heroic action for which he was posthumously awarded the Silver Star. His remains are up at Chosin still.

During the pre-dawn hours of December 6th, U.S. Marines, British commandos and remnants of the Army's 31st and 32nd Infantry, 7th Division, began burning extra gear, rations and clothing in preparation for departure from Hagaru. Elsewhere, teams of men got busy putting the town's huts and buildings to the torch—burning anything that might give shelter to the Chinese once we moved out. Forced from their homes, North Korean civilians poured into the streets to join the allied withdrawal, taking whatever possessions they could carry.

Witnessing such abject human misery was nothing new to those of us who served in the war. On a September afternoon during the Second Battle of

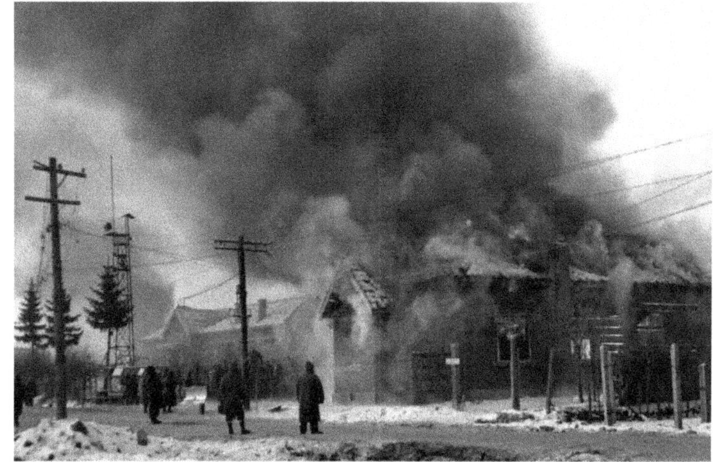

Hagaru aflame. Before withdrawing, men of the 1st Marine Division burn anything that might be of value to the Chinese Army.. (Photo by Sgt. William R. Keating, USMC)

Naktong, the platoon I was shadowing came upon a river of fleeing South Korean refugees; mostly women, children and babies. Some of those wretched souls were wounded, all of them were traumatized. More heart wrenching still was the sight of civilians hopelessly trapped in the crossfire of battle, not knowing what to do or where to turn, frozen like deer in headlights until they were finally gunned down. It's a sad fact of war that innocents get hurt and innocents die, but that doesn't make it any easier to swallow.

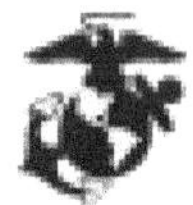

On December 6th, a miles-long convoy of some 10,000 allied troops began evacuating Hagaru-ri along a dangerous stretch of road christened "Hell Fire Valley" – a name bestowed by British Commandos following a deadly ambush there just days before. In short order our advance units began making enemy contact, and Walter Six and I hurried forward to capture the action. At the head of the column we found Marine infantry engaged in a furious firefight with Chinese entrenched on a rocky hillside. Flushed from their hiding places, the communists began clawing their way up the slope to escape, but most never made it. As they scrambled for their lives, our troops began picking them off one-by-one. Some Marines shouted with excitement as they pulled the trigger, others did their killing in a more business-like manner—just the deadly work of professional soldiering.

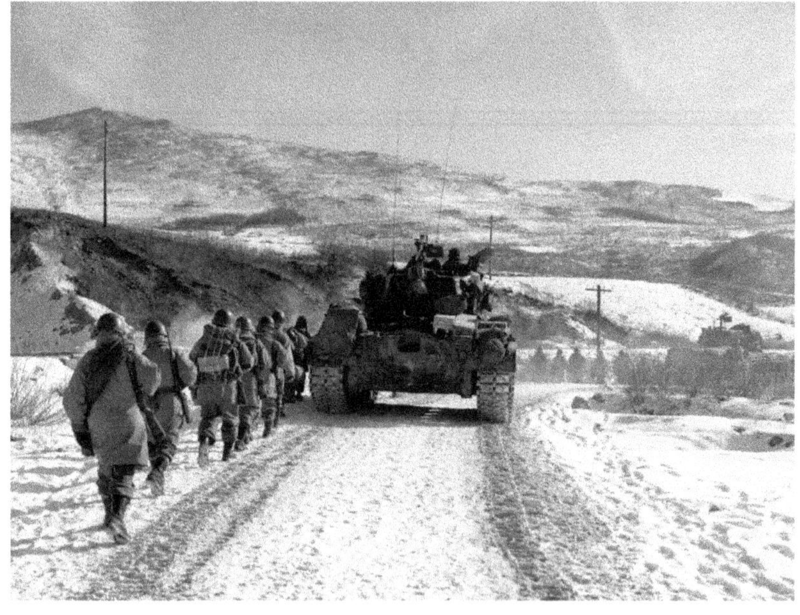

Men of the 1st Marine Division on the move from Hagaru-ri, December 6th 1950. (Photo by Sgt. Frank C. Kerr, USMC)

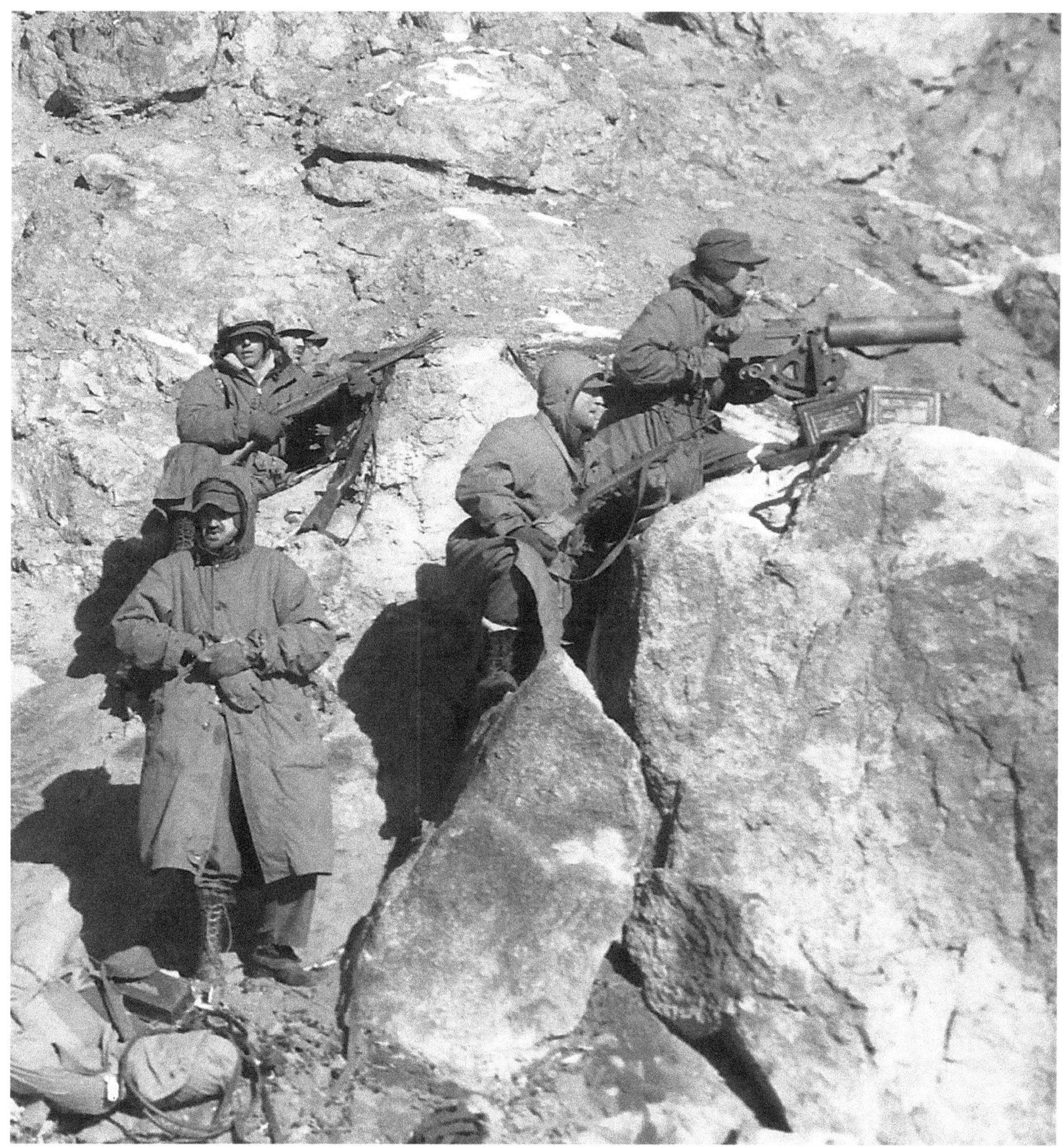

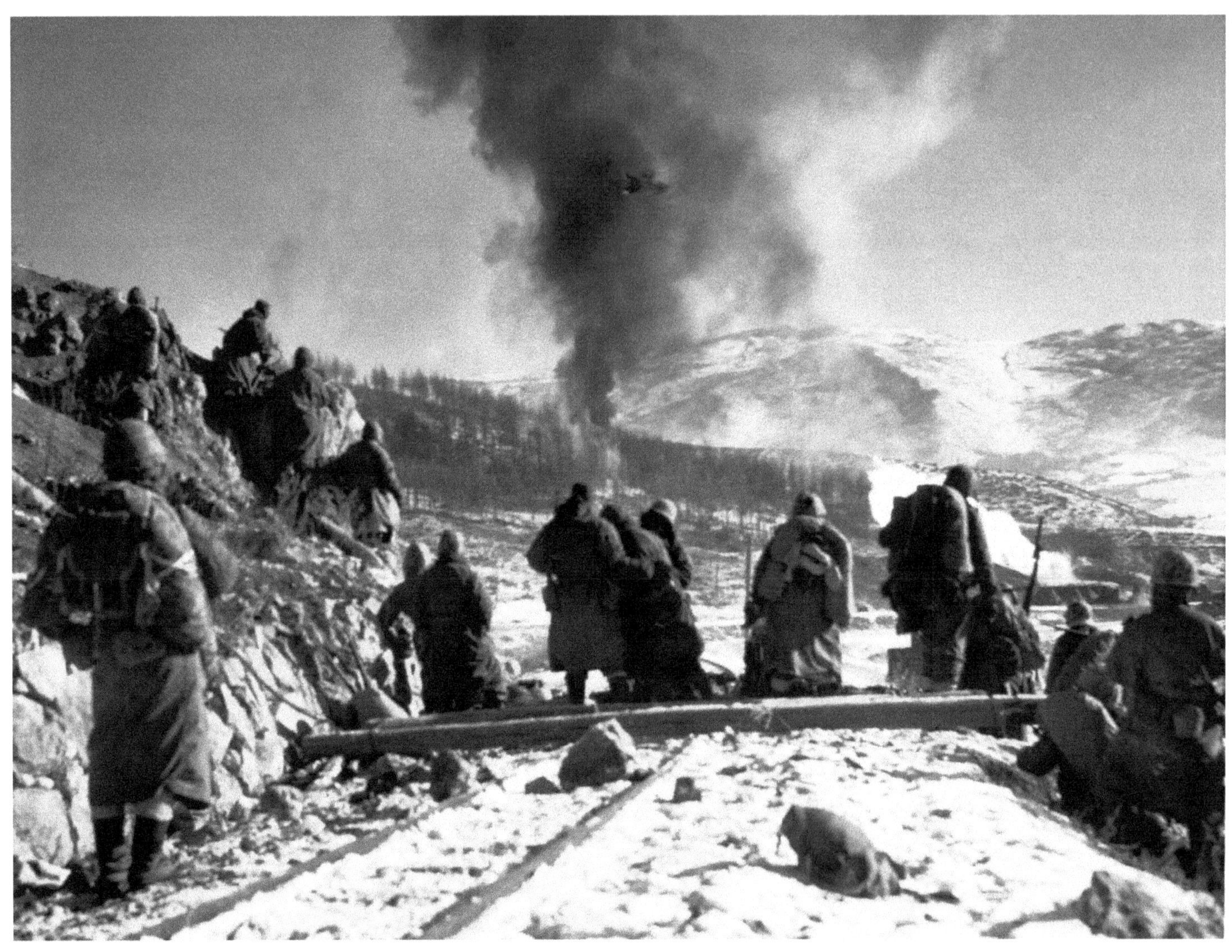

Previous page: 1st Marine Division infantrymen take to a rugged hillside to engage Chinese troops defending a roadblock on the road to Koto-ri, ***Above:*** Offering close air support to ground units, a Marine Corsair (partially obscured by smoke) drops napalm on the enemy position, allowing the allied column to continue its advance south. *(Photos by Sgt. Frank C. Kerr, USMC)*

Rallied by their officers, the Chinese found new positions higher on the slope until a Marine Corsair came swooping in and blasted the hill with napalm—a particularly vicious weapon of war and a godawful way for men to die. Even so, our troops were not in a charitable mood that day, and as the screams of napalmed soldiers echoed from the hillside, one Marine yelled back in a fury, "Burn you bastards!". Cruel words, it's true, but by its very nature war is an ugly, primal beast. Live with it long enough and it can devour you.

Having delivered its lethal payload, the Corsair buzzed low over the tactical air controller's jeep where Corporal Six and I were standing, then disappeared over the hills. Within seconds I heard the distinct chatter of a machine gun and felt the sting of a bullet as it grazed my face. Another round clipped Walter and a third went through the cheek of a Marine standing between us. As I was helping the injured man find cover, another spray of bullets peppered the jeep and the ground around us, prompting that wounded Marine to spit blood and rage toward the hills, "Damn it! If you're going to kill me, kill me, but stop trying to scare me to death!"

As combat cameramen, Corporal Six and I held one decided advantage over the infantry; carte blanche to move whenever and wherever we wanted. And at that moment, what we wanted was to move our butts back to the middle of the column where the action wasn't quite so warm. As it turned out, the middle was exactly where the Chinese decided to strike next. Sticking to their playbook, the assault came at night, announced with a flurry of hand grenades, followed by a series of bugles and whistles—signals from their officers directing the attack. Of a sudden the enemy was everywhere, ghostly shapes in quilted winter uniforms, firing rifles and burp guns, hurling grenades and screaming like men possessed.

Walter and I threw ourselves into a roadside ditch and returned fire, but bullets were coming in so thick and fast you could barely lift your head for fear of getting it blown off. Our outnumbered infantry battled furiously, but each time an enemy wave was beaten back, another would come rushing down from the hills. The number of Chinese soldiers was staggering, and it wasn't long before the fighting on that narrow stretch of dirt road was fixed bayonets and hand-to-hand.

Amid this battle frenzy, I became aware of someone setting up a machine gun behind me, but the action was so close and confused I couldn't be certain if he was friend or foe. "Are you a Marine!?" I called in the dark. The man never answered, but his weapon commenced firing in the enemy's direction so I figured he must be one of the good guys. When the Chinese broke off the ground assault, their mortars took over. As shells began raining down, I spotted one of their soldiers rushing my position and rose to take a shot. At that instant came the zip of an incoming mortar round, followed by a deafening blast that showered me in frozen dirt. A dying moan came from the machine gunner behind me. Hit by shrapnel, he was gone before I could reach him.

In time Walter and I realized we were the only able-bodied Marines left defending that bloody patch of turf. The bodies of dead Americans and Chinese lay piled in front of our ditch like sandbags, catching the bullets meant for us, and with our ammunition running low we figured it was time to make a dash for the opposite side of the road. My feet were like blocks of ice, and I stumbled rather than dashed across, but we both managed to find cover and hunker down for the next assault.

Fortunately for us that assault never came. Instead, the gray dawn revealed a remarkable sight almost too surreal to be believed. Across the blood-soaked snow, where the frozen dead lay twisted into grotesque shapes and the wounded begged for help, survivors from both sides wandered the battlefield in a daze, observing some strange, unspoken truce dictated by pure exhaustion. It was dreamlike and fascinating to watch, and the spell remained unbroken until a Marine bulldozer arrived to clear our destroyed vehicles from the road. As the enemy melted back into the hills, the wounded they left behind eyeballed us warily, expecting to be executed at any moment. But we were so preoccupied with our own casualties that we ignored them, not even bothering to confiscate their weapons until our somber work was done. Before long the wounded were secured, the dead catalogued, and our battered column was rolling again.

Though the Chinese Army had paid a heavy price in lives lost that night, they had succeeded in splitting the convoy in two. The forward section had continued on to Koto-ri while the rear was now leading the way. As our troops continued to advance, we came upon the remnants of a destroyed allied convoy. The frozen bodies of dead Marines, U.S. soldiers and British commandos lay sprawled along a scrapyard of smashed and looted vehicles. Here was the terrible aftermath of an enemy ambush that had earned this place the apt name "Hell Fire Valley." A passing Marine gave a shout and pointed toward a snaking line of Chinese infantry moving two abreast over a distant hill. A few of the men took shots at them but their targets were too far away, so they slung their rifles and fell back in line as the splintered column continued on toward Koto-ri—one step closer to the sea.

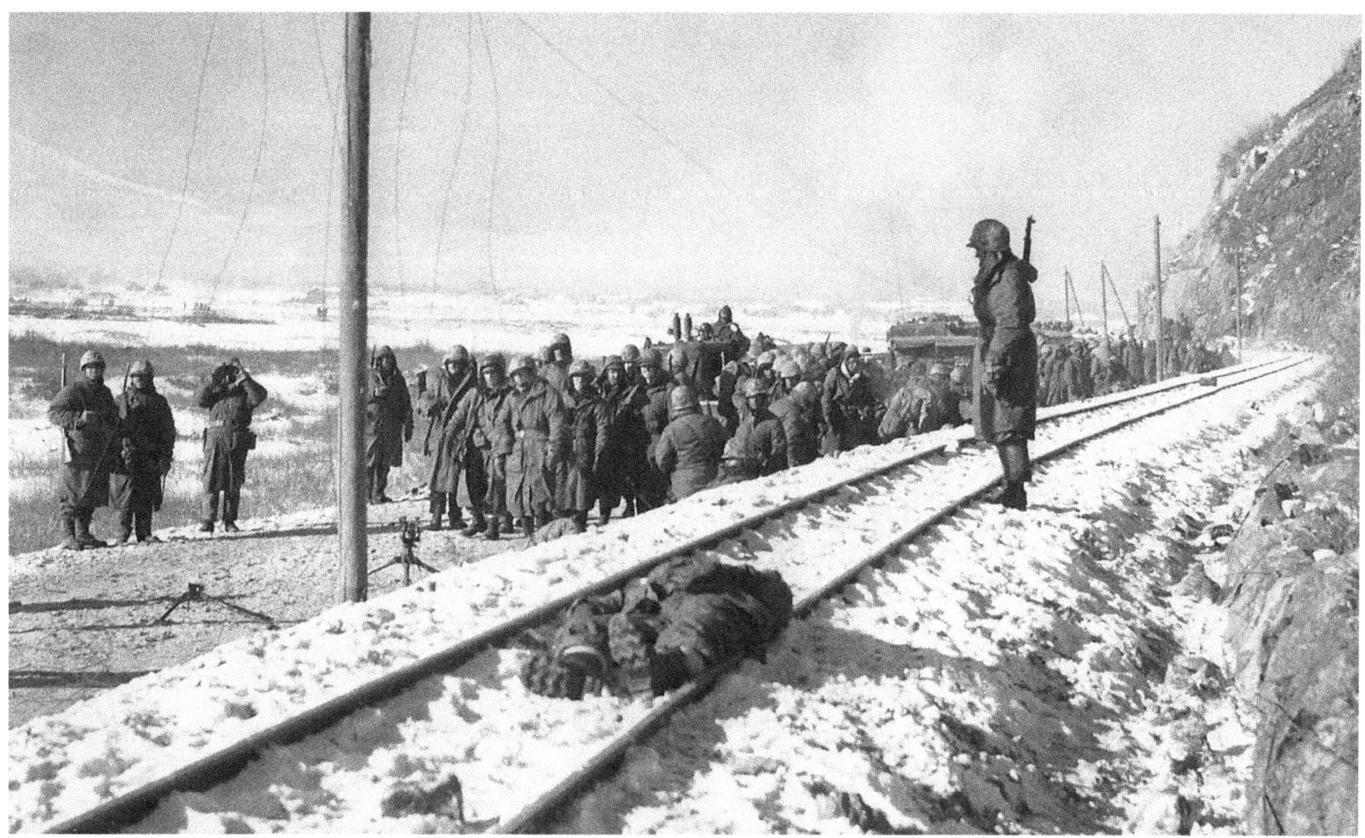

As a U.S. Marine stands sentinel, Leathernecks of the 1st Marine Division halt momentarily near the body of one of their own. December 6th, 1950. *(Photo by Sgt. Frank C. Kerr, USMC)*

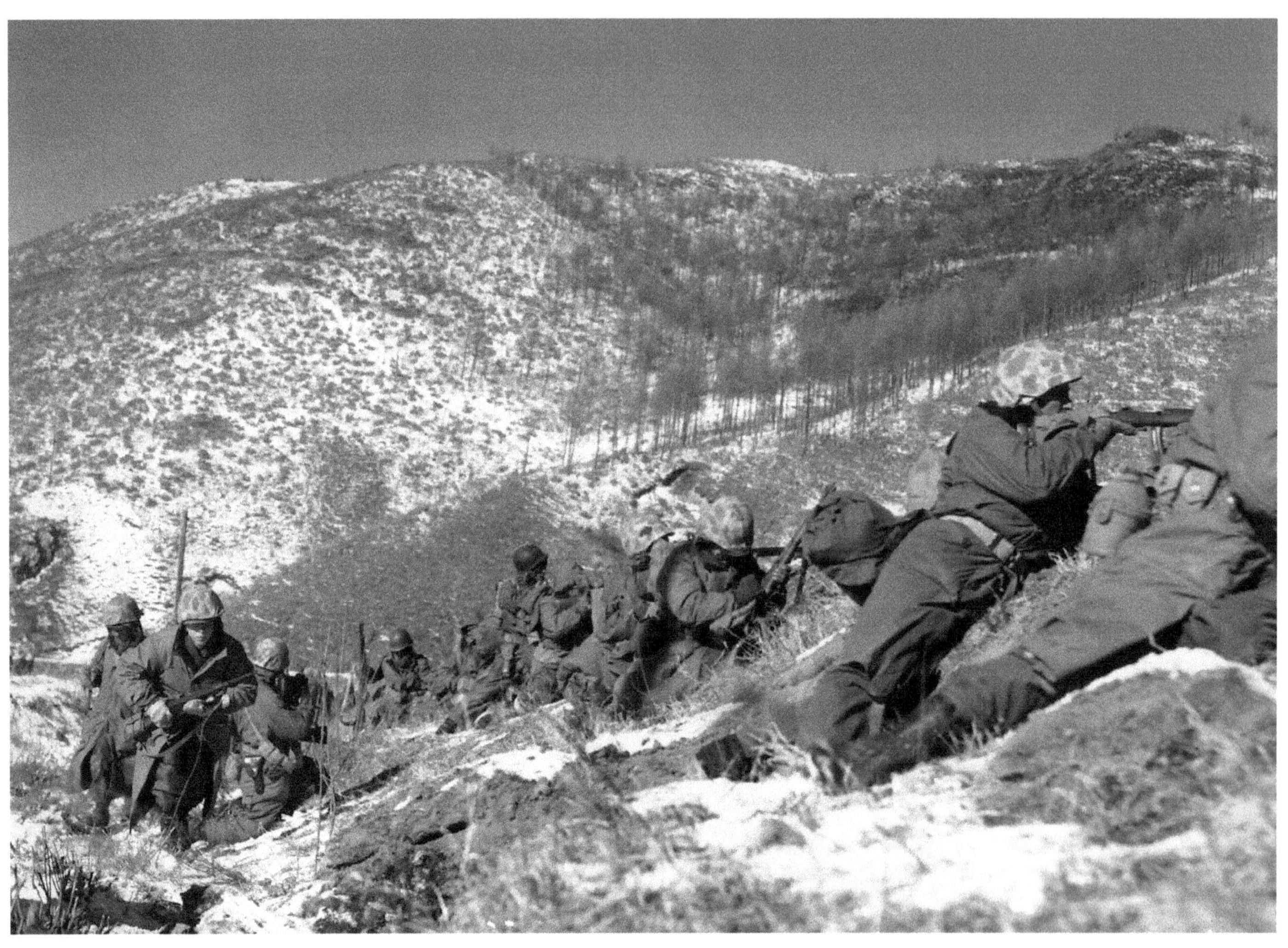

Marine infantry engage the enemy during one of the many ambushes aimed at slowing the allied advance from Hagaru to Koto-ri. *(Photo by Sgt. Frank C. Kerr, USMC)*

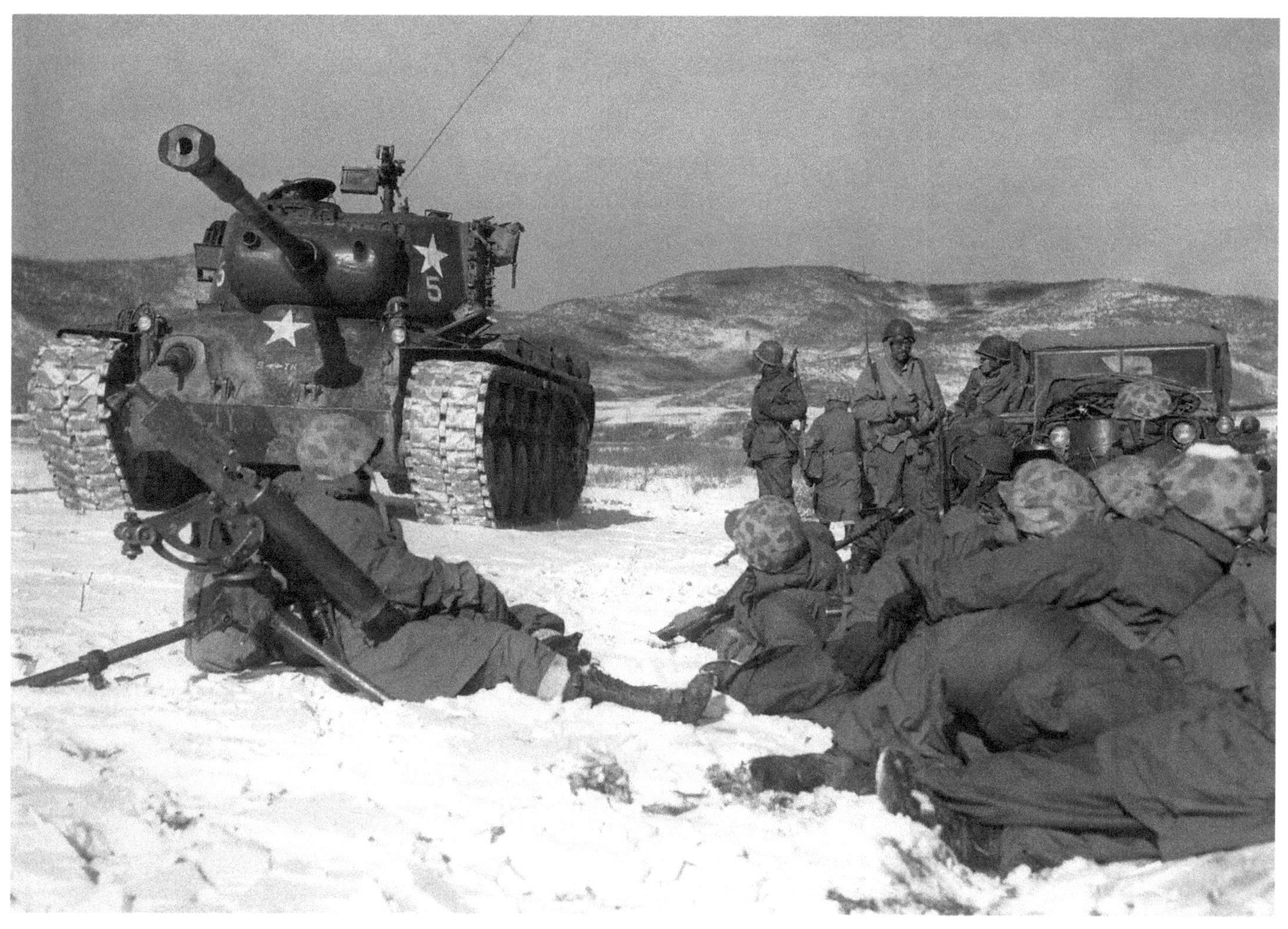

Following the ambush, elements of the 1st Marine Division pause to rest on the snow-covered roadside. *(Photo by Sgt. Frank C. Kerr, USMC)*

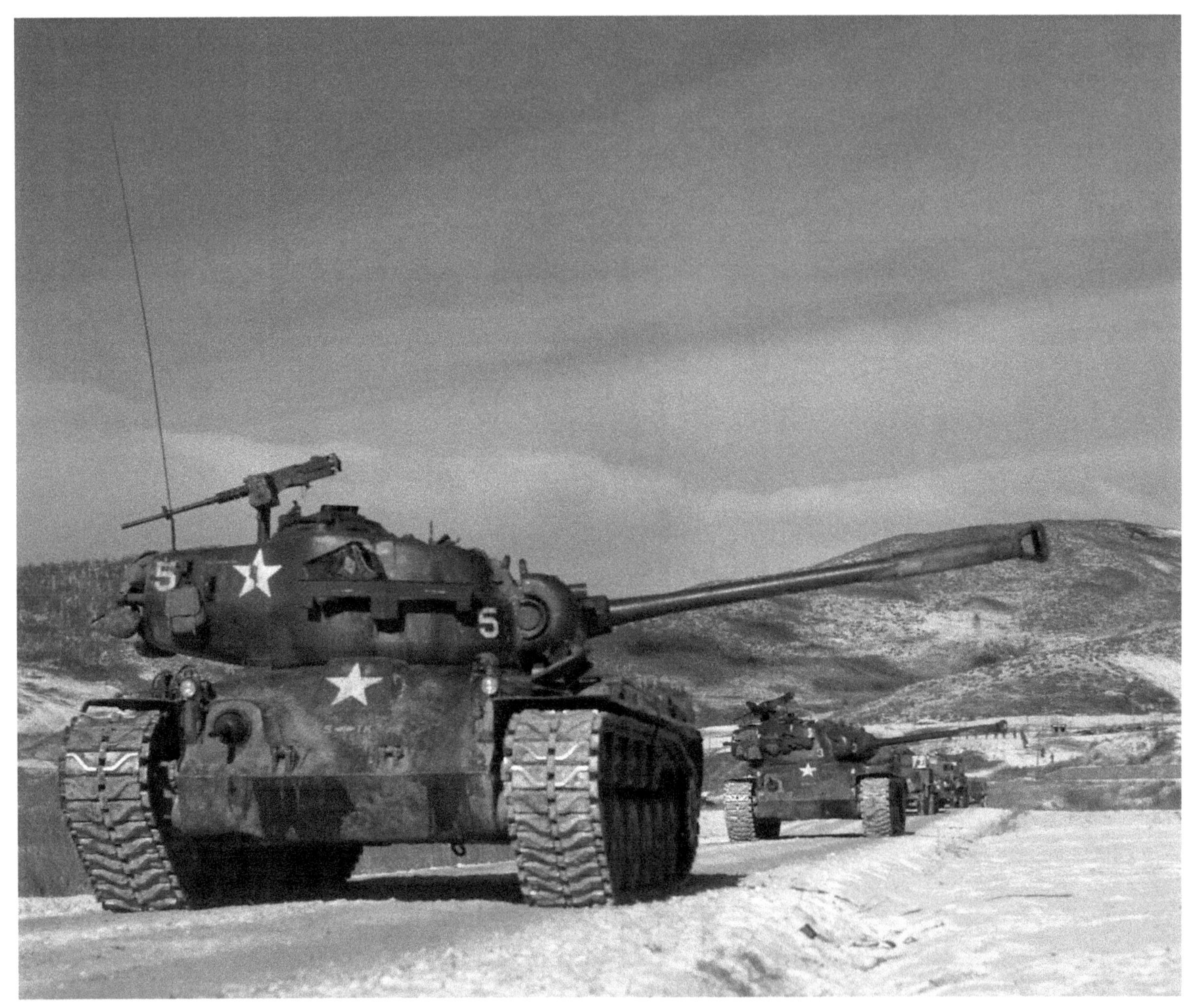

A column of Marine M-26 Pershing tanks roll south, keeping their turrets pointed toward enemy positions. During the breakout from Chosin, five Marine tanks would be lost to Chinese anti-tank fire.   ***Opposite page:*** U.S. Marines set up a firing line on the road from Hagaru. *(Photos by Sgt. Frank C. Kerr, USMC)*

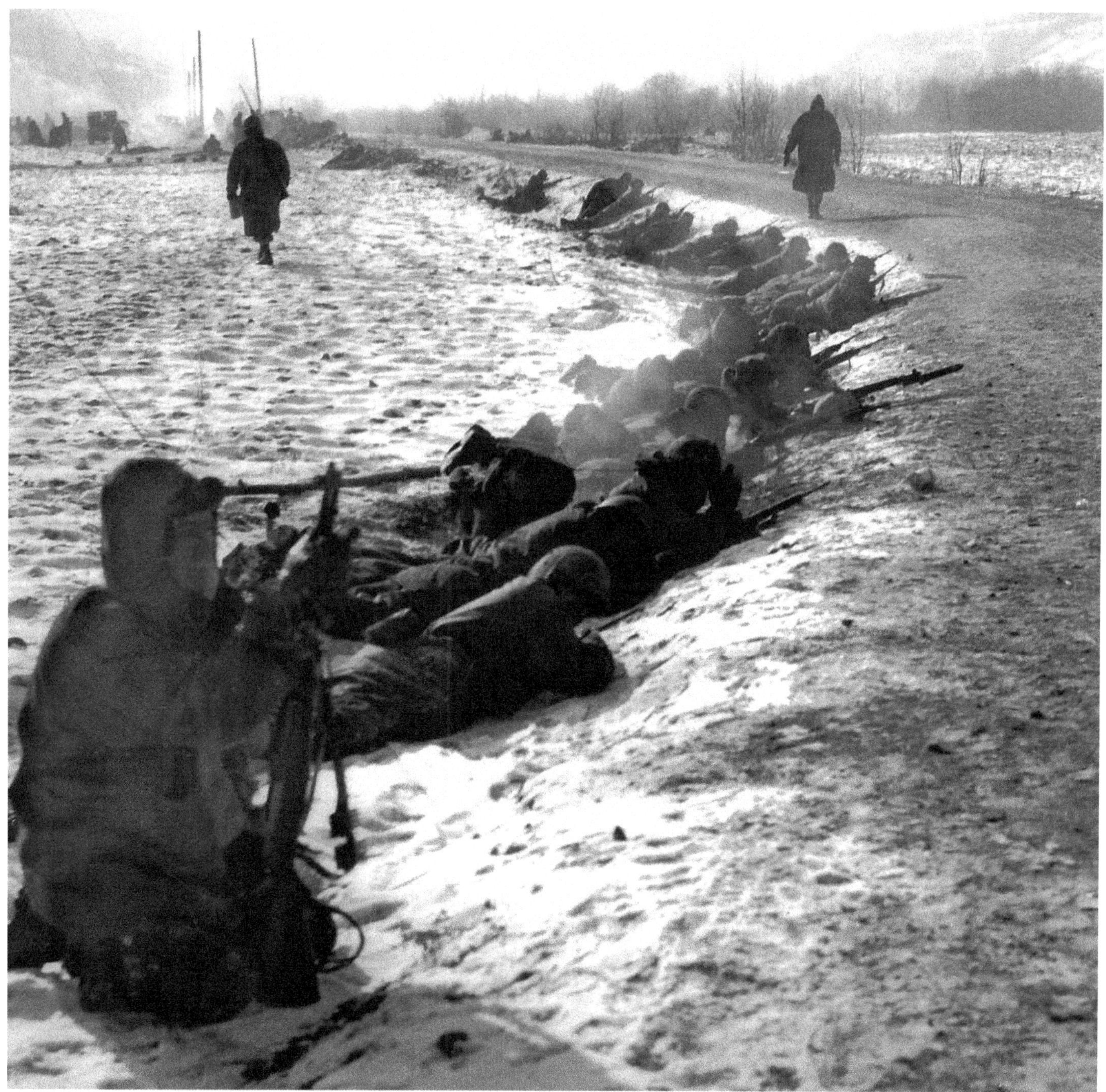

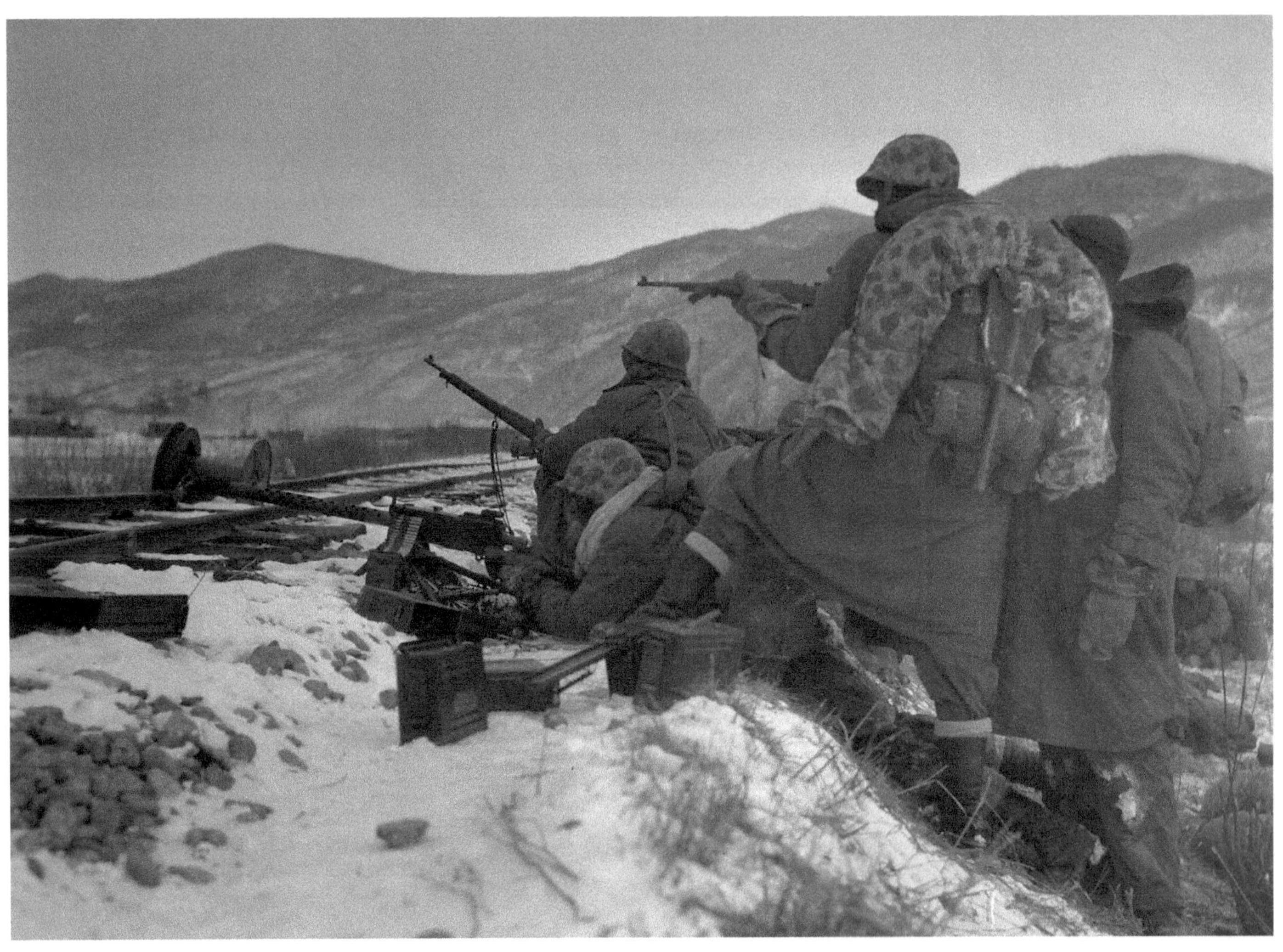

Marine infantry counter fire with fire when attacked by well-entrenched Chinese troops north of Koto-ri. *(Photo by Sgt. Frank C. Kerr, USMC)*

KOTO-RI

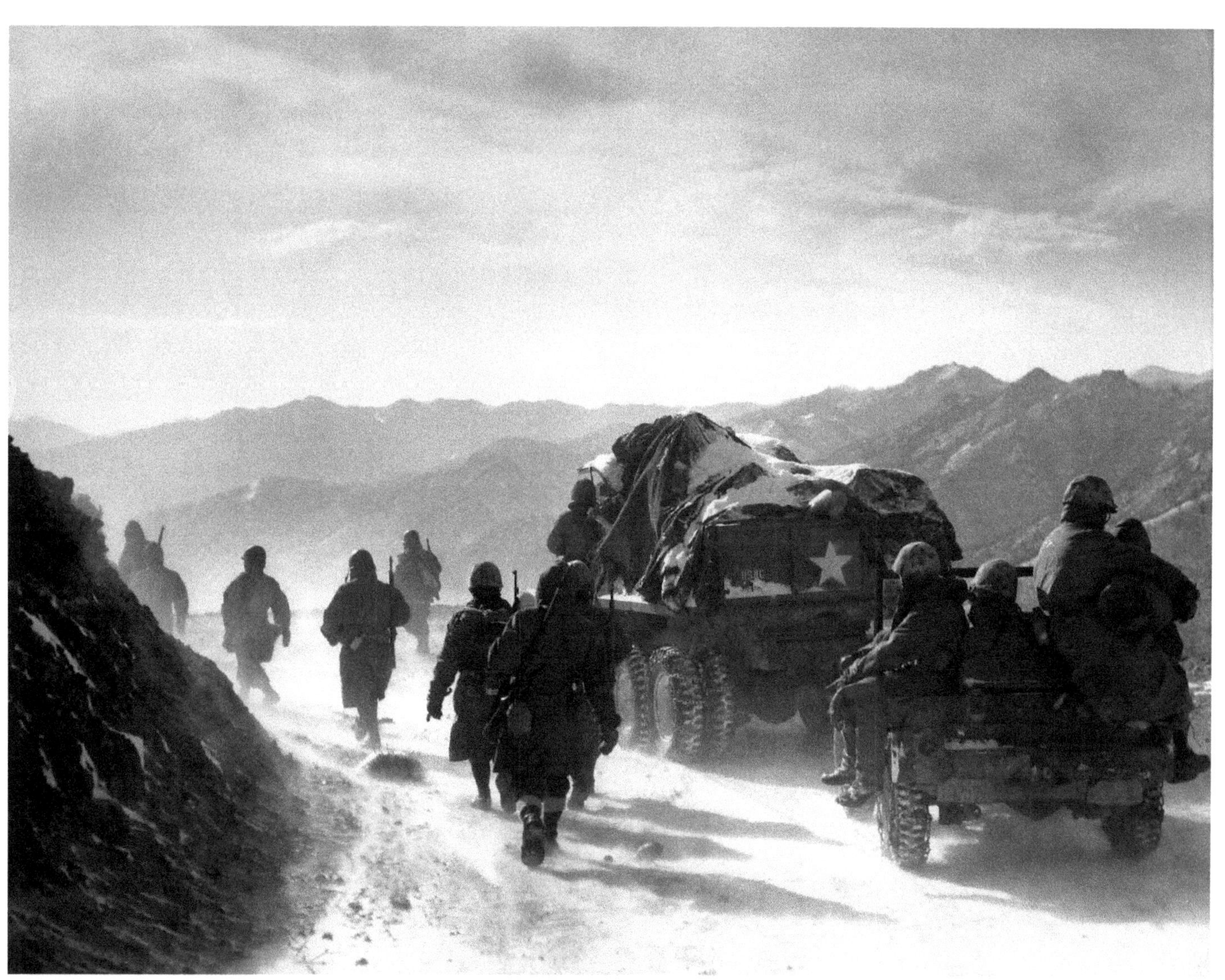

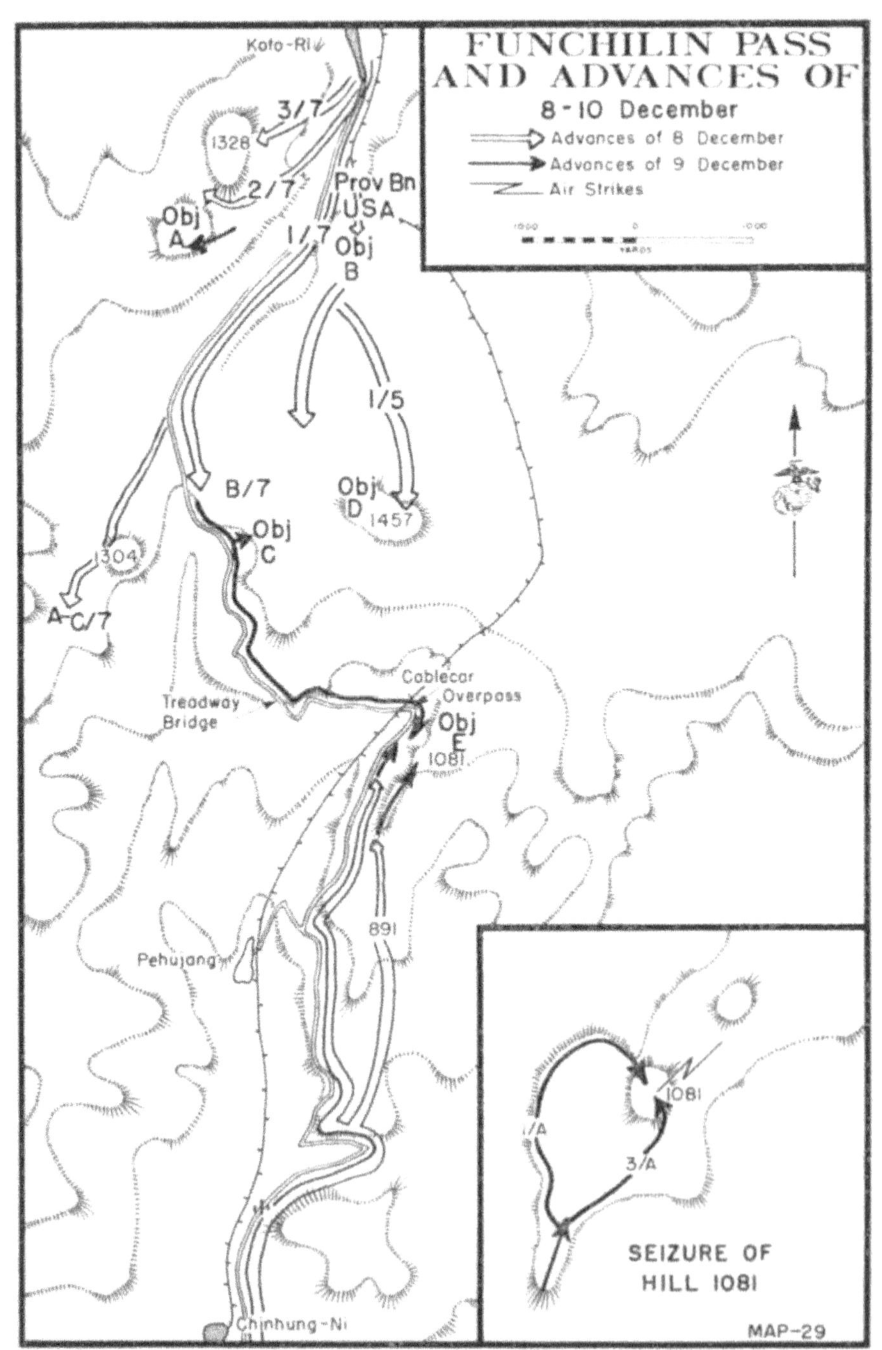

Koto-Ri
FUNCHILIN PASS
AND ADVANCES OF
8-10 December
Advances of 8 December
Advances of 9 December
Air Strikes
1000   0   1000
YARDS
3/7
1328
2/7
Obj A
Prov Bn USA
1/7
Obj B
1/5
B/7
Obj D 1457
Obj C
1304
A-C/7
Cablecar
Treadway Bridge
Overpass
Obj E
1081
891
Pehujang
Chinhung-Ni
1/A
1081
3/A
SEIZURE OF
HILL 1081
MAP-29

My first night in the hamlet of Koto-ri was spent in a tent with Marine correspondents, infantrymen, and a handful of British commandos. I was too tired for conversation and fell into a deep sleep until awakened by sporadic gunfire and a howling snowstorm blowing through the valley. This was bad news for all of us. Until the weather cleared, our troops would be deprived of critical air support and the ability to evacuate our wounded.

Around mid-morning I left the tent and walked the camp's perimeter, making pictures of burial parties going about their grim business in the storm, unloading the frozen corpses of allied dead from trucks and stacking them for burial. During my service in Korea I had seen so much death and dying that such horrors had become part of war's landscape. You saw it and moved on. But it wasn't always that way, and some deaths cut deeper than others. I think often of a close buddy from Pendleton who came over with the 1st Provisional Marine Brigade and was killed in a firefight with North Koreans at Pusan. He called me "Joe Combat" and joked I would be the first from our unit to get killed in the war. Damned if it wasn't him. We couldn't get our dead off the hill that night, but

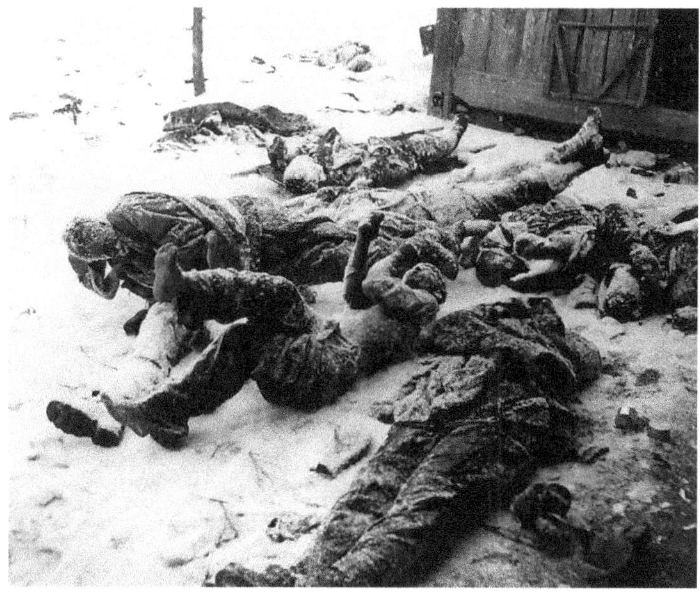

The frozen bodies of Marine dead await burial at Koto-ri. (Photo by Sgt. Frank C. Kerr, USMC)

the following day I found him lying on his back in the hot August sun with black ants parading through his eyes, nose and mouth. Like many men who got hit, he had that open-mouthed look of surprise on his face as if to say, "I can't believe this happened to me." I stood over that empty, ant-infested shell that was once my friend and thought… *is that it? Is that all there is?* For me, it was a simple but profound lesson on the impermanence of life, and one I'll never forget.

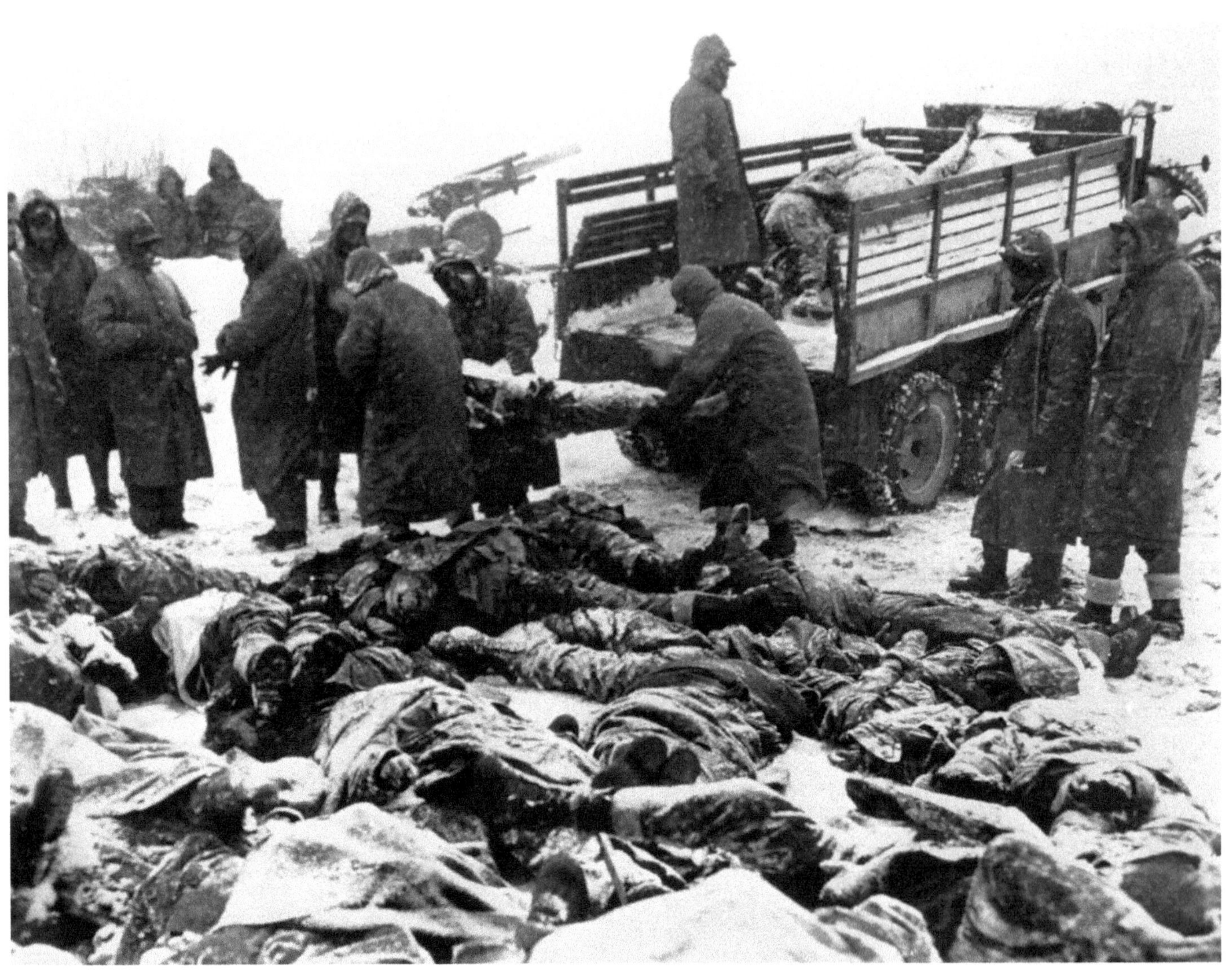

Solemn work. Allied dead are offloaded for mass burial at Koto-ri on December 8th, 1950 *(Photo by Sgt. Frank C. Kerr, USMC)*

That night at Koto-ri I took shelter with other Marines in a North Korean hut whose owner planned to evacuate with U.N. forces come morning and start a new life in the south. The man was all smiles as he tore planks from his home and burned them to keep us warm. By sunup the weather had cleared and I went into the hills at Funchilin Pass to photograph an infantry company guarding a bridge the Chinese had blown to keep the Division from escaping Chosin. They had done a thorough job of it, leaving our combat engineers the herculean task of constructing a new crossing.

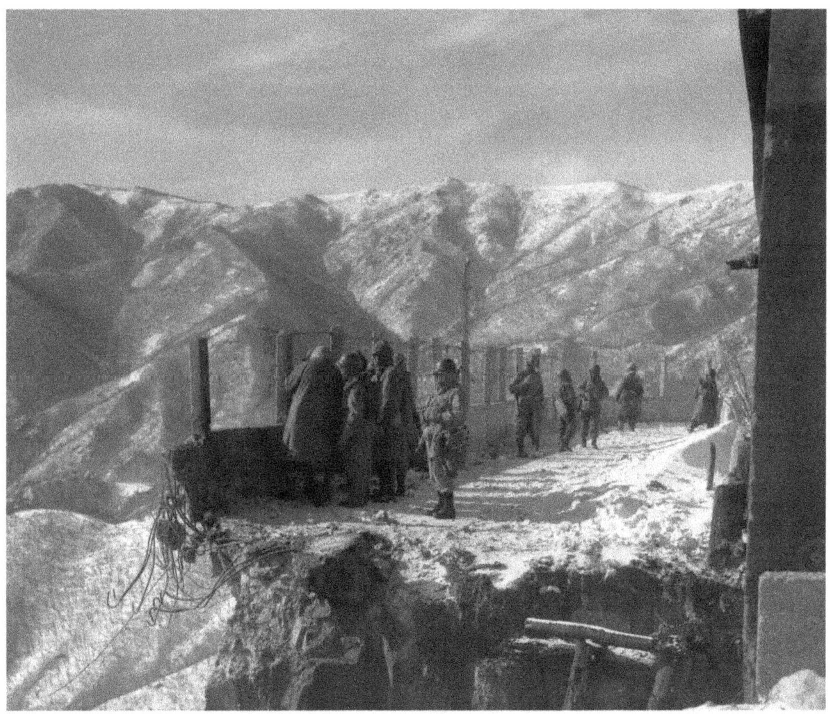

Men of the 7th Marines stand guard over a blown bridge at Funchilin Pass, south of Koto-ri. Combat engineers would span the gap with an air-dropped treadway bridge—a first in military history—allowing the column to continue its withdrawal from Chosin. (Photo by Sgt. Frank C. Kerr, USMC)

I lingered awhile, took a few more pictures along the road of cold and battle-weary allied troops, then fell in with a Marine lieutenant who was taking his patrol south to make contact with a relief force coming north. The patrol hadn't gone far before encountering a squad of Chinese soldiers who must have had their fill of war because they sent out a lone volunteer to surrender. The Marines were understandably wary, having learned from hard experience that it might be an enemy trick, but when the rest of those Chinese saw their buddy wasn't shot, they left their weapons and emerged with hands in the air and nervous smiles on their faces. Further down the road, after brief firefights, still more communists surrendered and were sent to the rear to join their comrades. For a time it seemed that

Marine patrol would capture the whole damn Chinese Army, until they bumped into an enemy concentration more stubborn than the rest. These soldiers were well emplaced and opened up with machine gun and small arms fire from two directions, wounding a couple of our men and sending the rest of us scurrying for cover. As the lieutenant was radioing for assistance, the relief force the patrol had been sent to contact was spotted coming up the valley. When the Chinese began maneuvering to ambush them, we took them under

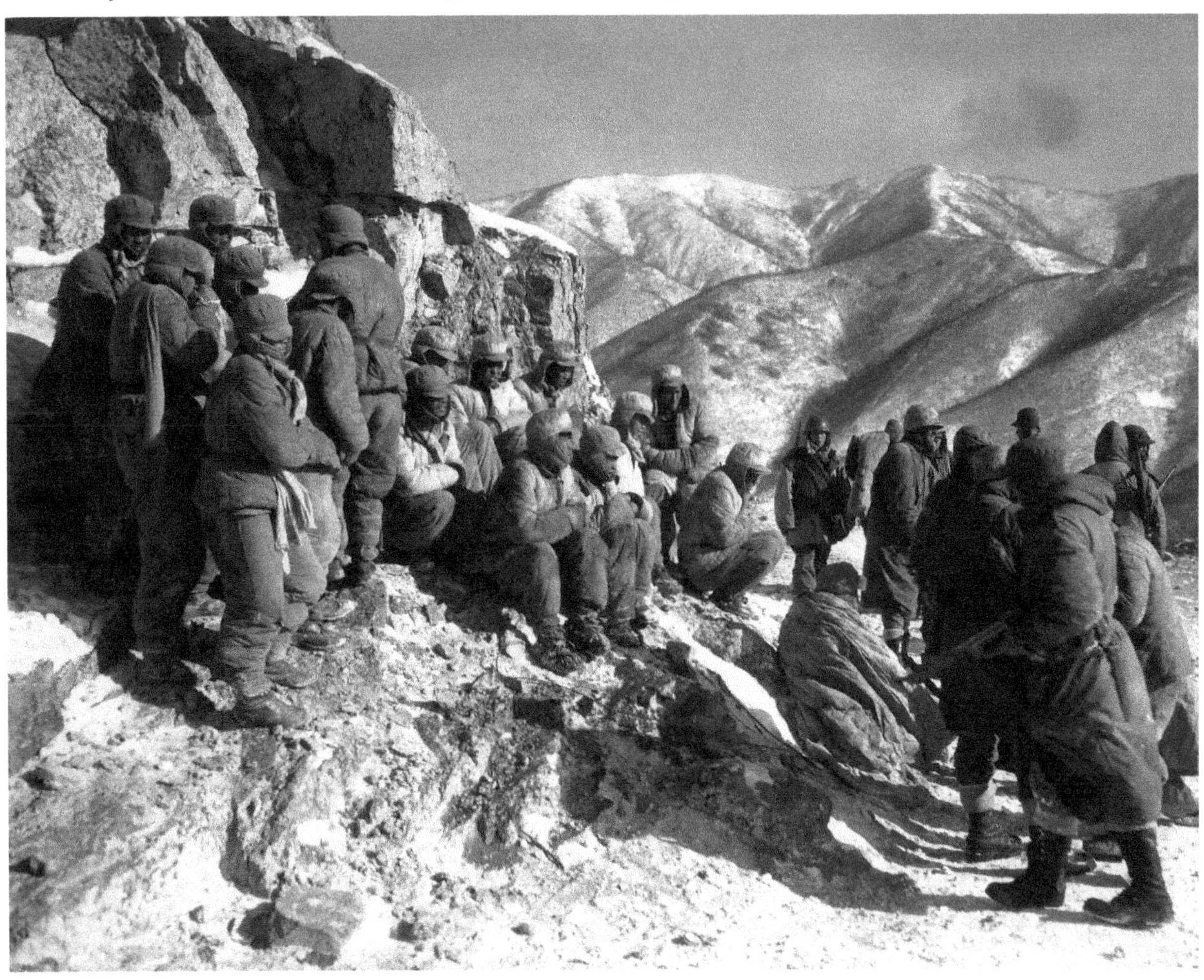

Captured Chinese troops wearing rags, sneakers and American footgear, wait for instructions after surrendering to Charlie Company, 7th Marines. *(Photo by Sgt. Frank C. Kerr, USMC)*

fire—an odd situation, caught in one ambush while firing on another. And if that wasn't confusing enough, the relief requested by the lieutenant now appeared on the ridge above us, moving to flank the enemy. Their arrival did not go unnoticed by the Chinese either, who quickly opened up with their machine guns, dropping some of those men and forcing the rest to hastily withdraw. It was looking like we would have to find our own way out of that mess, so the patrol disengaged and scrambled back down to the relative cover of the supply road.

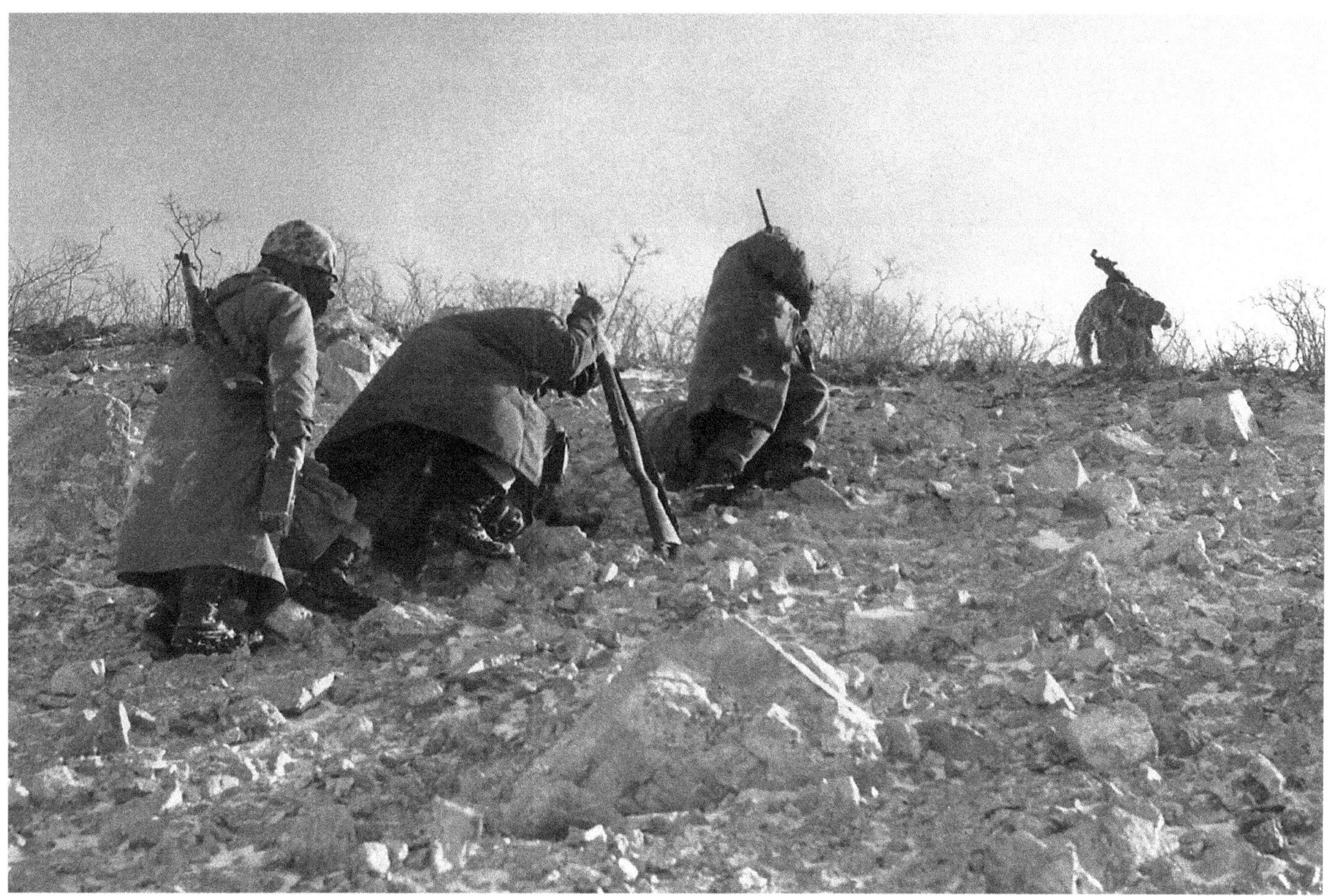

7th Marine patrol struggles up a hillside in an attempt to flank the enemy which is trying to trap them in the hills south of Koto-ri. *(Photo by Sgt. Frank C. Kerr, USMC)*

Once behind cover, the lieutenant paused for a head count and came up five Marines short. Back on the radio, he was letting his company commander know about the missing men when a short, elderly Korean woman came shuffling up the road. None of us quite knew what to make of this brazen old lady, so we stopped her at gunpoint and conducted a body search. The only contraband found on her squat little body was a can of C-ration sliced peaches concealed in her bosom that a Marine promptly confiscated, triggering a howl of protest from its former owner that must have been heard clear to the Chinese border. This was followed by a furious nonstop tirade, and though none of us spoke a lick of Korean, we were pretty sure she wasn't thanking us. To get her out of our hair, we sat her down with the prisoners, but that didn't shut her up. Those poor commies were looking mighty miserable, so to show a little mercy and keep some peace and quiet in the war, the lieutenant returned the can of peaches and sent the old woman on her way. She was still giving us an earful as she turned the corner, headed for the Chinese lines.

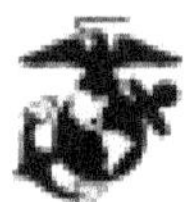

At dusk the patrol managed to slip away from the ambush and cut across the valley floor to the opposite slope, where we expended our last bit of energy clawing over snow and ice-covered rocks while the prisoners carried our wounded. Darkness had settled by the time we reached the windswept hilltop and shook hands with a rescue team sent to find us. They informed the lieutenant we were the first Marines to break out of the reservoir and that the road ahead was clear all the way to the coast. For us, it seemed, the worst of Chosin was finally behind us.

As we caught our breath and waited for transportation off the hill, an Army halftrack came rumbling up the road, driven by a young commander who looked fresh out of high school. He stopped to share his rations and chat a moment, lamenting that he had yet to see combat and wanting to know how close the enemy was. We assured him the bad guys were just around the corner, so he promised to give them hell and went on his way. In time we heard the distant, tell-tale chatter of the halftrack's guns and knew our eager young commander had finally found his war.

At a first aid station in the valley, we ate our first hot meal in days and were pleasantly surprised to find the patrol's five missing Marines. Apparently they had become separated during the ambush and found their own way to safety. I left the station with a full belly and was crossing through camp when I heard a familiar voice screaming bloody murder. Sure enough, there she was—the little old lady. She had defied the United States Marines and stood up to the Chinese Army, and now she was giving holy hell to some poor shmuck on sentry duty who had made the dumb mistake of confiscating her precious can of peaches.

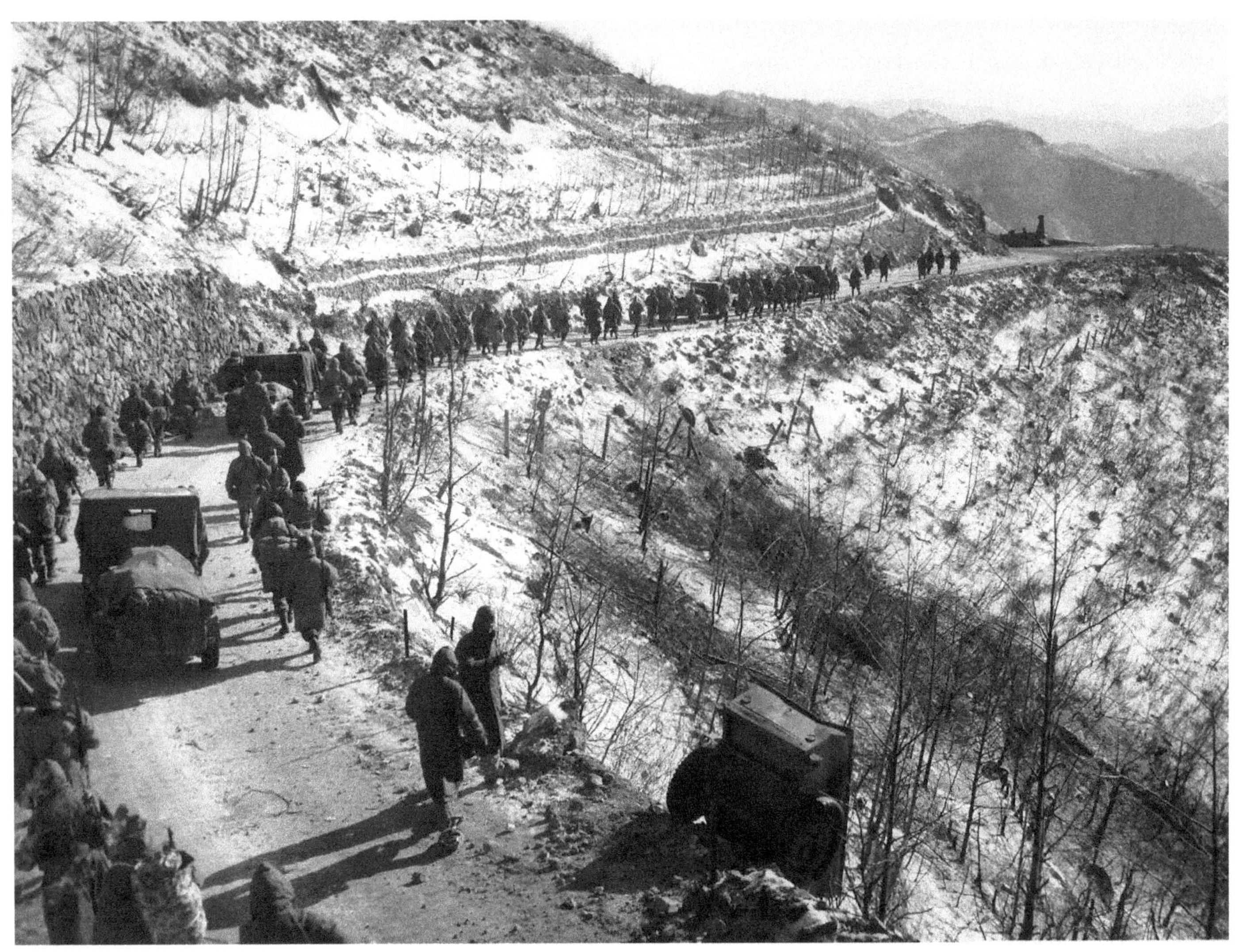

Through icy mountain passes, enemy attacks and continual roadblocks, the 1st Marine Division came down from Koto-ri in the company of U.S. soldiers, British Royal Marines and troops of the Republic of Korea. They brought out their wounded, their equipment, and tens of thousands of North Korean refugees. *(Photo by Sgt. Frank C. Kerr, USMC)*

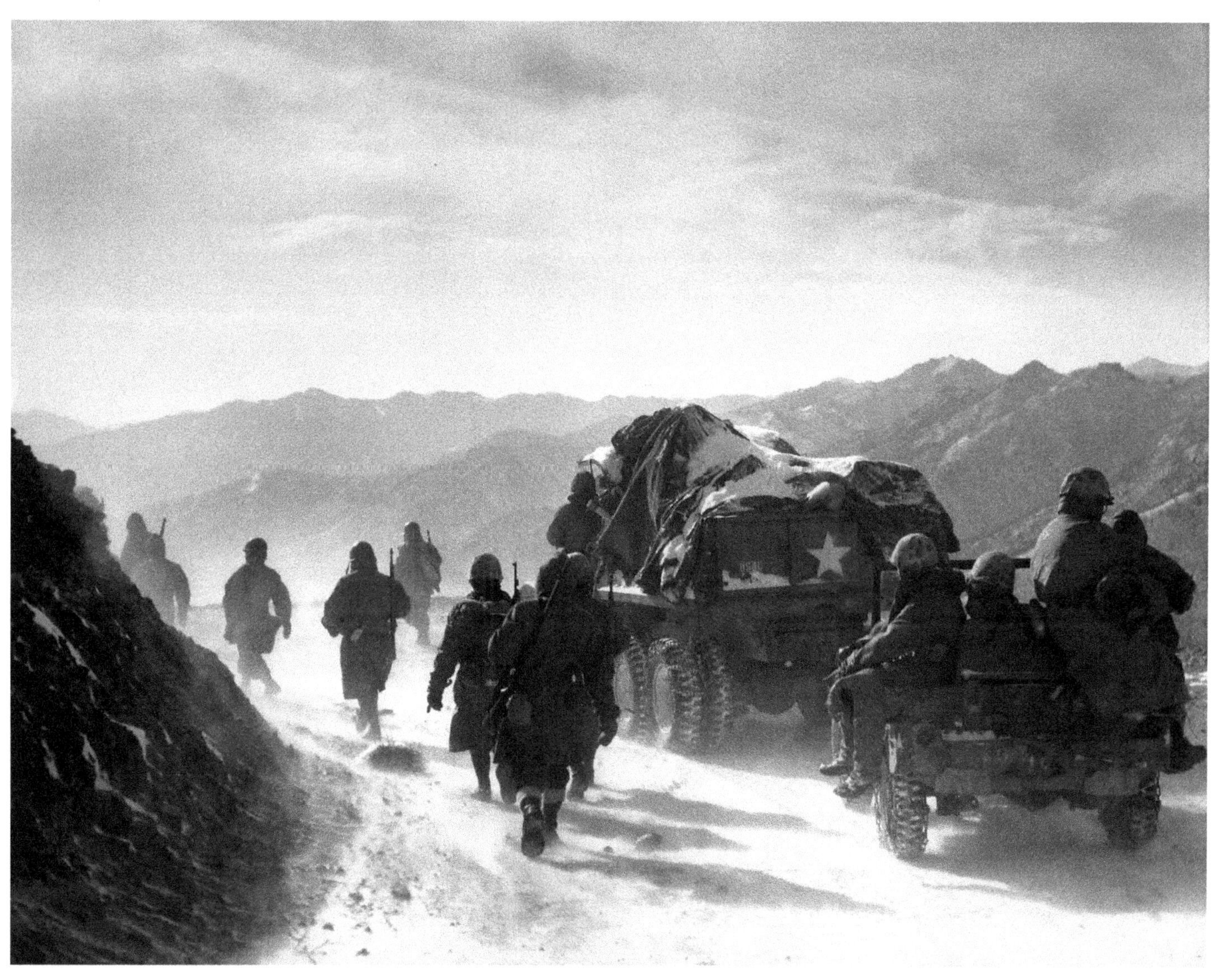

South of Koto-ri, December 1950. A mountain gale lashes allied troops with subzero cold during their historic breakout from the Chosin Reservoir. It has been estimated that windchill temperatures reached more than fifty below. *(Photo by Sgt. Frank C. Kerr, USMC)*

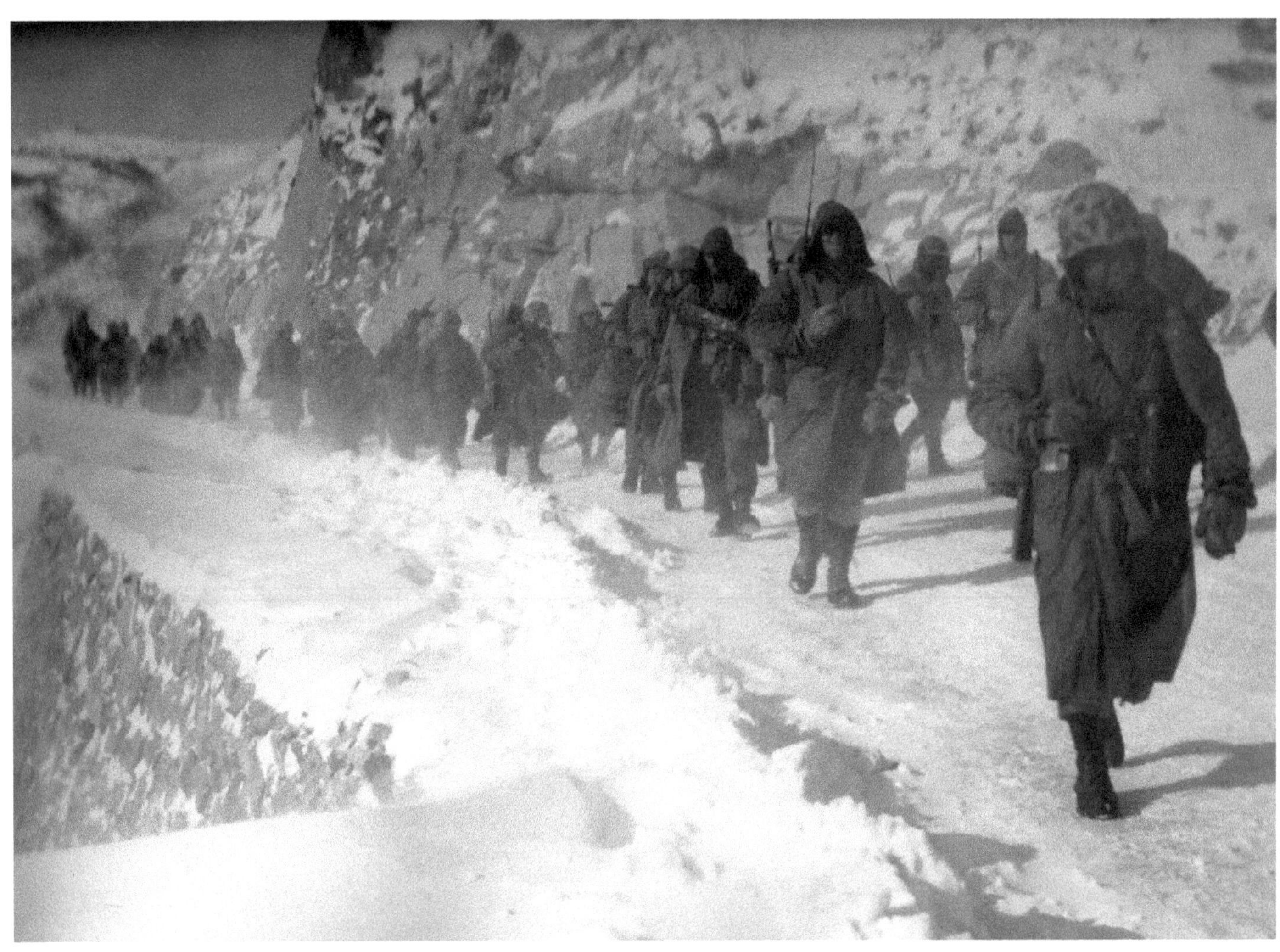

Battle-tested men of the 1st Marine Division make their way through blowing snow and a bitter Manchurian wind on the last leg of their withdrawal from Chosin. ***Opposite page***: Nearing the end of their long and arduous march to the sea, these tired Leathernecks smile for the camera before continuing on to the port city of Hungnam, and eventual evacuation from North Korea. *(Photos by Sgt. Frank C. Kerr, USMC)*

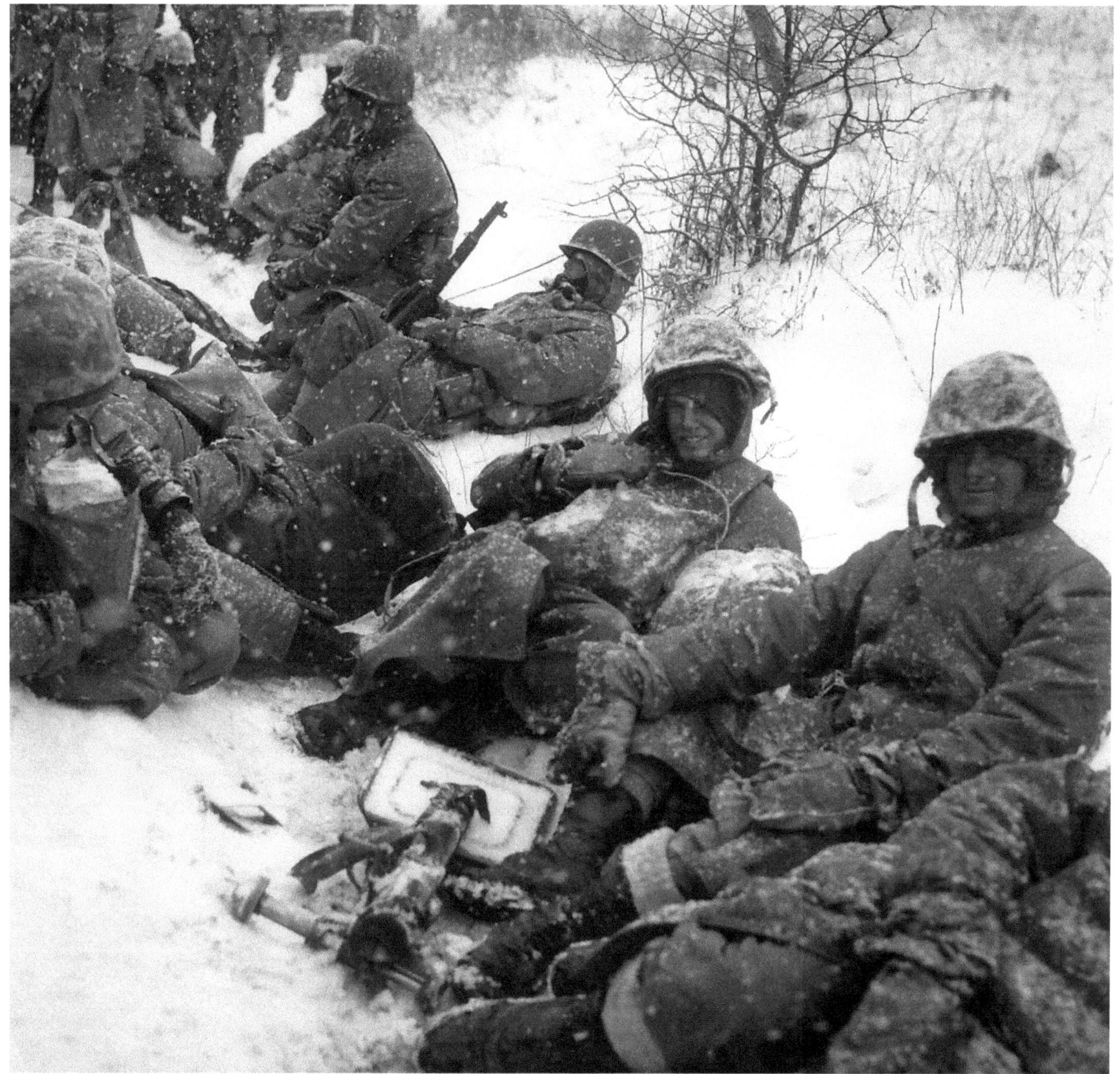

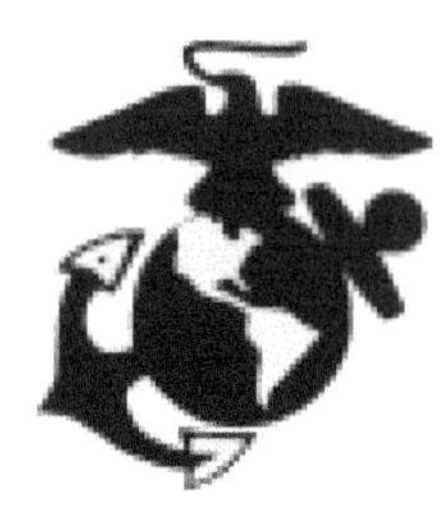

13 Dec 1950, USS General Randall, Hungnam, Korea

Dear Mom;

I guess you've probably read about the fight we had out here, it was really quite a show. When those damn Chinamen surrounded us I bet they thought they had a tiger by the tail. We really mauled a couple of their divisions. Now the wheels have us aboard ship and I don't know where we're going. I'm still okay though—not a scratch on me... I just might get out of this country all in one piece yet.

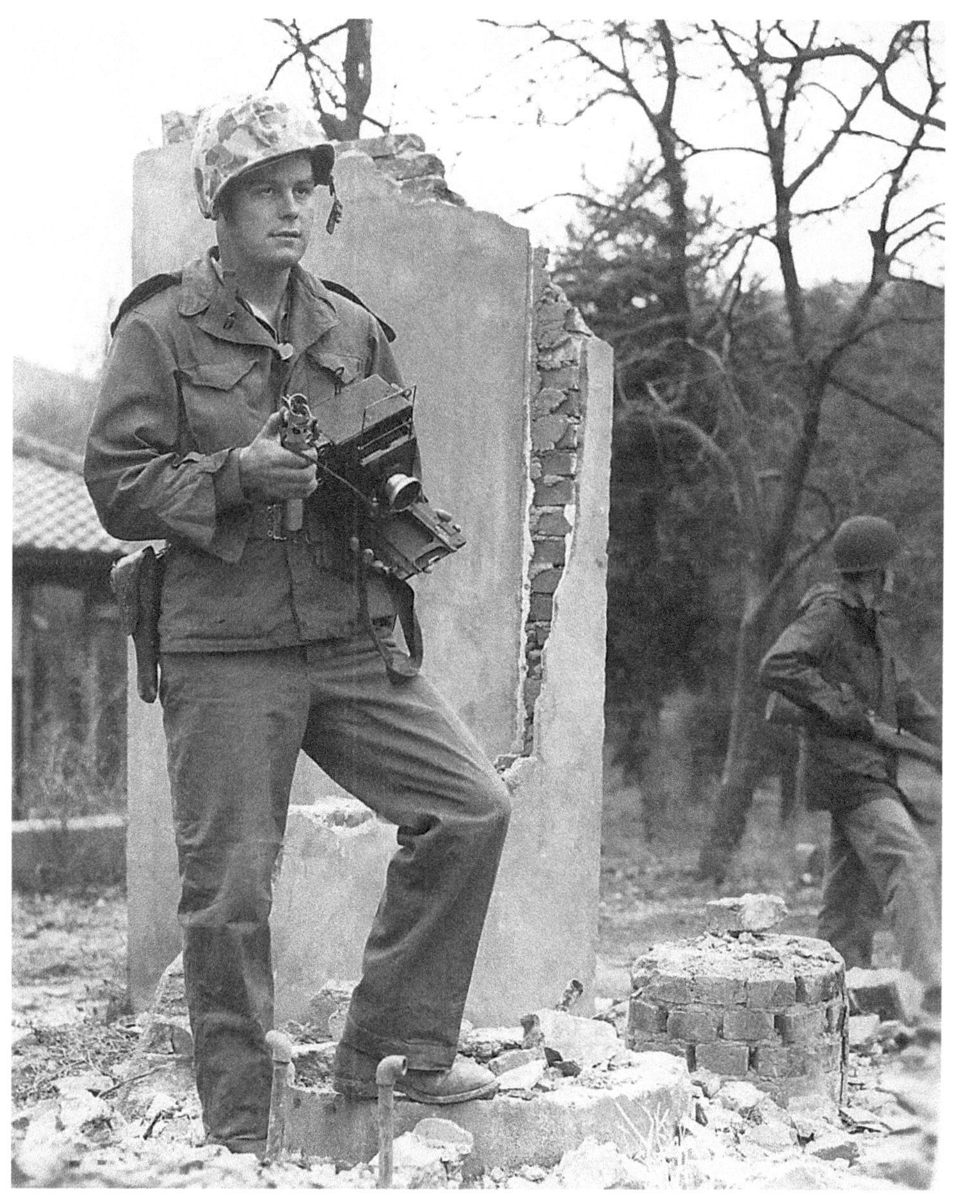

The author in Masan, South Korea following the Battle of the Chosin Reservoir. This publicity still, requested by Marine Corps Headquarters, was taken four months before Sgt. Kerr rotated home in May, 1951. *(Photo by Sgt. James Powers, USMC)*

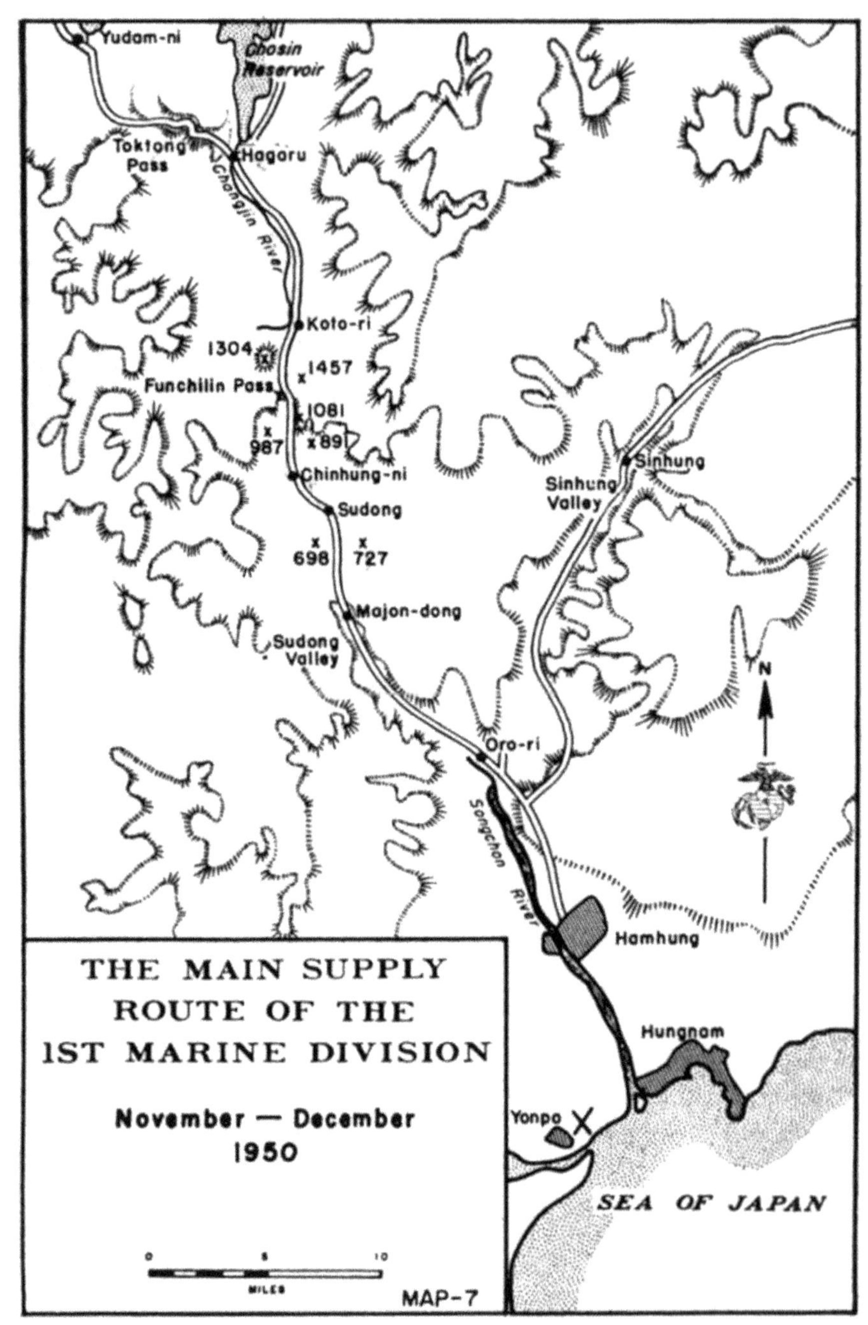

Yudam-ni
Chosin Reservoir
Toktong Pass
Hagaru
Changjin River
Koto-ri
1304
x1457
Funchilin Pass
1081
x89
987
Chinhung-ni
Sudong
698
727
Majon-dong
Sudong Valley
Sinhung
Sinhung Valley
Oro-ri
Songchon River
Hamhung
N
Hungnam
Yonpo
SEA OF JAPAN
THE MAIN SUPPLY
ROUTE OF THE
1ST MARINE DIVISION
November — December
1950
0   5   10
MILES
MAP-7

HUNGNAM

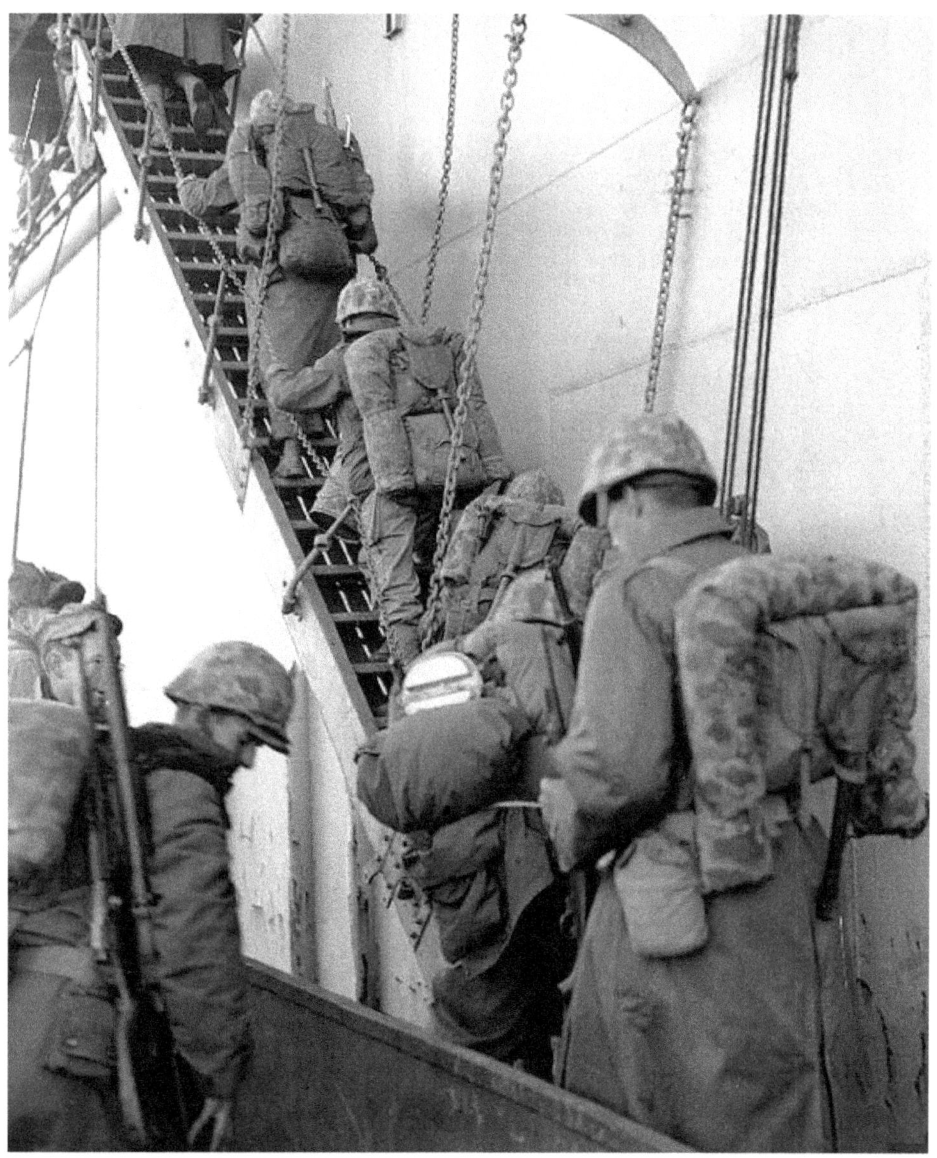

Department of Defense Photo (USN)

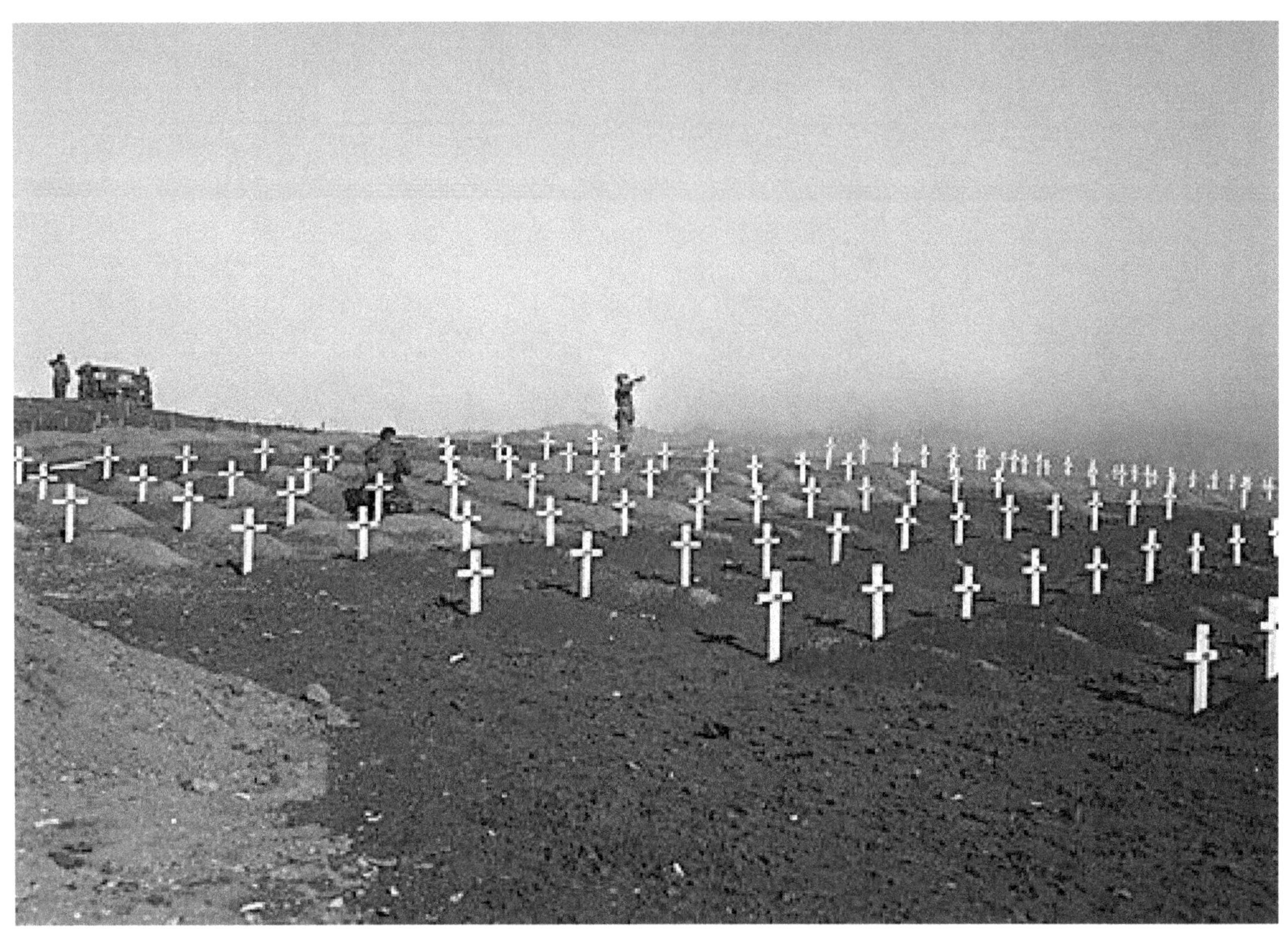

Following the Battle of the Chosin Reservoir, a lone bugler sounds taps over his fallen brothers of the 1st Marine Division, December 13, 1950. *(National Archives photo)*

There would be more hard fighting in the days ahead but I wouldn't be there to photograph it. On December 11th I was trucked with other U.N. troops into the port city of Hungnam, passing through an Army perimeter that was like entering another world. Photographers and war correspondents were everywhere, taking pictures and slapping the backs of unshaven, bone-tired men like they were conquering heroes. By nightfall the rest of the division was safely inside the perimeter and awaiting evacuation, having traveled the final twenty-three miles without food or sleep. Four days later the last of our troops would be safely aboard ships bound for Pusan in South Korea, along with tens of thousands of North Korean refugees.

The 1st Marine Division's epic breakout from the Chosin Reservoir was over, and so was my assignment covering that extraordinary campaign. At the photo lab I turned in the last of my exposed film then went looking for a bed. It had been two weeks of hardships and heartache almost impossible to imagine, yet through grit, discipline and *esprit de corps*, the Division had survived to fight another day.

As I write this, the memories of a time and place that profoundly shaped my life are so thick that it's hard to sort them all. Some I hope to forget, others I never will. I'll forever remember a quiet, pristine night in the mountains of North Korea, taking comfort knowing the stars were shining over places on Earth where people weren't cold, tired and hurting. I'll remember the worn photograph of a smiling young family and wondering what kind of husband and father that dead Chinese soldier had been to his wife and kids. And I'll remember a Marine machine gunner whose face I barely saw and whose name I'll never know, but who fought beside me one black night in a roadside ditch, and for the briefest moment before he was killed became my brother. We who were fortunate enough to return from that war will never forget those who died there. And though some may think it impossible, the men who fought at Chosin would tell you this; that once upon a time Hell did indeed freeze over… and we were there.

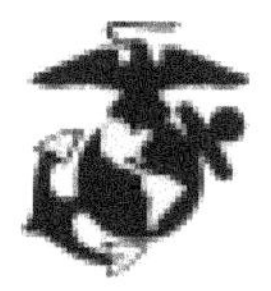

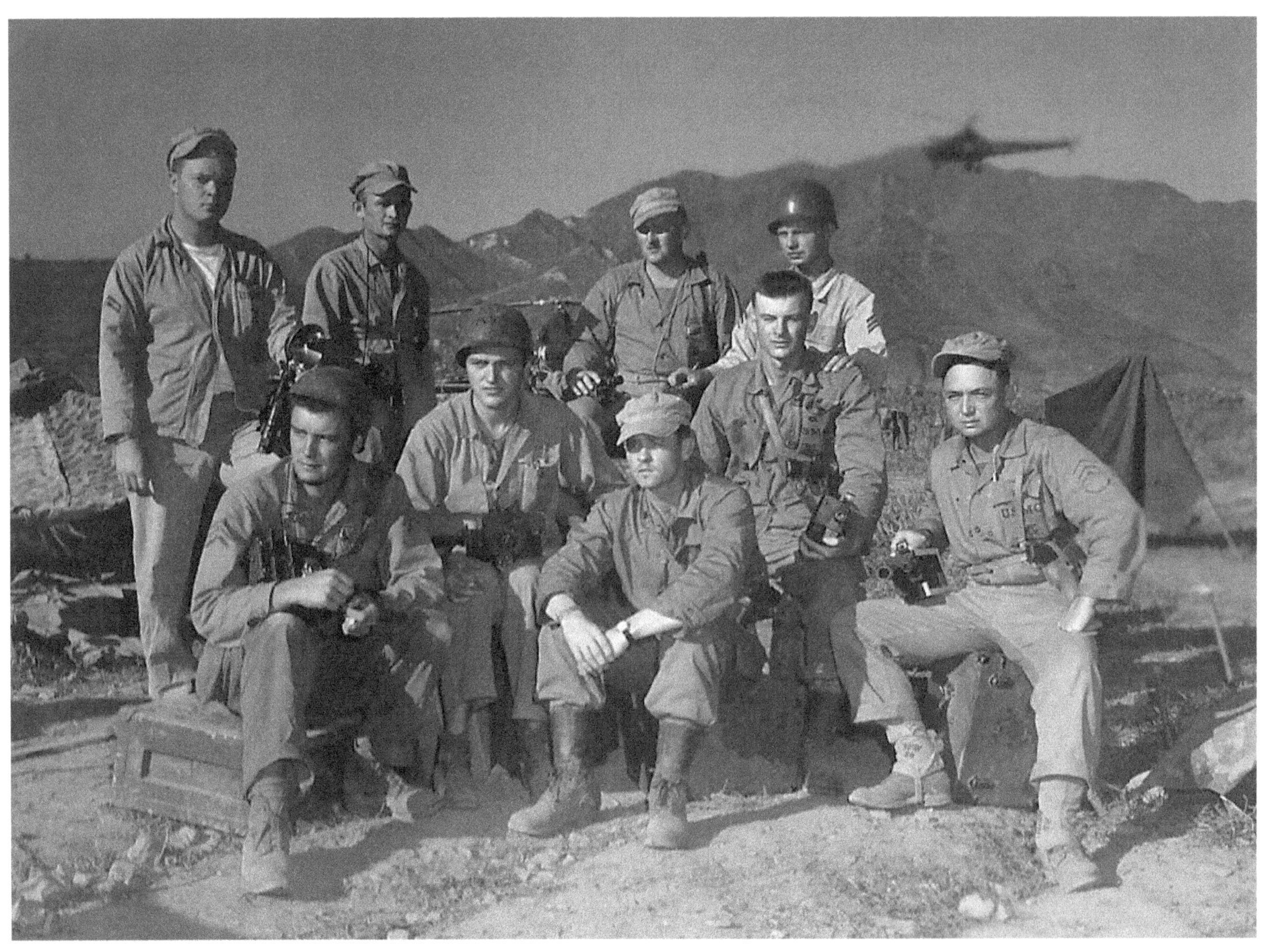

Sgt. Kerr (front left) and the Photo Section of the 1st Provisional Marine Brigade gather for a group shot during the early days of the Korean War. Not all came home. *(National Archives Photo, USMC)*

ABOUT THE AUTHOR

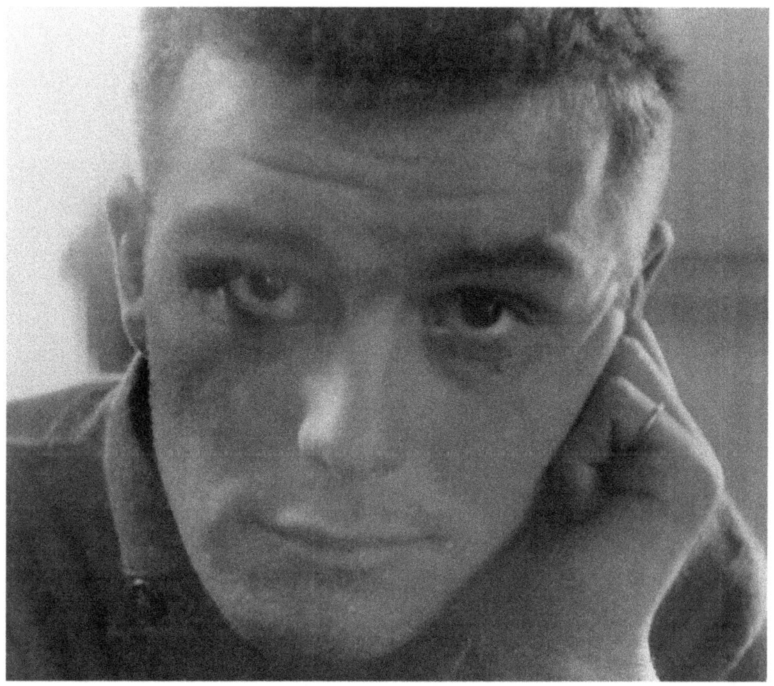

The strain of war. Sergeant Frank Kerr in Korea, circa 1950.

Frank Kerr enlisted with the United States Marine Corps in 1948 and went to war in 1950 as a combat photographer with the 1st Marine Division in Korea, where he was awarded the Bronze Star and Navy Commendation Medal for valor, and recognized by Commanding General Oliver P. Smith as the "ablest military photographer of the Korean theater". His photographs can be found in books, magazines, documentary films, and on the walls of the National Museum of the Marine Corps in Triangle, Virginia. He was co-founder of The Chosin Few, an international organization of veterans who served at the Chosin Reservoir, and led a three-man delegation to North Korea in 1991, seeking cooperation in recovering the bodies of American servicemen missing since the Korean War. He died in Massachusetts at age seventy-six from the long-term health effects of cold war injury, suffered during the Chosin campaign.

All proceeds from the sale of this book are donated to the nonprofit Marine Corps Heritage and Marine Corps Scholarship Foundations. For more information please visit www.allertonhill.com.

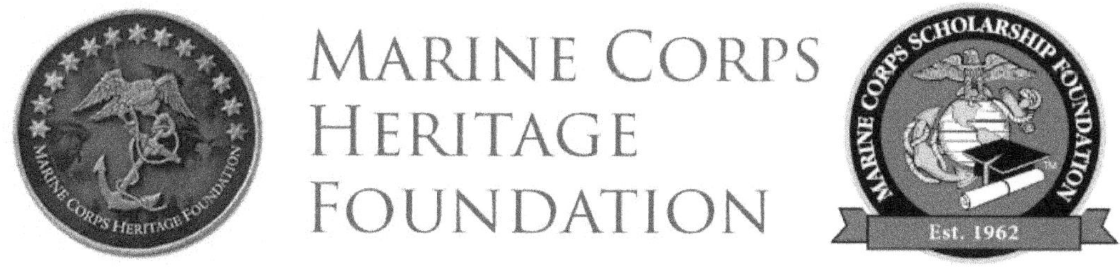